READING
JULIA ALVAREZ

Recent Titles in
The Pop Lit Book Club

Reading Barbara Kingsolver
Lynn Marie Houston and Jennifer Warren

Reading Amy Tan
Lan Dong

Reading Cormac McCarthy
Willard P. Greenwood

Reading Khaled Hosseini
Rebecca Stuhr

Reading Toni Morrison
Rachel Lister

Reading Joan Didion
Lynn Marie Houston and William V. Lombardi

Reading Nora Roberts
Mary Ellen Snodgrass

Reading Michael Chabon
Helene Meyers

READING
JULIA ALVAREZ

Alice L. Trupe

The Pop Lit Book Club

LIBRARIES UNLIMITED

AN IMPRINT OF ABC-CLIO, LLC
Santa Barbara, California • Denver, Colorado • Oxford, England

Library of Congress Cataloging-in-Publication Data

Trupe, Alice.
    Reading Julia Alvarez / Alice L. Trupe.
        p. cm.—(The pop lit book club)
    Includes bibliographical references and index.
    ISBN 978-0-313-38395-3 (hardcopy : acid-free paper)—ISBN 978-0-313-38396-0 (ebook) 1. Alvarez, Julia—Criticism and interpretation. I. Title.
    PS3551.L845Z94   2011
    813'.54—dc22   2011002498

ISBN: 978-0-313-38395-3
EISBN: 978-0-313-38396-0

15   14   13   12   11   1   2   3   4   5

This book is also available on the World Wide Web as an ebook.
Visit www.abc-clio.com for details.

Libraries Unlimited
An Imprint of ABC-CLIO, LLC

ABC-CLIO, LLC
130 Cremona Drive, P.O. Box 1911
Santa Barbara, California 93116-1911

This book is printed on acid-free paper ∞

Manufactured in the United States of America

CONTENTS

Preface   vii

Chapter 1   Julia Alvarez: The Life   1

Chapter 2   Alvarez and the Novel, Alvarez as
Poet   11

Chapter 3   *How the García Girls Lost Their
Accents* (1991)   21

Chapter 4   *In the Time of the Butterflies* (1994)   33

Chapter 5   *¡Yo!* (1997)   45

Chapter 6   *In the Name of Salomé* (2000)   57

Chapter 7   *Saving the World* (2004)   67

Chapter 8   Books for Young Readers   77

Chapter 9   Nonfiction   95

Chapter 10   Poetry   107

Chapter 11   Julia Alvarez and Contemporary
Issues   121

Chapter 12   Julia Alvarez and the Internet   131

Chapter 13   Julia Alvarez and the Media   135
Chapter 14   What Do I Read Next?   143

Notes   151
Bibliography   167
Index   177

PREFACE

With the publication of her first novel, *How the García Girls Lost Their Accents*, in 1991, Julia Alvarez achieved fame as a popular writer and a novelist worthy of critical notice. Her fiction has been translated into several European languages, Korean, and Turkish in addition to Spanish.[1] Her second novel, *In the Time of the Butterflies*, was dramatized in an award-winning made-for-television movie, and a stage play based on *How the García Girls Lost Their Accents* debuted in 2008. In 2002, Alvarez received the Hispanic Heritage Award for Literature, and in 2009, she received the F. Scott Fitzgerald Award, an honor she shares with such writers as William Styron and John Updike.

Julia Alvarez is, above all, a good storyteller, and the role of storytelling is an important theme in all of her work. Her stories are anchored in life experience—as an immigrant, a latecomer to the English language, and a latecomer to success. With one foot in the Dominican Republic and one foot in the United States, Alvarez writes about Latina women. Her characters find ways to reconcile competing cultural values and allegiances, largely without role models for the new pathways they tread. Elements of this story emerge in her poetry and nonfiction as well as her fiction for adults and young readers.

Alvarez established her reputation with her novels for adults, publishing five between 1991 and 2006: *How the García Girls Lost Their Accents*, *In the Time of the Butterflies*, *¡Yo!*, *In the Name of Salomé*, and *Saving the World*. Since 2000, she has established an equally solid reputation as a writer for young readers. Two of her novels for young readers, *Before We Were Free* (2002) and *Return to Sender* (2009), have received the Pura Belpré Award. She has published three picture books telling legends from the Dominican Republic. Less easily classified is Alvarez's lovely little parable, *A Cafecito Story*, a brief fiction about sustainable agriculture and fair trade with organic coffee growers in the Dominican Republic. The book grows out of her experience with her husband, Bill Eichner, in a coffee growers' cooperative and literacy initiative.

Poetry is her first love, though—a love that shows in the rhythms and images of her prose style as well as the volumes of poetry published between 1984 and 2004. Her essays are collected in *Something to Declare* (1998), and she has written a critical inquiry into the *quinceañera, Once upon a Quinceañera: Coming of Age in the USA* (2007).

Recurring themes echo throughout Alvarez's work, but each book frames them freshly. Dominant issues are immigration, freedom from oppression, women's roles in a patriarchal culture, family relationships, the importance of storytelling, and justice. Her semiautobiographical first and third novels, along with her first novel for young readers, are rooted in her family's flight from the Rafael Trujillo dictatorship in 1960, when Alvarez was a child. Their abrupt departure wrenched them from a comfortable life and plunged them into fast-paced English and anti-Hispanic prejudice in New York City. Alvarez and her sisters adjusted to their new language and culture, rebelling against conservative Dominican values and reveling in North American freedom in the turbulent 1960s. Clashes between their two cultures were internalized. Like many other contemporary immigrants and migrants, Alvarez maintained strong ties with her homeland, through her *familia* who stayed in the Dominican Republic, and much of her writing plays out the themes of continuing loss and divided identity.

Alvarez's love of language grew as she learned English, and she began writing poetry as she became a voracious reader.[2] She writes in English, but the rhythms of her poetry and prose are inflected by the Spanish of her childhood and her homeland's strong oral storytelling tradition.[3] The meaning and role of stories in our lives are recurring themes. Her work also shows the influence of the *testimonio*, the Latin American genre of personal narratives by those who have witnessed, and often suffered, significant historical events. The difficulties involved in speaking up and speaking out appear throughout her writing, whether the subject is love or protest against tyranny. What can be said and what must be kept secret? Whose memory of the past is right? Can there be one authoritative story of the past? These questions are intertwined with issues of identity and language. In her historical novels, especially, Alvarez resurrects silenced voices in narratives that bear witness to forgotten lives. Equally important, class divisions and unequal distribution of wealth in a global economy are recurring concerns, while the shadows of terrorism and exploitation hang over her recent writing.

Though Alvarez's writing focuses on individual lives, it is, above all, political. Situated at the dividing line between two cultures, straddling both, Alvarez uses her vantage point to give readers a fuller picture of America than they might encounter elsewhere.

This book is an introduction and companion to Julia Alvarez's work. A brief biography lays the groundwork for understanding important themes and aspects of her characters. A chapter on genre focuses mostly on Alvarez's novels, but her use of poetic form is also discussed. Each of Alvarez's novels for adults is discussed in a separate chapter, followed by a single chapter treating her fiction for younger readers. Chapters include plot summaries, analyses of literary elements, facts of interest in understanding the works, and discussion questions. A separate chapter is devoted to Alvarez's poetry, focusing on themes and structure. Two nonfiction books are discussed in a single chapter. These chapters on her works are followed with an overview of contemporary issues that Alvarez's writing addresses. Brief chapters on her Internet presence and dramatizations of her first two novels are included. The final chapter suggests other authors and works that a lover of Alvarez's writing may enjoy.

JULIA ALVAREZ: THE LIFE

Julia Alvarez was born in the United States in 1950. The second of four daughters, she was named after her mother, Julia. Her parents had met and married in the United States. Her father, a doctor, had lived in North America from 1937, after fleeing the Dominican Republic because of his involvement in a plot against its dictator, Rafael Leónidas Trujillo.[1] The family returned to the Dominican Republic when Julia was three months old, during a period when Trujillo promised reforms. Her childhood was spent amid her extended family in an atmosphere of privilege. Alvarez and the other children were insulated from the realities of the brutal regime under which they lived, until 1960, when her father's involvement in another plot to overthrow Trujillo was discovered.[2] He again fled the country with his wife and daughters, and Alvarez has lived in the United States since then, making her home in Vermont, where she began teaching at Middlebury College in 1988.[3]

In the Dominican Republic's capital city of Santo Domingo (called Ciudad Trujillo during the dictator's 30-year rule), the Alvarez family lived an upper-class life in the Tavares family compound, which encompassed her grandparents' and several aunts and uncles' homes. The whole family spent each July and August at her grandfather's seaside home until the summer of 1960, when they were under surveillance by Trujillo's secret police (the Military Intelligence Service, known as the SIM). The family compound supplied much companionship, with servants to perform household chores and care for children, and there were

1

cousins, as well as sisters, to play with. There were parties at which Alvarez recalls seeing her uncles perform flamenco on the dining room table, and they visited her father's enormous family in the country.[4] Alvarez would eventually discover her own voice by remembering the voices that dominated her early life.[5]

Alvarez developed a love of stories from an early age, when she was given the book *The Thousand and One Nights* (or *Arabian Nights*) as a child; she did not read other books, such as her school's Dick-and-Jane primer, which bored her.[6] Dominican culture was, and is, an oral culture. Even in the 21st century, 10 percent of its population is illiterate.[7] The family's history and identity were preserved through stories. Alvarez's first contributions were the stories she told to get herself out of trouble and avoid punishment—stories that she says her aunts would call "lies."[8]

Her mother's father, the head of the family, was a well-educated man who recited poetry in English as well as Spanish. The men of the family traditionally attended boarding school and college in the United States, and her grandfather had attended Cornell University.[9] Alvarez's mother, Julia, had attended boarding school in Massachusetts for two years.[10] A privileged child, Alvarez attended the Carol Morgan School, where she studied English. Before she began to learn English, Alvarez associated the language with secrets and anxiety because adults would speak in English to discuss matters the children should not know about.[11] Those who dared to criticize Trujillo, or perhaps make a joke that could be interpreted as critical, were likely to be jailed and were lucky to survive. Alvarez's grandfather was once imprisoned for two days in order to convince him to sell a piece of land to Trujillo's daughter at a low price.[12] More frightening than this was the knowledge that at any given time, a person might simply disappear; it could be years before the family members learned whether he or she was alive or dead. Even more frightening, the family members of any suspected opponent were equally in danger; they could be tortured or killed to put pressure on the culprit.

Although the children were unaware of their family's growing involvement in the opposition, their parents became increasingly anxious to leave the Dominican Republic, and Alvarez's grandmother went so far as to seek help from voodoo practitioners.[13] Papers for travel were difficult to get, so American friends established a fellowship to enable Julia's father to study heart surgery in the United States.[14] Adult family members first suggested to the four girls that a vacation in the United States would be fun, then on the eve of their departure allayed their anxiety by reassuring them that instead they were headed to the family's house at the beach, which was near the site of the new airport. Instead of taking a vacation, though, the family boarded a plane bound for New

York City. The abruptness of the transition and their inability to prepare for it left the children with a sense of displacement.

Alvarez was deeply affected by the sudden changes in her life. The family lived in a small apartment in significantly reduced circumstances, financially challenged until her father obtained his license to practice medicine in the United States.[15] American neighbors and classmates saw Alvarez as a foreign, underprivileged "spic" and taunted her. Though she knew how to speak English, it was a school version of English, and at first she had trouble understanding the fast-paced colloquial English of the New York City kids at her local Catholic school.[16] However, fascinated by the language, Alvarez quickly grew proficient, helped and encouraged by caring teachers. She became a voracious reader, escaping her situation as an unwanted foreigner in stories. The public library was a world of uncensored ideas, in contrast to the censored society she had left behind.[17] As she became a reader, Alvarez began writing stories to preserve memories of her homeland, completing her first poem in English within her first year in the United States. She states that she would not have become a reader and writer if she had not come to the United States.[18]

When her father received his U.S. medical license in 1963, the family moved to a house in Jamaica, Queens.[19] Her father put in long hours seven days a week at his clinic in the Bronx, serving Hispanic patients. The summer Julia was 15, she chose to work for him rather than visit the Dominican Republic with her sisters.[20] By this time, Julia was attending an expensive boarding school in Massachusetts, where she found role models in her teachers, and her love of literature blossomed. Walt Whitman was the first poet whose work she really loved, drawn to his claim to "contain multitudes"—a powerful message for a bicultural teen.[21] She tells, too, of the impact Langston Hughes' poem, "I, Too, Sing America," had on her, with its line, "I am the darker brother," and its conclusion, "I, too, am America,"[22] a theme that is echoed in her poem "All-American Girl."[23] Embracing English, Alvarez became a poet herself. By the time she was a senior in high school, she was writing essays and stories and keeping a journal as well; her senior project was a collection of poems she had written.[24]

Alvarez attended Connecticut College, where she received a poetry prize.[25] Then she transferred to Middlebury College, where she earned her B.A. degree in 1971, graduating *summa cum laude*.[26] For a brief period after college, she worked on an ecology newsletter, living at home with her parents.[27] To get more time to write poems and stories, she entered a master of fine arts program at Syracuse University in 1973,[28] earning her degree in 1975.[29] There she taught some poetry courses to undergraduates, an experience that paved the way for her to pick up part-time or temporary teaching jobs between 1975 and 1988, that sustained her while she tried to establish herself as a writer.[30] Later she would explain that "Struggling writers grow up to become college teachers with one or two slim volumes and occasional sabbaticals."[31]

Alvarez led an itinerant life as poet-in-the-schools in Kentucky, Delaware, and North Carolina, and as an English teacher at Andover Academy, the prep school that had absorbed its "sister school," Abbot Academy, her alma mater.[32] She moved from unsatisfactory, stressful high school teaching[33] to several temporary teaching positions at universities. Over a period of 13 years, she had 18 different addresses.[34] The difficulty of making a reasonable salary this way is underscored by her comment that she read library books instead of buying books, bought her clothes in second-hand shops, skipped professional haircuts, and drove a car that was falling apart.[35] Alvarez also continued to study her craft. In 1979–1980, she attended the Bread Loaf School of English, and she began publishing in literary journals.[36] At that point in her career, however, there was no indication of the popularity her books would later bring. It took her ten years to finish her first novel.[37]

Before multiculturalism came into vogue in education and publishing in the 1980s, Alvarez had difficulty finding a role model for her writing, until she read Maxine Hong Kingston's *The Woman Warrior*, published in 1976.[38] Kingston questioned the ways in which women were silenced in her Chinese American culture and wrote a new kind of bicultural narrative. Alvarez began to see possibilities for her writing voice: *How the García Girls Lost Their Accents*, like *The Woman Warrior*, grew out of a dual cultural identity. Both books challenge the older, conventional immigrant narrative of assimilation into a new, American identity.

Alvarez's academic life became more settled when she was offered a tenure-track teaching position at Middlebury College in 1988. There she completed *How the García Girls Lost Their Accents*, thinking of it as the book that would bring her tenure,[39] but it also launched her career as a well-known writer. This book, which has continued to be a popular success, was recognized with the Josephine Miles Award from PEN Oakland in 1991, the year of its publication, and designated as a notable book by the American Library Association in 1992 and one of "Twenty-one Classics for the Twenty-first Century" by the New York Librarians.[40] Its literary merit has earned it attention in the academic world as well. It is well established in literature courses in colleges and high schools.

Alvarez's personal life was as unsettled as her professional life until she was nearly 40. She married her first husband, a musician who was three years younger, during her senior year of college. After about a year of poverty, constant arguments, and estrangement from her parents, Alvarez went to the Dominican Republic to obtain a quick divorce, which was handled by a lawyer uncle.[41] She met her second husband, an Englishman who was living in the United States, while she was an itinerant poet in Kentucky. They were married in the Dominican Republic on an election day that ended in a military takeover of the country; the ceremony was performed by a general, who had the power to perform marriages when martial law was in effect.[42] This marriage, too, was short-lived; their expectations of marriage were drastically different.

In June 1989, she married ophthalmologist Bill Eichner,[43] and this companionship has proved lasting. The combination of her marriage, publication of *García Girls*, and tenure at Middlebury transformed her life. She settled in Vermont, becoming a stepmother to Eichner's two daughters and, eventually, a grandmother.[44] Her husband, who came from a farm background in Nebraska, is a passionate farmer.[45]

The success of Alvarez's first novel should not obscure her growing reputation as a poet in the 1980s and early 1990s. She received numerous awards and grants for poetry. Her poems were included in *The One You Call Sister: New Women's Fiction*, edited by Paula Martinac, in 1989, and *The Best American Poetry 1991*, edited by David Lehman.[46] After publication of her first and second novels, her collection of poems, *Homecoming*, originally published in 1984, was reissued in an expanded edition in 1996. She was awarded the Jessica Nobel-Maxwell Poetry Prize in 1995. Another collection of poems, *The Other Side/El Otro Lado*, was published in 1995. A small volume, *Seven Trees*, followed in 1998 and was later included in *The Woman I Kept to Myself*, published in 2004.

In the Time of the Butterflies, Alvarez's second novel, was published in 1994, to wide acclaim. With this book, she demonstrated her ability to write on historical and political topics as well as autobiographical themes. *In the Time of the Butterflies* was recognized as a notable book by the American Library Association in 1994, selected as a Book of the Month Club choice the same year, a finalist for the National Book Critics Circle Award in 1995, and listed as one of the Best Books for Young Adults by the American Library Association in 1995.[47] Alvarez's interest in the lives and deaths of the Mirabal sisters, known as *Las Mariposas* or "the Butterflies" in the underground movement that opposed the Trujillo regime, originated with the report of their deaths. She recalls the *Time* magazine issue, four months after her family's arrival in the United States, which she was forbidden to look at because it reported the murder of the sisters by Trujillo's agents.[48] Because her father had also been involved in the underground, this episode brought home to her the danger that she and her family had been in while they remained in the Dominican Republic. Her research for the book took her to many locations in the Dominican Republic, and she spoke with many people, most notable among them the surviving sister, Dedé Mirabal, and daughters of two of the murdered women.

The book had a tremendous impact on readers in the United States and the Dominican Republic, and this would lead to wider recognition in both of her home cultures. Alvarez tells about a call she received from a Dominican American, living in California, whose father had been a torturer while Trujillo was in power. His mother had told him not to read the novel, but he did and found it a transformative experience.[49] In 2001, the made-for-television movie based on the novel, directed by Mariano Barosso and starring Salma Hayek, aired.[50]

The two early novels firmly established Alvarez as an important American writer. In 1995, she was honored by the U.S. State Department for her contribution to the Dominican community.[51] In the Dominican Republic, a one-day conference on her work was held in 1995, and in 1997, the Dominican Republic Annual Book Fair was dedicated to her work. She was honored by Middlebury College in 1996 with the Alumni Achievement Award. She was also a recipient of an honorary doctor of humane letters from the City University of New York, John Jay College, in the same year.

Alvarez's third novel was ¡Yo!, a sequel to García Girls, published in 1997. One chapter has been dramatized and aired on PBS in 2005.[52] A volume of essays, Something to Declare, followed in 1998. In 1998, after achieving much success as a writer, Alvarez made the difficult decision to give up her tenured position as full professor of English at Middlebury so that she could devote more time to writing. Because she enjoyed teaching, she continued at Middlebury as writer-in-residence, her duties being to teach creative writing on a part-time basis and advise Latino students.[53]

Since then, Alvarez has published at least one book every year except 2003.[54] She published her fourth novel in 2000, In the Name of Salomé, a historical novel about a Dominican poet and her daughter, a lifelong educator in Cuba and the United States. It was chosen as one of the top 10 books of 2000 by Latino.com. In the same year, Alvarez published her first book for young readers, The Secret Footprints, a picture book. Recognition of her achievements continued with her selection in 2000 as Woman of the Year by Latina Magazine and receipt of the Hispanic Heritage Award in Literature in 2002. Her visibility as an important Dominican American citizen resulted in her being chosen to attend the inauguration in 2000 of Dominican President Hipólito Mejía, in the U.S. delegation headed by then–Attorney General Janet Reno.

Alvarez has been a regular visitor to the Dominican Republic over the years, preserving family ties as well as researching the topics she writes about. On one of these visits, on assignment from the Nature Conservancy, Alvarez purchased land with her husband to grow organic coffee.[55] Their Dominican farm near the mountain town of Jarabacoa would grow to 260 acres, and their coffee, Café Alta Gracia, is now distributed in the United States by the Vermont Coffee Company. The couple's goals for cooperative, fair-trade practices, along with sustainable agricultural practices, are explained in *A Cafecito Story*, published in 2001, and on the Café Alta Gracia Web site. In addition to implementing organic farming methods and campaigning for fair trade, Julia and her husband started a school for the community. *A Cafecito Story* is a short fictional text by Alvarez about a meeting between a farmer/teacher from the Midwest and a poor coffee farmer in the Dominican mountains that results in the development of an organic farming community much like the one Alvarez and Eichner started, followed by an essay by Eichner, explaining that they are not the couple portrayed but setting forth the principles behind their project. On her Web site, Alvarez lists it as "a green fable for young readers of all ages."

Much of Alvarez's writing in the past decade has been for young readers, though she also published a volume of poetry in 2004, a fifth novel for adults in 2006, and a nonfiction book, *Once Upon a Quinceañera: Coming of Age in the USA*, in 2007. She has published two more picture books: *A Gift of Gracias: The Legend of Altagracia* in 2005 and *The Best Gift of All: The Legend of La Vieja Belén/El major regalo del mundo: La leyenda de la Vieja Belén* in 2009. Her first book for intermediate readers, *How Tía Lola Came to ~~Visit~~ Stay*, was published in 2001. A sequel is forthcoming in 2010, *How Tía Lola Learned to Teach*.[56] Audiobooks of these are also forthcoming.[57]

Her novels for older intermediate to teen readers are *Before We Were Free* (2002), *Finding Miracles* (2004), and *Return to Sender* (2009). Both *Before We Were Free* and *Return to Sender* received the Pura Belpré Award, which recognizes high quality in the depiction of Latino experience in works for young readers.[58] *Before We Were Free* fills in gaps in the story of *How the García Girls Lost Their Accents*, focusing on the cousins left behind in the Dominican Republic and continuing the narrative of resistance to Trujillo through the time of the dictator's death and its aftermath. Alvarez says that she wrote it because of the dearth of literature for young readers that depicts dictatorship in the Americas.[59] The subject of her most recent book and second Pura Belpré Award recipient, *Return to Sender*, is the plight of migrant workers and the children caught in the current controversy over immigration. Set in 2005–2006, it chronicles the problems of illegal migrant Mexican workers on a Vermont dairy farm. Alvarez's interest was sparked when she was asked to help area schools by translating for their growing Spanish-speaking population.[60]

Finding Miracles (titled on the cover and on Alvarez's Web site without capitalization as *finding miracles*) is written for young adult readers. Its subject is a 16-year-old girl's questions about her identity as an adopted child from a small, unnamed Latin American country, questions that become impossible to ignore when a family of refugees from the same country moves to Vermont. All three of these novels show friendships between Latin American children and U.S. American children, and all three include scenes in both the United States and the homeland. One teen in *Finding Miracles* identifies their group of friends as "border-liners" in the high school setting, occupying the intermediate ground between two very different groups.[61] Later in the novel, this term is applied to those who straddle two cultures. In interviews as well as in this novel, Alvarez claims this position as the best one from which to see two cultures clearly.[62] Those who inherit dual cultural identities, she argues, are the bridges between cultures. She also comments that stories start from an in-between position.[63]

Alvarez's most recent volume of poetry, *The Woman I Kept to Myself*, was published in 2004. Alvarez notes on her Web site that, though it was her first collection of poems in nine years, she had been writing poetry all along, fitting it in around other writing. Also in 2004, she received an honorary doctorate in letters from Union College in Schenectady, New York.[64]

Alvarez's most recent novel for adults, *Saving the World*, published in 2006, bridges two worlds, making use of historical material. This novel, like *How the García Girls Lost Their Accents* and *¡Yo!*, features a protagonist whose life circumstances are much like the author's. As the protagonist imagines the life of a historical figure from the early 19th century, she tries to make sense of the world and her role as a storyteller in the aftermath of the September 11, 2001, terrorist attacks. Always interested in the role of stories, Alvarez, in the past 10 years, has increasingly treated storytelling as a political act.[65]

In 2007, Alvarez published a work of nonfiction, *Once Upon a Quinceañera: Coming of Age in the USA*, a finalist for the National Book Critics Circle Award in the category of criticism.[66] Its wide appeal is evident in that it was reviewed on the Web site Teenreads, and, like Alvarez's other books, it is available in Spanish as well as English. This is the first book that Alvarez was ever commissioned to write, and she had feminist reservations about her suitability for the project. The *quinceañera* is a "girly-girl" kind of celebration, a "wedding without a groom," that makes a princess of a 15-year-old girl. Alvarez's research interested her in the ritual's possibilities for supporting and guiding Latina girls, who are disproportionately represented in statistics for poverty, teen pregnancy, high school dropout rates, and suicide.[67] She reflects on her own experiences as a young woman as she analyzes the *quinceañera*, in the final pages assembling her own "court" of wise women to pass along what they have learned.

Some degree of resolution of her relationship with her mother appears in these final pages as well, when she writes of her admiration for her mother's "resilience" in moving back to Santiago after four decades in the United States to care for Dr. Alvarez, who was suffering from Alzheimer's.[68] In 2007, too, she accepted an award for her mother from the United Nations in recognition of Mrs. Alvarez's work on behalf of the elderly during her 23-year career as an alternative representative from the Dominican Republic.[69]

In 2008, a dramatization of *How the García Girls Lost Their Accents*, by Karen Zacarías, had its world premiere in a three-week run at Round House Theatre in Bethesda, Maryland,[70] and was subsequently staged in 2010 at the Miracle Theatre in Portland, Oregon.[71] Alvarez received a third honorary degree, doctor of letters, from the University of Vermont in 2008 as well.[72]

In recognition of Alvarez's achievement in literature to date, she was awarded the F. Scott Fitzgerald Award in October 2009, given at the annual F. Scott Fitzgerald Conference at Montgomery College in Rockville, Maryland. First awarded in 1996, the centennial of Fitzgerald's birth, this award puts Alvarez in prestigious company. Other recipients have included William Styron, Norman Mailer, and John Updike; other women recipients are Joyce Carol Oates, Grace Paley, and Jane Smiley.[73] Alvarez was also recognized at the National Book Festival in Washington, D.C., earlier the same month. In her remarks, Alvarez observed that reading liberates people, allows their imaginations to roam freely, and nurtures their compassion when they identify with others in stories. She opposed these ways of thinking to the suppression of thought and ruptured relationships enforced by the Trujillo regime, noting that the first steps a dictatorship takes are to confiscate books and outlaw gatherings. She states that there is only one reason for people to gather in a society that is not free: to be indoctrinated with the single story that the government wants everyone to accept and repeat. In the final analysis, then, to share stories through reading and writing is to be free.[74]

2

ALVAREZ AND THE NOVEL,
ALVAREZ AS POET

Julia Alvarez is primarily known as a novelist, though she is also well established as a poet. Alvarez is a storyteller, and each novel tells a number of stories. Her art is grounded in the strong oral tradition of the Dominican Republic and her "first muse," *The Arabian Nights*, which was the only storybook she read in her childhood in the Dominican Republic.[1] The episodic form of her novels and the storyteller's presence as a character are indebted to these early influences. Her sensitivity to the spoken word and poetic rhythm also manifests itself in characterization: each of her characters speaks in his or her own voice. An awareness of words' subtle shades of meaning, so essential in her poetry, permeates her fiction. Moreover, the complex and sophisticated structure she employs in each of her novels owes much to her development as a poet who uses formal verse forms.

Her novels for adults share several important characteristics. They incorporate multiple story lines and points of view. Their episodic plots leave gaps in the narrative. The story lines are discontinuous as well as episodic: one form of discontinuity is chapter-to-chapter alternation between two stories; a second form is reverse chronological order; a third form is the juxtaposition of narratives by different characters. Point of view, too, is discontinuous, with shifts between third-person limited and first-person narration, between present tense and past tense.

Most of her novels have multiple settings. Only the second novel, *In the Time of the Butterflies*, is set entirely in the Dominican Republic. In others, the action moves between the Dominican Republic and the United States; in two, there are scenes in additional locations as well: Cuba in *In the Name of Salomé*; and Spain, the Caribbean, Mexico, and the Philippines in *Saving the World*. The time element, too, is discontinuous or nonchronological. In two novels, *How the García Girls Lost Their Accents* and *In the Name of Salomé*, Alvarez uses reverse chronology, with the effect of underscoring a significant, pervasive theme: the role of stories and memories in understanding identity. Long periods of time are covered in the semiautobiographical novels, *How the García Girls Lost Their Accents* and *¡Yo!* (34 to nearly 40 years), and *In the Name of Salomé* (118 years). In *¡Yo!*, a degree of circularity is created in the opening and closing chapters, one by Yo's mother, one by her father, both revisiting Yo's early childhood storytelling.

Point of view is complex when Alvarez uses multiple narrators. The many characters in *¡Yo!* generally corroborate one another's narratives but sometimes give contradictory views of Yo, and the reader sees these narrators from other characters' perspectives as well as hears their (other characters') voices. Many of these characters also appear in *How the García Girls Lost Their Accents*. For example, the teenaged Lucinda goes out for the evening with her North American cousins in the first novel, and her brother Mundín worries about her reputation; Lucinda, a divorced mother, is a member of the party, along with Mundín's wife, in the chronologically latest chapter with which *García Girls* opens; Mundín negotiates the exchange of gifts in the story of childhood, "The Human Body." In *¡Yo!*, Lucinda speaks twice, telling her own story about boarding school with Yo and reflecting on it at Yo's wedding; the reader also sees her from Dexter's perspective in "the suitor's" chapter. These multiple appearances lend greater complexity to Lucinda's character, complicating the way that the reader reads her own featured narrative.

Moreover, stories are layered within stories, and their context contributes significantly to the reader's understanding of their truth and their meaning. The third chapter of *How the García Girls Lost Their Accents* is a collection of stories that the mother tells. One is told at a family dinner; one is told to a psychiatrist at the time of Sandi's commitment for an eating disorder; one is told about Yo's childhood before a poetry reading, to Yo's current lover, a relationship of which the mother is unaware; the reader learns the fourth story, about Sofía, when Sandi tells her sisters about their mother's romanticized retelling of the story, which the reader has read in the preceding chapter, to a stranger the mother met in the hospital. Whenever the mother tells a story, its truth is problematized, as Sofía points out in the prologue to ¡Yo!, in which the mother's version of a memory contradicts Sofía's memory, leading her to question whether everyone in the family is lying.[2]

In the Time of the Butterflies is framed with a 1994 visit by a North American writer to the home and museum of the Mirabal sisters, the subjects of the novel, who died in the 1960s. The writer interviews the surviving sister, Dedé, over the course of a single afternoon and evening. Each of the novel's three sections starts with a chapter about Dedé, beginning in the present, when reflection or conversation prompts a memory of the past. Similarly, the novel ends in the present, after the interviewer's departure, in an epilogue. Once the memories have been set in motion in each of Dedé's chapters, each of her sisters has a chapter in each section. Overall, the narrative moves forward chronologically from 1938 to 1960 in a total of 12 chapters. In the epilogue, Dedé adds events that follow the murder of her sisters, skipping over a few more years, and closes the narrative in 1994. The effect of the structure is to investigate memory and the role of the survivor as well as to tell four individual stories. Moreover, the presence of a listener complicates Dedé's telling; the reader is aware that she is telling the story at a particular time, in a particular place, to a particular audience—and some of what the reader knows comes from the character Dedé herself; the reader is privy to information that the North American writer is not privy to.

In the Name of Salomé tells two stories, one in chronological order and one in reverse chronological order. The central characters are the poet Salomé Ureña and her daughter Camila Henríquez Ureña. The earliest events are in Salomé's childhood in 1856, and the novel ends with Camila's death at age 79 in 1973. Alvarez moves back and forth between the two stories, after a prologue set in 1960. Salomé's story moves forward in time from her childhood to her death; Camila's story moves back in time from the 1960 prologue. Thus the two stories move toward convergence. The structure is highlighted by using titles of Salomé's poems as chapter titles. Each story has eight chapters, Salomé's identified by the numbers uno through ocho and each titled with the name of a poem in Spanish, Camila's identified by the numbers one through eight and each titled with the name of one of her mother's poems in English translation. The end of Camila's story, 13 years after the prologue, is told in the epilogue. In an interview, Alvarez comments that Camila's life follows a pattern opposite to her mother's; she was a late bloomer, so their stories were mirror images.[3] By setting these narratives against each other in chronology, Alvarez brings out the contrasts. In this novel, as in *In the Time of the Butterflies*, a protagonist in the present launches into the earlier story from a particular time and place, for a particular audience, her friend Marion, who is driving her to Florida.

Similarly, *Saving the World* moves back and forth between two stories with alternating chapters. The contemporary story, in a post-9/11 world, covers novelist Alma Rodriguez's life from one autumn to the following summer. The story of the past, focusing on Isabel Sendales y Gómez, begins in 1803, continues over several years, and then skips from 1811 to 1830 to conclude with Isabel's death. Within this framework, each narrative moves forward chronologically. The structure underscores the novelist Alma's development of Isabel's narrative, her transitions into the narrative coming at points when contemporary events prompt reflection or escape into the imagined past.

In addition to telling interesting stories, Alvarez interrogates the roles that stories and language play in our lives. Her protagonists are writers; alternatively, in *In the Time of the Butterflies*, a storyteller and a listener-writer interact. Her writer characters reflect on the roles their stories play, questioning whether writing is important, most explicitly in *Saving the World*. In all of her novels, characters consider what is truthful, in what ways life experience is transformed into fiction, and how versions of the same event may differ according to who is telling the story.

Her most metafictional novel is ¡*Yo!*, in which each chapter is titled with a literary term, calling attention to the way the reader's expectations of genre shape the telling of a story, the way that writers structure effective stories, and the relative importance of one element over other elements of fiction in any given story. The mother's story, "Nonfiction," gives one version of the story of the father's gun hidden under the closet floor; yet the mother's reliability as a narrator has already been called into question in the prologue. The father's story, "Conclusion," gives another version of the story and, moreover, pointedly gives the story a different ending, revising the story as a father's blessing. The incident is also alluded to in *How the García Girls Lost Their Accents* in the eventful chapter about the Garcías' escape from the Dominican Republic. In revising the ending, the father says that the story as he remembers it is factual, but that stories can be changed: "I can add my own invention—that much I have learned from Yo. A new ending can be made out of what I now know."[4] In this conclusion to the novel, the father's story balances the mother's, but it also elaborates on the prologue and Yo's radio interview comments on the way art mirrors life.

The relationship between fiction and life stories is complicated by the strongly autobiographical element in Alvarez's fiction, especially *How the García Girls Lost Their Accents* and ¡*Yo!* Many of the incidents in Yolanda García's life derive from Alvarez's own life, as she points out herself in essays, autobiographical reflections in *Once Upon a Quinceañera*, and poems, which tell the same stories in different ways. The nickname Yo puns on the first-person singular pronoun, I, and calls the reader's attention to the autobiography at the heart of her fiction. Though Alvarez's own life is not as explicitly evoked in other novels, autobiographical details give verisimilitude to characters throughout Alvarez's fiction. Presumably she is fictionally present as the North American writer who visits Dedé Mirabal in *In the Time of the Butterflies*. The writer protagonist of *Saving the World* has achieved popular success and dislikes the publishing industry's need to create "buzz" in order to sell books, has had her identity as a Latina writer discussed by critics, and gets interested in Isabel's story much as Alvarez herself did.[5]

This blurring of autobiography and fiction is central to the novels about Yolanda. *How the García Girls Lost Their Accents* ends with a paragraph in which Yolanda, or possibly Alvarez, speaks directly to the reader about the source of her art. *¡Yo!* begins with a prologue that focuses on the family's reaction to Yolanda's publication of semiautobiographical fiction. In essays and interviews, Alvarez comments on the family storm that her first novel stirred up.[6] By incorporating it in the sequel, she adds another layer of autobiographical truth to her fiction.

The structure of the first novel seems to be influenced by psychoanalytical practice: plagued by unsatisfied "cravings" in her 30s, Yolanda works her way back to a childhood incident that caused her to have nightmares that originated in fear and guilt. The traumatic memory, she says, is the origin of her storytelling. By working retrospectively to rediscover the painful past and analyze its meaning, she frees herself to begin healing and to reforge a new, stronger identity than the one that crumbled when her marriage ended. In the sequel, Alvarez seems to offer a different view of identity and of understanding the past as socially constructed.

Like the shifts in time and place in Alvarez's intricately structured novels, point of view shifts with pronoun use, as well as from character to character. In *How the García Girls Lost Their Accents*, most of the chapters are told in third person, but the perspective in most of the chapters is limited to one character's view of events or one character's story. The exception is the critical chapter with which part III begins, about the day of the family's escape from the Dominican Republic with the secret police on their heels. Within this single chapter, the point of view shifts rapidly, with third-person narration maintained in the first part, followed by two closing first-person narratives. The rapid shifts emphasize the fast pace of events and the turbulence of emotions. The chapter's final narrative is by Chucha, the servant who oversees the closing of the house after the family's departure; told in past tense, it emphasizes the finality of their departure. The novel also contains first-person narratives, several of them Yolanda's. Significantly, the novel ends with a paragraph of direct address to the reader, telling where the stories come from. Here, the writer-protagonist's and author's identities blend.

Similarly, throughout the novel, there are shifts between past-tense and present-tense narration. The first chapter, which takes place in 1989, is in the present tense, as is the second chapter, which sets out to tell the stories the mother has about each of her girls, stories that she tells and retells. Two chapters combine portions in present tense with portions in past tense: the chapter when Yolanda is hospitalized and the chapter about their escape from the Dominican Republic.

Like *How the García Girls Lost Their Accents, ¡Yo!* has a tripartite structure, though in this case, the novel has a prologue in addition to 15 chapters. Similar, also, is the pivotal first chapter of part III in *¡Yo!*: this chapter is told by the wedding guests, shifting from one point of view to another, sometimes in first person, sometimes in third person. Throughout the novel, some chapters are narrated in first person, some in third person, and some are in present tense, some in past tense. These variations help to distinguish characters' voices.

In *In the Name of Salomé*, Alvarez uses first-person, past-tense narration for Salomé's story and third-person, present-tense narration for Camila's story. The epilogue, focusing on Camila, is an exception to this rule: here Camila reflects on her life and claims her whole name, Salomé Camila Henríquez Ureña, for her headstone. Similarly, in *Saving the World*, Alvarez uses first-person, past-tense narration for the historical story of Isabel that unfolds in 1803–1830, and third-person, present-tense narration for the contemporary story of the novelist, Alma. The use of present tense gives immediacy to the modern or contemporary story, while the use of third person lends it verisimilitude: the reader is likely to believe what the narrative voice is telling about the protagonist's thoughts and feelings. Use of the first person and past tense for the historical story helps to draw contemporary readers into identifying with a long-dead woman in a dramatically different social context.

In the Time of the Butterflies introduces another layer of interpretation by framing the story in the writer's interview with Dedé and her reflections. Each chapter set in the present day is told in third person, using present tense and shifting to past tense when Dedé's thoughts turn to memories. Each of the other sisters' chapters is in first person and past tense. María Teresa's chapters take the form of diary entries, contrasting with her sisters' narratives. The first-person accounts individualize the three near-mythic sisters, who are so often referred to collectively as "the Butterflies" or "las Mariposas" or, simply, "the Mirabal sisters." The structure of Dedé's chapters conveys the sense that memory is a reliving of the past. Throughout these chapters, the reader has access to Dedé's thoughts, as the visiting writer does not. But in the epilogue, the reader finally hears her voice, as she reflects on what it means to be a survivor. These narrative choices serve Alvarez's project of demythologizing the sisters and bringing them to life as real women.

Alvarez began her writing career as a poet, inspired from an early age by Walt Whitman and Emily Dickinson, as she says in her poem "Passing On." Dickinson's slant rhyme, or approximate rhyme, is a feature in much of Alvarez's work, especially her early poems, and Whitman appears often, not only in allusions, but also in Alvarez's use of repetition and listing and, sometimes, in her rhythms. Other voices that echo in her poems are women's voices from her childhood, also mentioned in "Passing On." Allusions to a number of poets attest to her conscious working within the tradition of American poetry. Describing a typical work day in *Something to Declare*, Alvarez writes: "I drink my coffee in the study, reading poetry (Jane Kenyon, George Herbert, Rita Dove, Robert Frost, Elizabeth Bishop, Rhina Espaillat, Jane Shore, Emily Dickinson . . .). I like to start the day with a poem or two or three or four. This is the first music I hear, the most essential."[7]

Alvarez uses a range of verse forms. She makes extensive use of the sonnet (though the form of the sonnet can vary substantially in her sonnet sequences) and the ode. In "Why I Teach,"[8] Alvarez explains the way she pushes creative writing students, requiring them to practice traditional forms and techniques. She uses the same traditional forms and techniques in her own poems. Joined to her use of poetic conventions is an underlying awareness of the way a phrase or a line would sound in Spanish.

Alvarez makes impressive use of a difficult form to comment on the challenges of expressing herself exclusively in English in "Bilingual Sestina," with which she begins the volume, *The Other Side El Otro Lado*.[9] The sestina has six six-line stanzas followed by a final three-line stanza. Instead of rhyme, it uses a complicated pattern of repetition of the last word of each line. Alvarez produces a variation on the form, changing the form of the word (so that *said* at the end of the first line appears later as *say* or *saying*) and even translating it (so that *nombres* in the first stanza appears later as *nombre* or *numbering*). The use of this complex form ironically undermines the claim of the poem, that some of what she has to say cannot be said in English.

Homecoming[10] features two sonnet sequences, "33," which started out as a cycle of 33 sonnets to mark Alvarez's 33rd birthday, and "Redwing Sonnets," a cycle of 10 sonnets. The sonnet form is traditionally used for a meditation, especially on love or philosophy. Typical English sonnets follow either the Petrarchan, or Italian, model of an eight-line stanza followed by a six-line stanza, or the Shakespearean, or English, model of three four-line stanzas (quatrains) followed by a couplet that pithily sums up the poem. Also, the traditional sonnet in English uses the iambic pentameter line, employing five feet (pentameter) consisting of an unstressed syllable followed by a stressed syllable (the iamb). Contemporary users of the sonnet form often diverge from this model in significant ways.

Alvarez's sonnets in "33" sometimes follow the English model in rhyme scheme, although her quatrains do not complete thoughts but rather employ enjambment to carry the idea into the next line. For example, the eighth sonnet uses the conventional rhyme scheme of *ababcdcdefefgg*, and the first two quatrains end with, first, a comma and significant pause and, second, a period. However, the third quatrain and final couplet consist of six sentences, four of which begin in the middle of a line; the final line contains two complete sentences. The poem is about the vegetarian speaker's date at a steakhouse. The topic is the motive for dating. The speaker comments on her desire just to talk. The appetite for sex, and for love, is likened to the appetite for red meat; the possibility for love is an especially fine cut. A new sentence starts midline, in which love is contrasted with sex in terms of hunger. Instead of summing up the idea in a final couplet, Alvarez begins in the middle of the 12th line, but the final two-and-a-half lines work in the same way that the pithy final couplet traditionally does, stressing the bloodiness of the rare steak, the prominence of the body's needs. This sonnet generally uses iambic pentameter, with some lines in tetrameter, and is more metrically regular than many of her other sonnets.

Other sonnets in the sequence are variations on the Italian model of an eight-line stanza and a six-line stanza. In the 15th sonnet, the sentence break that occurs in the middle of the ninth line marks the shift from the first part to the second part of the poem. This sonnet shows skillful use of enjambment throughout in a discussion of loneliness, loss, and separation considered as a chronic illness; for example, the break between lines eight and nine emphasizes separation. The final two lines function as the pithy summation, but the sentence is punctuated as a question, not a statement.

In the "Redwing Sonnets," Alvarez experiments with enjambment. In the second sonnet, she continues an idea from the first sonnet, starting it with a relative clause to comment on the thought that ends the first sonnet, a sentence of five lines. She makes even more obvious use of enjambment to connect the second sonnet with the third, breaking mid-sentence after a phrase set off by dashes in the 14th line of the second sonnet. The second sonnet consists of one seven-line sentence, and a sentence that begins on the eighth line and ends in the middle of the first line of the third sonnet. Additionally, Alvarez uses slant rhyme, internal rhyme (within a single line), alliteration, and assonance (repetition of a vowel sound) effectively in the sequence, appropriately using sound to reinforce the theme that human utterances are like birdsongs.

The Woman I Kept to Myself uses the ode form of three 10-line stanzas in iambic pentameter. Odes can take a range of forms, their unifying characteristic being a focus on a serious subject, the musing on the topic showing an emotional rise and fall. The English Romantic poets adopted, and adapted, the ode form. Keats's odes typically use the form of three 10-line stanzas. Alvarez calls attention to her use of the form in the first poem of *The Woman I Kept to Myself*, after the *Seven Trees* poems with which the book opens. Its title is "Intimations of Mortality from a Recollection in Early Childhood," a direct allusion to Wordsworth's famous ode, "Intimations of Immortality from Recollections of Early Childhood."

Alvarez uses many allusions in her poetry, sometimes naming a poet (sometimes surprisingly, as at the end of "The Animals Review Pictures of a Vanished Human Race" in *The Woman I Kept to Myself*) or other writers (Austen, Dickinson, Eliot, and Woolf in "Abbot Academy" in the same volume). She uses actual quotation sparingly (an example being her poem titled, after Auden, "'Poetry Makes Nothing Happen'?"[11]) but more frequently embeds allusions, such as Prospero's line in *The Tempest*, "Lie there, my art," used without quotation marks or attribution to end one of the sonnets in the "33" cycle. Her allusiveness also takes the form of variations on famous titles (such as her "Ars Politica,"[12] after the tradition of poems titled "Ars Poetica") or lines like the seasonal reference in "Lunch Hour, 1971"[13] that echoes the opening of Shakespeare's *Richard III*. In addition to the English and American poetry she most frequently alludes to, Dante is an important figure, invoked in essays and fiction as well as in the last of the *Seven Trees* poems, which focuses on mortality.

In summation, structure plays an important role in Alvarez's work. It is the aspect of her fiction with which she most conspicuously experiments. Her poems are deceptively straightforward, often conversational, but their tight structure demonstrates her control and artistry.

The order of repeated words in the sestina form usually follows this scheme. In the first stanza, with ending words labeled *ABCDEF*:

Stanza 2: *FAEBDC*
Stanza 3: *CFDABE*
Stanza 4: *ECBFAD*
Stanza 5: *DEACFB*
Stanza 6: *BDFECA*

In Stanza 7, the tercet (or three-line stanza), the words are repeated midline and at the end of the line, reproducing the original order.[14]

DISCUSSION QUESTIONS

- What is the effect on narrative momentum, or on reader engagement, when Alvarez shifts perspective from one character to another or from one point of view to another? What is the effect on momentum when the reader encounters a chapter in the form of diary entries?
- One of Alvarez's achievements is to establish distinctive voices for different characters. The widest range of characters appears in *¡Yo!* Do you accept all of the narratives about Yo as equally true, given these differences?
- Some of the experiences that Alvarez writes about appear in both prose fiction and poems. What advantages does poetic form have in a poem like "Spic," which describes an experience that also shaped the chapter "Trespass" in *How the García Girls Lost Their Accents*?

3

HOW THE GARCÍA GIRLS LOST
THEIR ACCENTS
(1991)

Alvarez's first novel[1] is semiautobiographical, tracing a story very much like the Alvarez family's. The 15 chapters create a single narrative of the four García daughters' immigrant experience after a sudden, wrenching departure from the Dominican Republic. They leave behind an extended family, a way of life, and a country, as well as a language. The title emphasizes the role that language plays in their acquisition of American identities and the price they pay: their "accents" are "lost." With its emphasis on "how" the transition occurred, the title suggests that the stories are steps in a progression, traced back through memory in reverse chronological order. The structure follows the pattern of Freudian psychoanalysis: by reclaiming the past and understanding its meaning, one begins to heal traumas rooted in childhood experiences.

The García sisters may have "lost their accents," but they have not lost the sense of violation that Yolanda claims as the source of her art. They internalize their heritage: Dominican lives violated by the brutal dictator, Rafael Trujillo, who governed the Dominican Republic for 30 years. The threat of violence hovers at the edge of consciousness, affecting family relationships in ways that the girls cannot understand until later in life. On the day of their emigration, the threat becomes visible in their home when the secret police (SIM) come for their father.

In addition to disrupting chronological order, the stories disrupt the usual coming-of-age plot by deferring the protagonist's arrival to stable adult identity. Yolanda is still resolving questions of identity and home in her 30s. The García sisters remain bicultural rather than assimilate fully, making trips "home" to visit *la familia*, once the worst of the political turmoil has passed. Yet their teen years are notably "American," and they share their generation's styles, trends, and politics in the divided U.S. society of the 1960s. Their resistance to parental expectations is intensified by the patriarchal values of the culture they come from, with its limited options for women. Moreover, their parents' caution and conservatism are intensified by the habits of secrecy and silence imposed by the dictatorship. The sisters' rebellion against patriarchy is fueled by the sexual revolution, and the timing of their immigration, coinciding with adolescence, dramatizes the link between their freedom as young women and their freedom as U.S. citizens.

The stories start in 1989, with Yolanda's first visit to the Dominican Republic in several years, and end in 1956, with her traumatic memory of violation and terror. Most of the chapters are told in the third-person limited point of view, but some chapters are first-person narratives, including several of Yolanda's stories, most importantly the final one that focuses on the origin of her storytelling.

Part I opens with "Antojos" (cravings), when Yolanda's Americanization and lack of understanding of Dominican culture become evident at a family gathering, where she announces her desire to travel around the country alone. Yolanda is secretly contemplating a new life for herself in her homeland, craving guavas and craving a home. An elderly servant associates an *antojo* with domination by a spirit, giving a spiritual explanation for Yolanda's restlessness.[2] Her aunts warn of dangers in traveling alone: there are rumors of violence, her Spanish is rusty, and she looks like a North American—like a missionary, according to her fashionable cousin Lucinda.

Traveling in the mountains, she stops at a *cantina*, or bar, in a small village where her car is a novelty that attracts a crowd of boys. The *cantina* is decorated with an old poster advertising Palmolive soap, showing a blond woman in the shower, her mouth open in an expression that suggests an ecstatic cry to Yolanda. Yolanda satisfies her craving in a grove of ripe guavas that the boys guide her to, reached by driving down a deteriorating track. When she tries to return to the village, she discovers she has a flat tire, and little daylight remains. She sends the *cantina* owner's grandson, her only companion by now, for help from the big house she passed earlier. Alone, she is fearful when two machete-equipped workers suddenly emerge from the dense foliage, but when her tongue loosens in a flood of English, she mentions the owners of the big house by name and instantly gets their respect. They change the tire, refusing payment. Seeing the Palmolive poster again as she drives away from the village, Yolanda reinterprets the blond model's open mouth: the woman seems to be calling out to someone "over a great distance."[3] Too much distance lies between Yolanda and her homeland. She can satisfy her craving for guavas more easily than her longing for a unified identity and sense of belonging somewhere.

The second chapter, "The Kiss," dramatizes the gulf between the parents' and daughters' values in a story of transgressions. Several years earlier, the father, snooping through Sofía's dresser, found letters from the German lover she had met in Colombia. He screamed at her, accusing her of being a whore. His rage and frustration come from his belief that she invited violation; she feels violated by her father's invasion of her privacy. Sofía left home and married Otto, but her father was not reconciled until the birth of her second child, a son whom they have named after him. Sofía invites the whole family to her home for her father's 70th birthday celebration, to be followed the next day by her son's christening. She has spent weeks preparing, but her father takes her efforts for granted. Her frustration builds until she brings the evening's last game to an end by embarrassing him. He is blindfolded and made to guess the names of the women who kiss him. Each time he starts with "Mami," followed by his three oldest daughters' names—but he never names Sofía. Outraged by his continued rejection, she sits on his lap and tongue-kisses his ear, arousing him. He tears off his blindfold and sees the shameless look on his youngest daughter's face that he remembers from their confrontation over her love letters, the look that proclaims her freedom from his values.

In the third chapter, the mother tells a story about each of her girls. Carla's story is about wanting red sneakers that her family could not buy for her. Yo's is about being left behind on a New York City bus, where her parents find her reciting a poem to strangers, a story that the mother tells to her neighbor at a poetry reading, who happens to be Yo's current lover. Her story is about separation, compensated by sharing poetry. The third story is told to a psychiatrist when the parents commit Sandi to a psychiatric hospital, ostensibly for an eating disorder. Convinced she is turning into a monkey, Sandi reads constantly to acquire as much understanding of being human as she can in the time left to her. This story conveys the trauma caused by loss of language and identity. Sofía's story is the mother's romanticized version of her marriage, a version that omits the confrontation over the letters. Sandi reports this episode of storytelling to her sisters, who have gathered for the birth of Sofía's first child, a daughter. As the sisters talk, the mother arrives with Carla's and Sofía's husbands, and, as the mother begins telling a story to the infant girl, the chapter ends, "Everyone listens to the mother."[4]

The chapter "Joe" is about Yolanda's breakdown after leaving her husband, who calls her Joe. Yolanda watches her psychiatrist from her hospital window when he goes to play tennis, flashing back to the end of her marriage when she became preoccupied with language. Language play with her husband turned unpleasant because they "didn't speak the same language"[5] and communication dissolved into babble. Yolanda felt her identity was fragmented by his list of pros and cons for marrying her. Hospitalized because of her constant, compulsive speaking in riddles and quotations, she has an allergic reaction to certain words, including "love" and her own name. As she watches Dr. Payne, her own pain gathers at a point in her stomach and bursts forth as a black bird, like Poe's raven, which escapes through her window and attacks the doctor, leaving her heart "an empty nest."[6] Experimenting with the words that cause her allergic reaction, she ends with an outpouring of words that rumble like thunder as she reflects, "There is no end to what can be said about the world."[7]

The last chapter in part I, "The Rudy Elmenhurst Story," depicts an earlier failed romance in Yolanda's college years. Despite the sisters' talk about being "wild," she stops short of sexual intimacy. She becomes involved with Rudy Elmenhurst after helping him write a sonnet for English class, not realizing that it is full of double entendres, which her classmates immediately recognize. He pressures her nightly for sex, using distressingly crude language. After his parents visit, treating her as a new cultural experience for Rudy and patronizing her with a compliment on her unaccented English, Rudy confesses his expectation that she would be more "hot-blooded"[8] than Anglo girls. Hurt, Yolanda walks away from their relationship. Five years later, he calls her, but again he wants only sex and dismisses her need for emotional intimacy as "hang-ups" he expected her to have shed. After kicking him out, she drinks his expensive Bordeaux from the bottle like "a decadent wild woman."[9]

This episode marks a significant point in Yolanda's "loss of accent": though speaking unaccented English, she is deaf to its nuances in her peers' language, as she is resistant to their casual sexual involvement. Moreover, she crashes head-on into crude stereotypes about Latinas. Rudy Elmenhurst is the first in a series of unsatisfactory men who cannot understand her bicultural identity. At the beginning of the story, her aspiration to wildness is contrasted with Sofía's actual wildness, the behavior that will result in Sofía's conspicuous violation of family expectations. The emptiness Yolanda feels during her hospitalization, when she is unable to find someone who speaks the same language, is still with her when she tries to satisfy her cravings at age 39, the distance between her two cultures symbolized by the blond woman on the Palmolive poster.

Part II, working back from 1970 to 1960, begins with "A Regular Revolution," focusing on all four sisters. It is now clear that the family will not be returning "home," and the father becomes a U.S. citizen. Though they are outsiders at their expensive boarding school, the girls are reconciled to the United States by their new freedom from parental control. The parents, seeing changes in the girls, arrange summer visits to the Dominican Republic, and respond to improper behavior by threatening to send the girls "back home to help set [them] straight."[10] Fifi's smoking, Carla's use of depilatory cream, Yoyo's reading about women's bodies, and Sandi's all-night "calculus tutorial" are skirmishes in "a regular revolution."[11] When the mother finds Fifi's marijuana, Fifi is punished with a year in the Dominican Republic. The next summer, her sisters find her unrecognizable, a "Spanish-American princess"[12] with a boyfriend who tells her what she can wear and does not allow her to talk to other men or leave the house without his permission. Fifi's transformation, Carla says, is "a borderline schizoid response to traumatic cultural displacement."[13] They get the old Fifi back by exposing her improper dating behavior, which shocks their elders. This time, her punishment is to return to the United States. Paradoxically, just when the sisters have won their revolution, they are trapped again by love when Tía Carmen defends them to their mother and "revives the old homesickness."[14] They are like the caged monkeys in an experiment who refused to leave when the cage door was opened. Though Fifi regards her sisters as traitors, they feel justified in releasing her to a future of her own choosing, a future that is also a wilderness awaiting her exploration. Freedom is a paradoxical gift: there are no guidelines, as well as no restrictions.

The chapter "Daughter of Invention" explains the bond between Yoyo and her mother in an episode of invention with the English language that challenges the father's Spanish accent. Laura, who tries to invent a gadget to make a lot of money, finds idiomatic English challenging: "Necessity is the daughter of invention" is her rendering of "Necessity is the mother of invention."[15] Yoyo, in contrast, rapidly becomes a fluent writer in English. However, when asked to deliver a speech on Teachers' Day, she struggles to write one. Her father's efforts to help, when he recites his high school valedictorian speech, are hampered by her difficulty in understanding his formal Spanish.

Finally, Yoyo finds inspiration in Walt Whitman—"He most honors my style who learns under it to destroy the teacher"—and writes freely, "sound[ing] like herself in English."[16] But her father is so dismayed by the disrespect he hears in her speech that he tears it up. When she accuses him of being like the dictator they left behind, his anger is as disproportionate as her accusation, and he chases her to her bedroom, where he tries to break the lock. Later, her mother comes to help her, and together they craft a combination of complimentary clichés in "a speech wrought by necessity and without much invention."[17] In apology, her father gives Yolanda a good typewriter with every accessory her mother could have envisioned, acknowledging her writing ability.

Adjusting to their new freedom of expression is as difficult for the parents as adjusting to English after their restricted lives in their homeland, like those of the caged monkeys. As English becomes their daughters' language, inevitably the girls express American ideas, as the quintessential American poet Whitman did. In this story, Yolanda explicitly links political tyranny with patriarchy, a link that explains why the generational battle is so heated: losing their accents means choosing values that differ from their parents'. Moreover, because words are so important to her, she experiences her father's destruction of her speech as an attack on her as a person.

In the chapter "Trespass," Carla's story, which occurs only a year after their arrival in the United States, links violation with sexual development. When she encounters a pedophile, she associates his exposure of his genitals with her classmates' insults, vulnerable in both situations because of her young woman's body and her status as a foreigner. This chapter illustrates the difficulties of interactions with authorities when one's English is too limited to explain a crime, especially one involving sexual acts and male bodies. Additionally, Carla's fragile self-confidence in finding her way through the New York City streets to school suffers a setback because the incident occurs on her long walk along a stretch of empty land, fenced off with a "No Trespassing" sign that Carla at first interpreted as a reminder to be good, remembering the phrase from the Lord's Prayer.

At home, two all-American-looking, gun-bearing policemen ask her what occurred, what the man looked like, and what kind of car he drove. Her difficulties in reporting take several forms: the policemen's gruffness reminds her of the boys who taunt her on the playground about her English and her body; she lacks English words and the knowledge to describe the male body and the act of masturbation that she witnessed; she is already repressing details of the experience and cannot remember what the man looks like; and she does not know enough about American cars to identify the model. Her trauma is intensified by the officers' questioning. Afterward, all she wants is to return to the security of her

Dominican Republic home, where the people around her loved her, and to childhood innocence.

Yolanda's first-person narrative, in the chapter "Snow," depicts Cold War tensions during the Garcías' first year in the United States and simultaneously illustrates the cultural knowledge embedded in language. Learning English words is not enough; concepts are equally important. At school, Yolanda participates in air-raid drills and learns about nuclear fallout; on television, President John F. Kennedy speaks gravely about the possibility of war during the Cuban missile crisis. When Yolanda sees her first snowflakes, she thinks the snow is nuclear fallout and cries out, "Bomb! Bomb!"[18] The teacher reassures her that these are simply the beautiful snowflakes that she has been taught are as individual as "irreplaceable" people.[19] Cold War anxiety is another form of living with terror, like living under a dictator.

In Sandi's narrative, "Floor Show," she learns to manipulate adults through her awareness of sexual transgression and regains some sense of control that has been lost in the family's reduced circumstances and neighbors' expressions of prejudice. The father's mentor takes the whole family out to dinner, and the mother impresses on the girls their sense of obligation. They are too poor to pay their own way, with Dr. García's income limited until he is licensed to practice in the United States. Dressing up and taking a taxi for the first time since their arrival reminds the girls of their life in the Dominican Republic. Sandi is intrigued that the restaurant's Spanish décor, food, and flamenco floor show are valued as an expensive evening's entertainment, contrasting this attitude with their neighbors' complaints about their loud Spanish conversations and smelly foreign food.

Dr. Fanning's wife drinks too much and kisses Dr. García when he accompanies her and Sandi to the restrooms. He is nonplussed, not wanting to offend her because he needs her husband's help. Then she joins the flamenco dancers onstage, entertaining the rest of the diners but embarrassing her husband. After the floor show, a dancer brings a basket of flamenco-costumed Barbie dolls to the table, offering them for sale, and Sandi takes advantage of the situation by telling Mrs. Fanning that she and her sisters want dolls. Sandi at first refuses to thank Mrs. Fanning for the gift, but then, prodded by her mother, she holds her doll up to the woman's cheek, makes a kissing sound, and says, "*Gracias.*"[20]

This section of the novel brings out the challenges of assimilation. The García girls have accents in the years 1960–1970. They encounter prejudice, but as they acquire the new language, along with deeper cultural knowledge, they leave their first language and values behind, along with their childhood innocence and sense of safety. They adapt, but their acculturation creates a gulf between them and their parents, between them and their family "back home."

Part III, spanning from 1960 to 1956, shows the pivotal period of their escape and the girls' earlier childhood world, a world that generally felt secure but held hints of adult knowledge and dangers, so that the traumas with which they wrestle as adults are shown to have roots even deeper than their abrupt emigration, roots in the oppressive class structure, patriarchy, and totalitarian government, as well as in transgressions they committed or witnessed.

The story set in 1960, "The Blood of the Conquistadores," is about the whole family on the day they escape from the Dominican Republic. This complex, fast-paced story is told mostly in present tense, with a shifting point of view told in third person except for two closing first-person, past-tense narratives by Fifi and the servant Chucha. This complexity reflects the atmosphere of emergency when Trujillo's secret police, the SIM, arrive. Dr. García goes into hiding, his wife entertains the SIM, the older children are sent to another house in the compound, their father's friend from the American embassy arrives, and Chucha, a practitioner of *santería*, works a protective spell for the children before they leave for the United States.

Yolanda is on the alert after seeing her father slip silently down the hall. Previously beaten for boasting about her father's illegal gun, she knows now to keep family secrets. The mother intimidates the SIM officers with her social position, treating them as honored guests, but she sends the two oldest girls to their aunt's home as soon as possible. From there, a call has gone to the U.S. embassy, bringing their American friend to confer with the girls' uncles and arrange a quick, secret trip to the United States. All the while, Yolanda and Sofía are still at home with the SIM officers, Sofía resisting molestation. In her first-person retrospective narrative, Sofía says that she was too young to remember anything except the ritual that Chucha performed, praying over the girls. Chucha has the final word, telling how the servants have closed up the house and lending a special note of finality to the narrative with her habit of sleeping in her coffin, preparing for death. Lying quietly, she listens to her heartbeat and the blood rushing through her veins like something she has forgotten to turn off.

Thus the chapter ends with an emphasis on blood. "The blood of the conquistadores" runs through the children's veins, but the blood that has been shed by the conquerors, including Trujillo, is also suggested. Chucha is a survivor of the massacre of thousands of Haitian residents that Trujillo ordered.

The García girls' childhood Eden is filled with forbidden knowledge—the threat of violence, or violation, coming usually from men outside the family. The girls are fascinated by the arts from an early age—musical instruments, painting sets, and modeling clay—but their attempts to develop these interests are linked with disobedience and pain, hence with guilt. Later in life, they associate banishment from their Eden with guilt for transgressions: lying, spying, witnessing forbidden scenes, and pushing boundaries of sexual propriety.

The adults in this wealthy family purchase gifts for the children from FAO Schwartz, New York City's famous toy store. Yolanda's story, "The Human Body," revolves around an exchange of gifts, which results in guilty knowledge of the body when her cousin Mundín offers his modeling clay and transparent "human body" doll in return for seeing her genitals. Their reenactment of the biblical Fall is made explicit through several details. Mundín shapes his clay into a snake to tempt Yoyo. She knows she's doing wrong, remembering the nuns' teaching about Adam and Eve's sin. Negotiations are carried out in the forbidden coal shed, intensifying Yoyo's awareness of wrongdoing. When an aunt discovers them there, Yolanda excuses their transgression with the lie that they saw the *guardia* lurking around the compound, a lie that sends the adults into a frenzy of hiding things and lets the children off the hook.

Sandi's discovery of the human body comes in "Still Lives," when her art lessons end in shock and pain. She and her cousins begin lessons with the German-born wife of a Dominican sculptor after the adults notice Sandi's gift for drawing. But she is bored by Doña Charito's strict limits on their drawing, so she wanders outside the house, eventually discovering the mentally disturbed sculptor at work in his studio, naked and chained. She witnesses him mounting a realistic sculpture of a woman, his penis erect. When he sees her, he lunges at her, and she falls, panicked, breaking her arm. She loses her drawing ability but not her artist's temperament, now frustrated. Yet, when the artist's new crèche is unveiled at the cathedral at Christmas, she discovers that the sculpted Virgin's face is her own, wearing the expression she wore when she looked through his window. Sandi's story links forbidden sexual knowledge to what is holy as well as to art.

Carla's story, in "An American Surprise," recalls her moral dilemma over a disappointing gift that she gives away to the maid, Gladys, causing Gladys's dismissal. The gift is a mechanical bank in the shape of a haloed Mary who rises heavenward when a coin is inserted. Carla feels guilty about giving away the bank, and she is sad when Gladys leaves. When her bank is restored, she humors her father by putting a coin into the bank, only to discover that it no longer works—Mary rises only halfway and remains stuck.

The final and chronologically earliest story, "The Drum," is Yoyo's. In her conclusion, she claims the stories as her own art. Her drum is linked in memory with stealing a kitten from its mother. The cat's litter is in the coal shed, which Yoyo associates with a host of spirits that their laundry maid claimed to see. She is not sure of the rules governing taking kittens as pets; above all, she fears that the mother cat will hurt her if she takes the black kitten she has named Schwartz. She seeks advice from a stranger, whom she at first speculates may be the devil. Initially, she accepts his adult knowledge that she must wait another seven days; the kitten will die if she takes it from its mother too soon. But when she hears his gun go off in the orange grove, where shooting is prohibited, she dismisses his stricture because he himself is breaking rules. She hides the kitten in her drum, beating the drum to cover the kitten's mewing and to keep the mother cat from pursuing. The noisy gun frightens the mother cat away, and when Yoyo, disturbed by the kitten's meows, tosses it out the window, the mother cat is nowhere to be seen. The police are called, and the trespassing hunter's gun is silenced, but Yoyo does not know the injured kitten's fate. She begins having nightmares of being threatened by the mother cat. Even after she gives her drum away, she is haunted by the cat for years.

After the move to the United States, she stopped dreaming about the cat, she says. Speaking directly to the reader, she summarizes the major changes in her life, saying, "You understand I am collapsing all time now so that it fits in what's left in the hollow of my story?"[21] She tells how she began writing about the events of childhood, troubled by "story ghosts and story devils" and insomnia.[22] Her art is ultimately rooted in a sense of "a black furred thing lurking in the corners of [her] life" that grieves over violation.[23] Ultimately, because the girls were torn suddenly from their homeland—the source of their security but also the source of danger—their pain and sense of dislocation leave all of them craving something they have lost. The girls, like the kitten, have been rudely taken from the mother—their motherland and their mother tongue—and then thrown out to fend for themselves.

Linking oppressive patriarchal values with violent political oppression, at the threshold of sexual maturation, the girls define freedom in sexual terms and in terms of speaking out: they will not be silenced. Thus, asserting their individuality and rights as women becomes a duty of citizenship. This assertion, however, leaves them unsatisfied in many of their relationships, due partly to Anglo Americans' prejudices. The García girls seek to overcome their outsider status through their

In *Something to Declare*, Alvarez describes her family's sudden departure from the Dominican Republic and its long-term effect: "For weeks that soon became months and years, I would think in this way. What was going on right this moment back home? . . . I would wonder if those papers [allowing the family to leave] had set us free from everything we loved."[24]

Santería is a Caribbean religion that blends elements of African religion with Christianity. Most practitioners of *santería* are baptized Catholics. Chucha, who has a prominent role in Alvarez's novel for young adults, *Before We Were Free*, predicts the future and invokes protection from the saints as well as spirits.[25]

acquiring of the language—that is, by losing their accents. Once they have succeeded, they find that their Spanish has been tinged with an American accent. Loving *la familia*, they are no longer part of it in the way that they were before emigrating, and the result is a desire that can never quite be satisfied.

DISCUSSION QUESTIONS

- How does leaving the Dominican Republic affect each of the sisters individually? What particular challenges does each García girl face in adjusting to the United States?
- What is the impact of immigration on the parents? How does their status change? What effect does this have on their authority over their daughters?
- A number of chapters deal with transgressions, violations, or invasion of personal space. What is the cumulative effect of these episodes?

4

IN THE TIME OF THE BUTTERFLIES
(1994)

In the Time of the Butterflies[1] was a critical success, nominated for the National Book Critics Circle Award. Based on the lives of the three Mirabal sisters known as *las Mariposas*, or the Butterflies, this political and historical novel brought home to U.S. readers the impact of totalitarianism close to home in the Caribbean. In the Dominican Republic, it helped to counteract lingering silences about Trujillo's three-decade dictatorship. The Mirabal sisters had been involved in the underground, imprisoned, and released after an international inquiry into treatment of political prisoners in the Dominican Republic. On their way home from visiting their still-imprisoned husbands, the women and their driver were murdered on Trujillo's orders. After they were beaten and strangled in a cane field near a lonely mountain pass, their bodies were placed in the car and it was pushed off the road to simulate an automobile accident. Instead of destroying opposition with this action, Trujillo solidified the opposition, and he himself was assassinated only six months later. The women, already respected and secretly supported, became legendary in death.

Alvarez's imagination was captured by the sisters who had captured the imagination of most Dominicans. She felt a strong personal interest in them because of her father's involvement in the underground, which impelled their own flight to the United States. The Mirabal sisters' murder occurred only four months after the Alvarezes' emigration, when Alvarez and her sisters were complaining daily that they wanted to go home to the Dominican Republic. When their father brought home the issue of *Time* magazine that reported the Butterflies' deaths, Alvarez was forbidden to read it.[2] The parental ban underscores the silence about Trujillo and the SIM that her parents continued to maintain in the United States.

The Mirabal story began to engage Alvarez's imagination as a writer in the mid-1980s, when she was writing a paragraph-long text for a feminist press.[3] Doing research in the Dominican Republic, she met Noris, daughter of the oldest Mirabal sister, and visited the Mirabal home, now a museum and home of the surviving sister, Dedé. She let the haunting topic sit after completing her assignment. Then, after publication of *How the García Girls Lost Their Accents*, she was invited to the Mirabal home by Dedé, and this meeting convinced her to write a novel about the women. The Butterflies had become legends, and Alvarez wanted to recoup their memories as real, breathing women.[4] Although she did substantial research, her gift for imagining their thinking and feelings made fiction, rather than biography, the logical choice.[5]

As in her first novel, Alvarez tells the story through a multivoiced narrative, each chapter told by one of the sisters; only Dedé's narrative is mostly in third person. The structure is tripartite, with an epilogue. Each section has four chapters, one focusing on each of the sisters. Part I covers 1938–1946, part II 1948–1959, and part III 1960. The occasion for telling the story is set up in the chapters on Dedé, covering an afternoon and evening in 1994 when a Dominican American writer visits the museum, Dedé's home, and this framing device begins each of the three parts, with a third-person narrative that shifts from the present into Dedé's memory of an earlier year, triggered by some question or comment. The epilogue begins with Dedé's brief first-person account of the aftermath of her sisters' deaths, followed by a shift to the present: her conversation with niece Minou and a reflection on what it all meant and what it means to be the survivor who tells the story. This layering of the narrative, with the presence of a visitor and a window into the survivor's present-day life, gives added depth and complexity to the characters and their legacy, as it lends authenticity to the novel.

The Mirabal family background is woven into the story. The four sisters were the daughters of Enrique Mirabal Fernandez and Mercedes Reyes Camilo. Don Enrique was a successful farmer and small businessman who owned a shop, coffee mill, and rice factory on the northern coast of the Dominican Republic. He was from a small town in Santiago, but when he married, he made his home near his wife's family, in Ojo de Ague.[6] Their oldest daughter, Patria Mercedes, was born in 1924 on the anniversary of the country's Independence Day, February 27, her name being the word for "fatherland."[7] Patria was deeply religious, and her parish priest, as well as her mother, thought she might have a vocation as a nun. The second daughter, Bélgica Adela, known as Dedé, was born March 1, 1925.[8] Dedé is portrayed as the accommodating sister, good at math and an able business assistant to her father. The third daughter, Minerva Argentina, was born March 12, 1926. She loved learning, especially poetry and art, and she aspired to be a lawyer. The fourth daughter, María Teresa, also known as Mate, was born several years after Minerva, on October 15, 1936. Tagging along after Minerva, she was drawn early into keeping Minerva's secrets.[9]

In the novel, Dedé's first memory is evoked by her American visitor's question about how she lives with the tragedy: she answers that there were many happy times. She remembers an evening in 1943, before all their troubles began, when they were all together. Their father pretended to foretell the future, a future in which Dedé would bury them all. A negative remark about the future ruined the mood, triggering the fear everyone lived with of being overheard and reported by Trujillo's spies. As she went to bed on that long-ago night, Dedé felt a frisson of fear because her father had not prophesied futures for her sisters. The next chapter is Minerva's, beginning their story in 1938, when the girls go away to the convent school, Immaculada Concepción. Her future underground activity is rooted in what she learns there about Trujillo. The chapter begins with an anecdote at home on the farm: Minerva tries to free a young rabbit from her cage, but the creature is too frightened to leave the security of its cage. Minerva later comes to see Dominican citizens as similarly caged in their own country. Her school friend, Sinita, tells family secrets in exchange for Minerva's explanation of women's maturation. Sinita's secrets are stories of Trujillo's murder of all the men in her family and the loss of their fortune. These disturbing stories are connected for Minerva with the onset of her first menstrual period. "Complications" is the term used by the nun who lectures the girls on "personal hygiene," and Minerva's understanding of her country is "complicated" by the knowledge Sinita imparts, linked in her mind with her menstrual flow as instances of spilled blood. Later, another school friend, convinced she is in love with Trujillo, is taken away and set up in one of his houses for mistresses, where she bears his child and is left behind when he moves on to another young woman. Minerva is fully disillusioned when this chapter ends, in 1944.

María Teresa's (Mate's) story is told through diary entries. Her first "little book" records her awareness of Minerva's association with political dissidents during her own first year at Immaculada Concepción, Minerva's last year there. When Minerva's radical friend, Hilda, is arrested,

María Teresa must give up her diary, with its incriminating details, to be buried at home with other papers. Patria continues the story, ending part I with a narrative of her crisis of faith in 1946. Falling in love at 16, Patria marries the farmer Pedro Gonzalez, known in the family as Pedrito. After bearing a son and a daughter, her third pregnancy ends in stillbirth, causing her to question her faith. Her mother initiates a pilgrimage to a shrine to the Virgin Mary (the Virgen de la Altagracia [high grace], or *Virgencita*, who is the patron saint of the Dominican Republic as well as the special protector of women). All of the women need the pilgrimage. Minerva is restless, unable to pursue her dream of studying law; Patria is grieving; Mate suffers from asthma; Dedé is not suffering but needs to make a decision about her future; and their mother admits that their father is involved with another woman. At the shrine, Patria's faith is restored. Her faith and love for her children will ultimately impel Patria's political involvement, in contrast to Minerva, whose motive is outrage at injustice, and Mate, whose involvement begins in admiration of Minerva.

Part II opens, again in the present, with Dedé's reflection on the way her sisters' memory has been glorified, and mystified, by the family's servant Fela, who has set up a shrine to them and claims to be possessed by their spirits. Minerva's daughter Minou visits Fela regularly. Dedé is recalled from her reverie by her visitor's question as to when their "problems with the regime" started.[10] Though their open conflict with Trujillo is generally dated to an incident at the Discovery Day dance in 1949, Dedé starts earlier, with Minerva's involvement with Virgilio (Lio) Morales. Minerva met Lio when Dedé was becoming romantically involved with her cousin Jaimito Reyes, whom she would marry. Lio taught medicine at the university in the capital (Santo Domingo, known as Ciudad Trujillo from 1936 to 1961).[11] He was involved in political agitation against the regime, which meant that Minerva must see him secretly, aided by Dedé and Jaimito. Dedé was taken with Lio, too, but she could see a safe future in marriage to a man her family approved of, and she thought she loved Jaimito. Lio asked her to deliver his letter to Minerva, inviting her to join him in exile, but Dedé destroyed it, ambivalent about whether she acted out of jealousy or the desire to protect her sister.

In the next chapter, Minerva narrates her discovery in 1949 of her father's second family, the four daughters of his *campesino* mistress. She also discovers that he has withheld Lio's letters. Avoiding a breach in their relationship, she is able to continue supporting his second family discreetly when the round of imprisonments begins. At the Discovery Day dinner-dance, Trujillo flirts with Minerva, who at first uses the occasion to petition for the opportunity to study law in the capital. But when he becomes physically aggressive, she slaps him. A driving rainstorm breaks up the party, and the younger men—Jaimito and Pedrito—convince Don Enrique to use it as the excuse for leaving early, rescuing Minerva. Trujillo does not forgive offenses like this. The last portion of this chapter, narrating the aftermath of the confrontation, is called "A Rainy Spell." Don Enrique is arrested, despite his letter of apology to Trujillo. Moreover, Minerva has pretended to Trujillo that she does not know Lío, and her lie is uncovered when Lío's letters are found in the purse she left behind. With her mother, Minerva goes to the capital to petition for her father's release, and they are held under house arrest in their hotel. Plausibly, she attributes her lie to fear of offending Trujillo. But when she refuses to visit him unaccompanied, thereby turning down the implied invitation to become his mistress, her father's release is delayed by several weeks. Though Don Enrique is eventually released, his health is broken; he has suffered a heart attack shortly after his arrest. Before letting them leave, Trujillo throws dice with Minerva; the stakes are law school if she wins, her body if he wins, and they arrive at a draw. The family drives home through "torrential rains" that hold the whole country in their grip, washing away any effort at protest.[12] The chapter's ending echoes the end of Minerva's chapter in part I, in which Minerva views the road through a windshield blurred by the bodies of moths, as though looking "through a curtain of tears"[13] after a narrowly avoided confrontation with Trujillo.

María Teresa's narrative in part II covers 1953 to 1958, again in the pages of a journal, this one infrequently kept. It begins with Don Enrique's funeral. Mate's writing ability is illustrated in her composition of a letter for her mother to send to Trujillo, hoping to placate him by notifying him of her husband's death. Mate also takes credit for writing Minerva's speech praising Trujillo, a speech that finally wins her entry to law school. Once there, Minerva joins the resistance. Mate and Minerva live together in the capital, even after Minerva marries Manuel Tavarez Justo, known as Manolo, an active resistance member, and bears a daughter, Minou. When Minerva completes her degree, she is awarded a diploma but refused a license to practice law, showing the limits of Trujillo's concession. Mate accompanies Minerva when she rejoins Manolo in Monte Cristi on the country's northern coast. Living with the sister she has admired for so long, Mate is drawn into the resistance and meets her future husband, Leandro Guzmán, whose underground name is Palomino. Minerva is already known as Mariposa, so Mate becomes the second Mariposa. The chapter ends with her wedding announcement in February 1958.

In the final chapter of part II, in 1959, Patria also joins the resistance, but her involvement is an outgrowth of her compassion and motherly love as she comes to believe that only the resistance can rebuild what has been destroyed by Trujillo's violence. Nelson, her oldest child, is increasingly drawn to his uncles' politics. The Dominican underground takes fresh inspiration from the victory in Cuba of Fidel Castro, his brother Raúl, and Ernesto Guevara (Che) over the dictator Batista. Patria is inspired to name her third surviving child, conceived at the time of the Cuban revolution, Raúl Ernesto. Minerva recognizes the name as a sign that she can trust Patria. Pedrito is sympathetic to the underground but fears confiscation of his land; he becomes active when Patria tells him that Nelson does not want to be a farmer like his father. Her radicalization comes when, on a religious retreat, she witnesses ordinary Dominicans slaying resistance members, acting as reinforcements for Trujillo's soldiers. She is haunted by the sight of a 15-year-old boy killed before her eyes, thinking that he could easily have been her own child. She helps unite Catholic antiregime elements with the secular underground, and the organization that includes the three Mirabal sisters takes the name of the Fourteenth of June Movement, commemorating the failed uprising that galvanized Patria.

Part III focuses on 1960, ending with the sisters' last journey. In the novel's present time, it is dusk, and the American visitor meets Minou, Minerva's daughter, just before leaving. Dedé faces the question of why she refused to join the movement, recalling how close she came in 1960. She backed out because she feared that her husband would leave her, taking their three sons, if she became involved, and they took a second honeymoon on the eve of the arrests. First to be rounded up were Leandro, Pedrito, Nelson, and Manolo. Pedrito's home was destroyed, his fields were dug up, and his buried guns were confiscated. Patria and Mate were staying at their mother's house when they learned of Minerva's arrest; then Mate, too, was arrested. From that point on, Dedé was involved. With Jaimito, she traveled frequently to the capital to work for the release of family members. She helped her mother and Patria smuggle small comforts and money to her sisters. Together they cared for Minerva's and Mate's three young children. From this time forward, the sisters were aware of neighbors' and strangers' whispered support of the Butterflies and warnings of danger, which Minerva would ignore, convinced that international attention to Trujillo's human rights abuses would protect her. This chapter ends with Dedé's recollection of how she started using her memory game to fend off despair over the family's tragedy. She links the "dark night" of their imprisonment and deaths with the poem Minerva often recited, beginning, "The shades of night begin to fall, and the traveler hurries home, and the campesino bids his field farewell."[14]

Patria's final chapter covers January to March of 1960. She struggles to hold on to her faith, remembering Christ's resurrection on the third day, as she works for Nelson's release. She attempts to bargain with God, offering her life in exchange for her son's, a bargain that may be said to be fulfilled when her life is taken later that year. In the meantime, however, she placates the local SIM officer, Captain Peña, treating him kindly so that he will share information with her, and, later, learning that he has acquired her husband's land, she pressures him to lend his influence to her cause. From Captain Peña she learns that Pedrito turned down the offer of a pardon and restoration of his land in return for divorcing her. Minerva and Mate are also offered pardons that they turn down. But when Peña obtains her audience with Trujillo, Patria is not ashamed to do whatever it takes to win her child's release.

María Teresa's final chapter spans March to August of 1960 and depicts prison life in another series of diary entries. She and Minerva are imprisoned with over 20 other women, some of them political, some ordinary criminals. These distinctions break down over time, as they share their experiences as women. All the women are susceptible to occasional emotional breakdowns. The political prisoners are made instruments in the pressures put on their husbands, stripped and brutalized before the bound men. Minerva's resistance lands her in solitary confinement repeatedly. Still, Minerva's and Mate's conditions are eased by the family's gifts, delivered by a guard they call Santicló (Santa Claus), a relative of their half-sisters. Minerva's kindness toward their father's second family has had the unexpected benefit of opening a channel for communication. One of the smuggled gifts is Mate's new journal. Some of its pages are torn out, pages that presumably record rape or torture. Mate thinks she may have been pregnant with her second child when she was imprisoned, but an episode with the guards has aborted it. When representatives of the Organization of American States (OAS) arrive to investigate prison conditions, Mate is able to smuggle out a political statement, hidden in her heavy braid, but she keeps her torture private. After the OAS visit, the women political prisoners are released. Mate fears that Minerva will again refuse—having turned down the earlier offer of a pardon because a pardon would suggest they have done something wrong. Separated from her infant daughter, Mate fears a complete breakdown if she must continue in the hell of prison. However, at this juncture, even Minerva is ready to choose release over a political statement.

Minerva's chapter ends part III, covering August to November 25, the date of the sisters' murder. This moving narrative shows the heroic Minerva acting more bravely than she feels. Home again, at first she must rest daily. She has been diagnosed with tuberculosis, and she comes out of prison with pneumonia. Now she loves the simple things in life, her children's touch, the taste of food prepared at home. However, Minerva is aware that she has reached legendary status, and she must put on a courageous front; gradually her interest in politics returns. Although the OAS has imposed sanctions and an American warship is reputed to be anchored off the coast, Trujillo is still in power. The family lives with secret police (SIM) guards on their grounds, allowed to leave home only to attend church and, eventually, visit the imprisoned husbands. Because all of the family cars have been confiscated, they must hire a car any time they want to go somewhere. They develop a friendship with one brave driver who helps them sneak in visits to doctors associated with the underground, from whom Minerva learns that their movement has been largely destroyed. It is expected that Trujillo's own associates will eliminate him the next year. An uncle reports that at a local gathering, Trujillo claimed, "My only two problems are the damn church and the Mirabal sisters."[15] The events that follow are apparently a response to his statement. Manolo, Pedrito, and Leandro are transferred to another prison, closer to their home but reachable only by a treacherous mountain road. This is where the ambush will occur, but Minerva's narrative ends at the beginning of their last journey home, when they plan to follow a truck over the mountain in the threatening rain. She feels, as they leave, the way she used to when the girls played "Dark Passages" in the garden outside their own home, slightly scared but reassured by the lighted windows of home.

The epilogue is Dedé's first-person account. She begins with stories she heard in the aftermath of her sisters' deaths, when a steady stream of visitors came to tell her any detail of her sisters' last day that they could share, bearing testimony. Over time, Dedé constructed a coherent narrative of their end. As her sisters traveled up the mountain, they passed the truck; when the truck driver reached the scene of the ambush, they and their driver were already in custody. Patria ran from the soldiers to call out a message to her family, and the truck driver, frightened, drove away. Dedé cannot help but wonder why he did not stop to help. Later, more information came out at the trial, after Trujillo's death. Sentenced to 30 years' imprisonment (20 years for the man who only stood guard), the murderers were freed during the period of revolutions that followed the end of the dictatorship. At first, Dedé was informed that her sisters had been killed in a car accident. When she went to Santiago to prepare the bodies for burial, she could see that her sisters and their driver had been clubbed and strangled before being returned to the vehicle and pushed off the mountain road. Cutting off Mate's braid to keep, she remembered her father's prediction that she would bury the rest of the family.

Dedé rode home in the back of the truck with the four coffins, witnessing the tribute of many people who threw flowers into the truck. She was reckless, accusing the SIM of being "assassins," and Jaimito told her that her martyrdom was "to be alive without them."[16] As Dedé and her mother looked after all the children and Trujillo's regime gave way to a short-lived presidency, her grief became manageable, but it was like living cancer-free after a mastectomy: something had been destroyed so that the rest could live. She remembers the radio commentator who equated dictatorship with pantheism because "The dictator manages to plant a little piece of himself in every one of us,"[17] a description that Dedé would later associate with cancerous cells in a healthy body. Manolo, resisting the military government that deposed their democratically elected president, died three years after his wife, fighting in the mountains. Pedrito regained his land and married a much younger woman, but he was never the same man after prison. Leandro decided against joining Manolo in the mountains and went into the construction business. Dedé has witnessed all of it, wanting to believe her sisters' deaths accomplished something. At some point, instead of listening to others' testimonies, she became the keeper of the story, "the oracle" who could make sense of what had happened.[18] At the end of this day, having again retold and relived the tragic story, she considers doing something new: go north, see maple trees in the autumn. Lying in bed, she thinks how often she feels the presence of spirits in her insomnia—sometimes hearing the tread of Trujillo's boots, more often hearing her sisters' light footfalls. The absence of her cancer-infected breast has come to symbolize all of her losses.

This novel is a *testimonio*, a story that bears witness to lives destroyed by a violent tyrant. In Alvarez's hands, the *testimonio* takes on a feminist cast and, additionally, comments on the value of stories and memories. By focusing on the significant moments of the Mirabal sisters' lives as women, Alvarez emphasizes the high cost of their courage. Minerva's politicization comes with her first menstruation; her resistance to Trujillo's sexual desire results in the first Mirabal imprisonment; Minerva's and María Teresa's commitment to the resistance movement coincides with falling in love, marrying, and bearing children; Patria symbolically names her youngest child and joins the underground because she wants to protect children; the dictator's invasion of private lives is like cancer and the destruction of the dictator like removal of a breast. These parallels show women as doubly vulnerable where an oppressive patriarchal society is ruled by an oppressor.

Don Enrique, their father, is shown through his sentiments and actions to be complicit in the oppressive social system that limits women's opportunities. He resists sending all of his daughters to school and fails to support Minerva's goal of studying law. When Trujillo wants Minerva, Don Enrique counsels her to placate the dictator, even though this would result in her rape. He, too, has a mistress, to whom he doles out money, but he never thinks of sending his illegitimate daughters to school; it is his legitimate daughters who help the younger girls avoid becoming victims like their mother. Ultimately, Don Enrique is powerless to protect his family because of the tight hold that Trujillo keeps on the country through imprisonment, torture, and secret deaths.

The secrecy that surrounds Trujillo's crimes, along with glorification of the dictator, is enforced through the normalization of spying throughout the society. The widespread spying is symbolized by the picture of Trujillo that is required by law to be displayed in every home. Ordinary citizens act out of a misguided sense of civic duty, out of a desire to curry favor, or out of fear of retribution when they inform on their neighbors or allow their daughters to be carried off or turn a blind eye to government-sanctioned violence. The church, too, is complicit with corrupt power, accepting the patronage and gifts of Trujillo and his henchmen in return for their silence about his sins. It is only when resistance becomes widespread and the dictator's crimes inconcealable that the church unites in opposition, helping to crack the code of silence that has made oppression seem normal.

In Alvarez's postscript to this book, she points out that making the Mirabal sisters into legends, investing them with superhuman courage, runs the risk of reproducing the ways of thinking that led to the pseudo-deification of Trujillo as well as holding them up as heroes others cannot hope to imitate.[19] She meant to humanize them, and this is what she has succeeded in doing.

In 2009, Dedé Mirabal published her memoir, *Vivas en su jardin*. It has not yet been translated into English.

The date of the Mirabal sisters' death, November 25, was designated the International Day Against Violence Against Women at an international women's conference in Bogotá, Colombia, in 1981, and was adopted by the Organization of American States in 1994.[20] In 1999, the United Nations recognized November 25 as the International Day for the Elimination of Violence against Women.[21]

DISCUSSION QUESTIONS

• The Butterflies are often spoken of collectively. How does Alvarez characterize each sister as an individual? What elements of each sister's narrative give her a distinctive voice? What effect is created by presenting Mate's voice entirely through diary entries?

• Has Dedé come to terms with her losses? Is she burdened by her role as the storyteller who keeps her sisters' memory alive? How does she feel about their legendary status in the Dominican Republic?

• What is the effect on the reader of coming to each sister's story through the framework of Dedé's memories in 1994 and of her retelling the story to a visitor who is an outsider? Does this give their narratives more or less authority?

5

¡YO!
(1997)

In *¡Yo!*,[1] Alvarez continues Yolanda García's story. Having claimed authorship at the end of *How the García Girls Lost Their Accents*, Yo is now established as the author of a popular semiautobiographical novel, and *¡Yo!* begins with her family's reaction to publication of material from their lives, reworked as fiction. In contrast to the ending of the first novel, where Yo speaks directly to the reader, Yo never speaks directly in this novel. Instead, the reader views her from 16 perspectives, ranging from family members and lovers to Dominican servants, a New England landlady, and a stalker. The cumulative effect is a complex, sometimes contradictory, portrait that suggests that identity is socially constructed through interactions with others. The title is a triple pun: Yolanda is nicknamed Yo; *yo* is the first-person singular pronoun in Spanish; and the word is an attention-getting exclamation. This punning emphasizes the writer-protagonist's obsession with words—their multiple meanings as brought out in different contexts. The thread that ties all the stories together is Yo's passion for writing.

Like *García Girls*, *¡Yo!* is told episodically in fifteen chapters divided into three parts. To this structure is added a prologue. Each chapter has a title from the terminology of literary study ("poetry," "confrontation," "characterization," etc.). The prologue and part I use the terminology of literary genres, part II the language of fiction writers' techniques, and part III the language of formal literary analysis. These titles sharpen the focus on Yo as a writer. Each chapter is further identified by the character

45

whose perspective is represented, in terms of the speaker's relationship to Yolanda ("the mother, "the student," etc.). In contrast to the reverse chronology of *García Girls, ¡Yo!* is a chronological narrative, but both the first and last chapters—one by Yo's mother, one by her father—are anchored in Yo's childhood, and both are about punishments administered when she told stories, or lied. Both emphasize the risks of speaking out in the Trujillo era, when a child's imaginative exaggeration could endanger family members' lives.

The prologue ("Fiction"), told in first person by Sofía, shows the family's anger over Yo's fictional portrayal of them. They feel betrayed, dismissing her explanations of how "art and life [mirror] each other."[2] Their mother has even threatened to sue her. Yet the mother herself is a fiction-maker who transforms life stories, as Sofía discovers when her mother tells a family story differently from the way Sofía remembers it—or else "everyone in [the] family is lying."[3] However, the family is reconciled by the birth of a baby, and Sandi leaves a long message on Yo's answering machine in "her one chance to say all she wants without someone in the family cutting in with their version of the story."[4] In this identification between *García Girls* and Yo's successful novel, Alvarez blurs the distinction between "art and life" rather than clarifying it, and sets the stage for a narrative built of multiple versions of truth, weaving a web of connected but disparate views. With characters commenting on their lives as characters, the prologue could easily be titled "Metafiction," rather than "Fiction."

Part I opens with "Nonfiction," the mother's story about her imaginative child that illuminates her own character as well as the trauma Yo experienced in leaving the Dominican Republic. The mother feared arrest in her homeland and, later, deportation from her adopted country. In the Dominican Republic, Yo's discovery of her father's illegal gun, hidden in the floor of her parents' closet, made her parents anxious that Yo would betray the family, given her proclivity for making up stories and embroidering the truth. In the United States, Yo did tell stories in school, resulting in a visit from a social worker. The mother had once unintentionally terrified her children by dressing up in her fur coat and pretending to be a bear and subsequently used this incident to frighten them into good behavior, though Yo soon learned the truth, while exploring her parents' closet. Another punishment, specifically for lying, was hot pepper sauce on the tongue. A third punishment was being locked in a closet. When the mother locked Yo in with the fur coat after the family moved to the United States, Yo panicked at the return of the bear.

At school, Yo told "disturbing" stories about children being locked in closets, made to eat lye, and set upon by bears.[5] The mother, hoping to win the social worker's sympathy and forestall deportation, told her stories about torture and disappearances in the Dominican Republic, leading the social worker to conclude that Yo had witnessed such horrors. The misunderstanding established a political explanation for the girls' fears that excused the mother. Though incensed by Yo's publication of family stories, the mother illustrates how stories change and how nonfiction can be transformed into fiction and fiction taken for nonfiction. Ultimately, this explains how one trauma enables a writer to imaginatively experience other traumas.

"The cousin" Lucinda's story, "Poetry," is about her competition with Yo for a boy's attention, which she won by submitting the winning poem to the school's literary magazine competition. When Yo left her diary where her mother could read it, the mother's report of the romance to Lucinda's parents ended Lucinda's education in the United States. Lucinda was convinced that Yo's exposure of her secret was a deliberate act of revenge. Twenty years later, Lucinda feels vindicated, even though she knows the García girls look down on their female cousins as "Barbie dolls,"[6] because she is a successful businesswoman and mother, while Yolanda has led her life only on paper.

In "Report," "the maid's daughter" tells how Yo made her the subject of an anthropological study for a school assignment. Coming from the Dominican Republic as a child, Sarita was treated almost like a little sister by the García girls before they left for boarding school. Sarita attended public school, where rumors of her exotic origins and wealth circulated because she was met after school by a woman in a maid's uniform—her mother. Yolanda attended school with Sarita to study her "acculturation" and, discovering the rumors, added her own imaginative details, but Sarita felt undermined rather than bolstered. Yo's written report further made Sarita feel that something had been stolen from her: her life no longer seemed to be hers. She exacted compensation from Mrs. García, asking for help with tuition at the Catholic school the García girls had attended. This move transformed Sarita's life: she eventually became a doctor. Twenty years later, their class difference is clear in their life choices: with her initiative and drive, Sarita has achieved success, in contrast to Yo, whose upper-class background gave her the luxury of a prolonged search for identity and an insecure life as a writer.

"The teacher," Mr. Garfield, Yo's occasional confidant and mentor, depicts her 15 years of wandering after college. The chapter title, "Romance," may describe her haphazard heroic quest or his love affair with a colleague that ends with his lover's death from AIDS. When Yo visits her teacher on the eve of his retirement, he tells her to tear up his letter of recommendation and do what she really loves; she should gather her stories and poems for book publication. Thinking of the time he wasted in his own life, he responds to her terror of failing by saying, "You don't have a choice."[7]

"The stranger," Consuelo, is an illiterate Dominican who enlists Yo's help in composing her "Epistle" of advice to her daughter, who is working in the United States. Yo ultimately refuses to write Consuelo's recommendation that her daughter remember her marriage vows and stay with her abusive husband. Instead, Yo starts a fresh letter that affirms Consuelo's pride in her daughter and encourages her to seek help from an agency. The words Yo writes, Consuelo feels, are the ones that truly were in her heart. Once Yo has committed to her career, she is in a position of power: putting her intuitive gift to work, she can wield words to shape life decisions and actions.

In part II, which begins and ends in the Dominican Republic, Yo lives a writer's life, productive if not yet successful. Her American identity, as seen by Dominican servants, is stressed at the end of part I and the beginning of part II, while part II ends with an American view of her Dominican identity. Don Mundín's caretakers' story opens part II, in which Yo's inspiration as a writer is linked with the mystical voices that a spiritual healer hears ("Revelation"). This chapter introduces a theme of listening—and interpreting what one hears—that is woven throughout the rest of the book.

The caretaker's wife, María, regains her lost capacity to hear the saints' voices a year after her small son's death by drowning in her employer's pool. Rightly or wrongly, María has held the wealthy family responsible for her loss, believing that the lives of the poor are subordinated to the desires of the rich. The locals are skeptical about Yo's reasons for choosing a retreat, and her American disregard for class distinctions puzzles them. She invites the steward's family to dinner, offering to give the children swimming lessons, unaware of the previous summer's tragedy. María has seen Yo standing in her tower room, apparently listening for voices, and she begins to wonder if this lady, like María herself, is marked by the saints. While the children splash in the pool, María climbs to Yo's tower room. When she looks up, the sunlight blinds her, as if she were in her saints' presence; looking down at the view of her village, she sees her own place in the world. As she does so, she hears her drowned son's cry, rejoicing in the way he "can float."[8] María's revelation, with which the story ends, links the writer's inspiration with holy inspiration.

"Motivation," as presented by "the best friend," links Yo's writing to the body and emotions, in contrast. Tammy and Yo live together one summer, participating in the same therapy group and writing poetry. At the end of the summer, they invite Yo's male acquaintance and Tammy's current lover to a dinner party. Afterward, as the men sleep off the alcohol they have imbibed, the women cope with insomnia by sharing poems. Usually unwilling to share her writing with men, Yo makes an exception when the men shuffle in, but before she reads aloud, she asks that they dress as women, and the men obligingly comply. Tammy realizes that she has found a muse, a man she can be friends with, and a best friend in this poetry-sharing gathering where all her needs for understanding and companionship are met.

"Confrontation" follows immediately after this summer of writing. "The landlady," Marie, rents her apartment to Yo after her husband leaves her for another woman. At first Marie is suspicious of Yo's apparent foreignness, then imagines she and Tammy are lovers, but Marie grows to like them. When her husband, a drinker with a temper, moves back in, he begins hitting Marie. A confrontation is inevitable. Yo cannot write with the sounds of violence in the background, but she cannot yet afford to move, and the husband threatens to sue if she breaks her lease. A rainstorm brings matters to a crisis: the roof leaks, and Yo's typed manuscript pages are ruined. Marie and Yo join forces, both crying—Yo over her ruined books and finished pages, Marie over the ruin of her love. Together they bag the husband's belongings, put them out in the rain, and wait for him on the porch. His belongings remind Marie of "a ladder to escape out of a fairybook tower,"[9] and she is saddened by her sense of waste—the years, the emotional commitment—while Yo listens to the rain as if recovering her ruined pages. Yo connects with Marie through her compassion, as she did with Consuelo and María in the Dominican Republic.

"Variation," from "the student's" perspective, spans several years between Yo's early teaching career and her achievement of tenure. Football player Lou Castellucci takes Yo's creative writing class to impress a beautiful English major. His writing is transformed when he reaches inside himself to express his hurt after his father left, and Yo is impressed by his best story, about the only game he ever lost. Several years later, married to the English major, a father and successful businessman, he returns for a reunion. Browsing through Yo's book of short stories in the college bookstore, he recognizes the kernel of his story in her story about a Hispanic boy and briefly considers initiating a class-action suit, speculating that she has plagiarized other students' stories, too. Later, Lou encourages his wife to read a story aloud, not revealing the connection between his teacher's story and his own. Afterward, he asks whether it's a little too sentimental—the grounds on which his story was rejected by the college literary magazine. She says no, it isn't. It calls up her own memory of loss, which she shares with Lou. Like the prologue and Sarita's story, this chapter comments on the transformation of life experiences through art. Yo's story is a variation on Lou's, but in her surer hands, it gains power. Stories are not the exclusive property of their tellers, Alvarez implies, but are there for everyone to build on, each person finding personal meanings in them.

"The suitor," Dexter, is overwhelmed by Yo's Dominican identity in "Resolution." Yo discourages Dexter from accompanying her to the Dominican Republic, where her uncle is running for president—she does not want a scandal, and she does not want her family to assume they are engaged. He does not really understand what she tells him about cultural differences until he arrives, posing as a Washington reporter covering the Dominican election. This lie—Yo's suggestion—is the same kind of lie she tells her father every time she spends a weekend with Dexter. With an American view of family and adult sexuality, Dexter does not understand why a grown woman should have to lie to her family. Then he sees them in action. Every night he tries to cross the compound to Yo's room, only to be waylaid by some relative and drawn into an alcohol-fueled male gathering. Even the children, who catch him smoking pot, seem more sophisticated. Out of his depth with this Latin American intrigue, he feels like a boy among men. He realizes his relationship with Yo is not heading toward a more serious level. At home, Dexter has seen Yo as an American with an exotic tinge; here, he sees her as Dominican and knows she will never separate from her family.

In part III, Yo finds a new, stable life. The first chapter, "Point of View," about her wedding to Doug, is narrated by "the wedding guests," shifting from one character to another, and mixing third-person limited and first-person narratives. This pivotal, complex chapter appears in the same position as *García Girls'* pivotal chapter, with similar shifts in point of view. This narrative of Yo's wedding brings together many of the friends and family members introduced in earlier chapters. It is framed by the minister, Luke, who reflects on the uncertainties and tensions in Yo and Doug's union, represented by the guests' differences.

Doug's daughter, Corey, is sullen, her dreams of her parents' reuniting ended by the wedding. Doug and Dexter are contrasted in an incident that shows Yo's maturation in her choice of husband; Doug is a family man, doctor, and part-time farmer. Doug frees a trapped sheep from a fence, while the flamboyant Dexter pretends to protect Lucinda from the sheep. Sarita and Tía Flor provide counterpoint to each other: Sarita explains that a limousine was the only available transportation from the airport, while Tía Flor thinks Sarita is flaunting her success and resentfully remembers that Sarita's mother claimed Flor's husband was Sarita's father. Lucinda contradicts her earlier perspective, admitting that she forgave Yo many years earlier. Tammy reassures Yo, who is worried about the tensions: Corey won't talk to her, and the aunts pass judgment on the maid's daughter and Yo's lesbian friends. Tammy also relinquishes her status as best friend, hoping that Doug will now be Yo's best friend.

The minster closes the chapter by narrating the ewe's release. Seeing the incident in a biblical light, Luke thinks of the sheep as sent by God to lead these descendants of the prophet Abraham to worship, with the gray-clad Yo as the angel of the Lord, lifting her hand in welcome. The gathering illustrates the kaleidoscope of Yo's life. The chapter encapsulates the novel as a whole, the disparate points of view revealing the tensions and contradictions in Yo herself.

In his opening view, Luke envisions Yo as quilting her life from these diverse perspectives. Each piece in a quilt retains its integrity, juxtaposed rather than interwoven with other pieces, joined to form a pleasing pattern. If Yo's life is stitched together, the thread is writing, or storytelling. Yo's storytelling and her wandering reinforce the Old Testament image of Abraham's people, similarly clannish and nomadic, telling their history in stories. They are blessed and united, however briefly, by Yo's angel call to ritual.

In the next chapter, "Setting," Yo returns to Mundín's house to write and meets "the night watchman," José, hired by the steward when José is about to lose the land his family has farmed for generations. José pities the American lady for her childlessness and, blessed with several children, considers offering Yo the child his wife is carrying when Yo mentions that she is considering adopting. Briefly, he dreams of the opportunities his child would have in the United States but is both relieved and disappointed when she decides against adopting. In explanation, she invites him to her tower room to show him her writing. When she discovers that he is illiterate, Yo immediately begins teaching him his letters. By the time she leaves, he can write her name, as well as his own, and he names his new daughter Yolanda.

"Characterization," from the perspective of "the third husband," illustrates the continuing challenge of Yo's divided, bicultural identity when she returns to the United States, showing how Doug comes to terms with it. Tensions erupt when José begins calling Yo collect. Sixteen-year-old Corey, staying with them on her way home from a summer in Spain, accepts his first call, and José suggests that she marry him so he can live in the United States. Yo's description of José's poverty wins Corey's sympathy, and for the first time in two years, Doug sees his wife and daughter united in a cause—although a cause that he opposes. He thinks of the two women as "the soft underbelly"[10] of the United States, the spot where it is vulnerable to penetration. The calls continue: José plans to fly to New York and wants to know what he should do once he gets there. Truly alarmed, Doug puts his foot down—no more accepting collect calls—and precipitates a crisis. Corey explodes, and days of shouting and slammed doors follow. Eventually, Corey brings up her parents' divorce, the Pandora's box they have kept closed.[11]

Yo blames their conflict on Doug because he removed the charm she usually keeps in her stepdaughter's room, which he has dismissed as Dominican superstition, and she says they need to get rid of José's gift, a handful of soil meant to keep Yo connected to the Dominican Republic, which instead has connected José to their family. The solution is to dig it up from their garden and take it away, to free them from control by spirits so that they can act rationally with José. Doug digs up some dirt from his garden and bags it for later disposal. Then Yo reconsiders, concluding that José would not have attempted spirit manipulation.

Doug, however, feels that José poses a threat to his family. When he takes a call from José, in his limited Spanish, he identifies himself as Corey's father, tells José there will be no marriage, and threatens him with the police. He is unhappy about threatening a needy man; it undermines his self-image as someone who helps others. But José's calls stop, and peace is restored. Although the problem has been resolved without dumping the Dominican soil, Doug finds he wants to be rid of it: this bag of soil has come to represent his anger and frustration with Corey, with Yo's absences, and consequently, with the Dominican Republic itself. José's calls are a concrete representation of the claim this other culture makes on his wife, periodically separating her from him; this is why his anger was disproportionate. It is time to move on, so Doug disposes of the soil in the dumpster behind the hospital.

As Corey's visit ends, they make plans to spend Christmas with Yo's family in the Dominican Republic; Doug suggests buying land there and employing José. Dreams of sharing his love of the land with a less fortunate man redeem his self-image. Now, instead of resisting and resenting the Dominican Republic's hold on his wife, he has arrived at a desire to be with her wherever she is, joined in whatever enterprise captures her sympathy.

This happy ending is followed with the chilling narrative, "Tone," told by "the stalker." He speaks in first person, addressing Yo, with whom he has been obsessed for 25 years. In earlier encounters, he has cut off her braid, trapped her in her apartment by flinging himself against her door, and set fire to her apartment. His violence derives from his history as a victim of abuse. Posing as a magazine interviewer (in a twisted echo of Dexter's pose as a Washington reporter in the Dominican Republic), he gains access to her hotel room, bringing along childhood comfort foods and his hunting knife, along with a collection of her books that he has cut up and rearranged.

Yo attempts to calm him, talking and talking until he screams at her to shut up. He rocks himself, crying, and then hurls her mutilated books across the room, shocking Yo into silence. After his anger is spent, he puts away the knife and insists that this time she will listen to him. That is all he wanted the last time he came close, when he sat outside her apartment door. The chapter ends with Yo's look of skepticism, shared with her sister, just before she gives him her full attention, with a penetrating look that takes him back to the beginning. This will be the critical test of Yo's belief that stories save us. But the reader does not actually find out whether the stalker's story saves him or Yo or her sister.

The final chapter, "Conclusion," by Yo's father, also tells a story of Yo's being violently silenced. As a child, watching a cowboy program on television at a friend's house, she told her friend's father, who was a general, that her father had a lot of big guns. He would kill all the bad people, including the sultan in his big house—a detail from her favorite book, *The Arabian Nights*. The general questioned her very seriously, and she responded by assuring him that even Trujillo and he would be killed if he did not stop tickling her. Because she was sitting on his lap when she told the story, molestation is suggested as well. Yo's story could easily have resulted in family members' imprisonment and death, as private citizens were prohibited from owning guns and any threat to Trujillo was taken very seriously. At home, her parents questioned her but could not determine the truth from their frightened child. Bent on putting an end to her dangerous storytelling, the father whipped Yo with his belt while the mother held her, running the shower to cover her screams. Then he went out to leave his rifle with a trusted friend, whose name he never revealed, even decades after Trujillo's assassination.

The father revisits this painful memory because it is time to break his silence in order to free Yo from self-doubt about her life's work. The worst consequence of a story Yo can imagine today is a bad review, he says, but the worst consequence he and his wife imagined was their loved ones' torture and death. After waiting most of the night for the secret police to arrive, they finally realized they would not be arrested. The father went to Yo's bedroom to comfort her, but she shrank from him in terror, and afterward he found it difficult to speak about the incident.

Recently, in her letters, Yo has been asking her father for details of his life story, and he repeatedly finds himself telling her "the whole story"— stories he did not want to share with anyone.[12] Then Yo stops writing for several weeks, and his wife explains that Yo is depressed because she has never borne children, having heard a lecturer argue that this is "committing genetic suicide."[13] The father writes to tell Yo that he is proud of her, indirectly suggesting that her books are his grandchildren. In response she telephones, and, at the close of the conversation, he promises her his blessing.[14]

This retelling of the story is his *bendición*, with a different ending that conveys what he has learned over many years. In his new ending, the father is ready to sacrifice his child's happiness, as in the biblical account when Abraham was ready to sacrifice his son's life, but, like Abraham, the father now spares the child. Blessing her rather than whipping her, he tells her that her gift is to preserve "the way back" for a family that will be separated from its history unless it has a story—the story she can tell.[15] His blessing ends the novel.

The parents' framing narratives focus on the origin of Yo's storytelling and their desire to silence her lies. Both narratives connect their fears as citizens in a totalitarian regime with their punishments, the punishments that inspire Yo's fears, which appear in different guises in her stories. The price of dictatorship is the silencing of all narratives except one official story. The Dominican Republic was held hostage by the dictator (as Yo has been held hostage by the stalker). The parents could not silence Yo. Yo keeps opening Pandora's box, which Doug alludes to, ending silence about family tensions, family fears, and family transgressions. Exposing lies, squabbles, and small betrayals as well as the deeper threats of violent secrets in Dominican society, Yo exorcises troubles—but sends them out into the world.

But in sending out stories, Yo also casts herself as Scheherazade, who must continually invent new stories to stay alive. Do stories save lives? Some of the stories told in *¡Yo!* suggest that stories can endanger lives. Certainly they can threaten relationships. Moreover, listening is ultimately as important as telling stories. The caretaker's wife, María, knows that she must listen for the voices of the saints and the departed; the stalker claims to want only a listener. The stalker is driven to tell his story, like Coleridge's ancient mariner, perhaps expiating his sins, perhaps seeking absolution through sacrificing a victim.

¡Yo! also retells stories and rewrites endings. Yo's fear of the fur coat echoes her fear of the black furred thing at the end of *García Girls*. The writer herself can choose an ending, can change the conclusion, as the father does in *¡Yo!*, and the writer can revise a life. The story may be retold in fiction or poetry, as report or romance. Whatever her genre, the storyteller employs revelation, motivation, confrontation, and so forth, changing the point of view or the setting or other elements, finally—but only provisionally—reaching a conclusion. Only death will silence her, as Alvarez suggests in her poem "Why I Write."[16]

The story of Abraham's willingness to sacrifice his son and heir, Isaac, at Jehovah's request is told in the book of Genesis. At the last minute, a ram appeared in a thicket, and Abraham substituted the ram for the boy, with the Lord's approval.

Together these narratives render a fuller picture of Yo than she could create by speaking in her own voice. At the same time, the novel's construction of an identity from different perspectives suggests how difficult it is to give a full picture of any individual. Each narrator's view is shaped by expectations of the genre he or she employs. Stories change with retelling. Each story leaves gaps. And each story touches on many other stories in the web of relationships in which each individual is involved.

DISCUSSION QUESTIONS

- What kind of a person is Yo, as developed from this composite picture? Are there contradictions in her depiction through these multiple narratives?
- Do stories belong to the people who live them? Is it fair for a writer to make use of another's life experience to write fiction?

6

IN THE NAME OF SALOMÉ
(2000)

In the Name of Salomé[1] takes its subject from the Dominican Republic's literary history, the Dominican Republic's first national poet, a woman of color, Salomé Ureña (1850–1897), and her reticent daughter Camila Henríquez Ureña (1894–1973), a college professor in the United States and Cuba. As depicted by Alvarez, both women resist restrictions on their lives and ambitions. The fiercely patriotic Salomé is a political poet in a period of turmoil and revolution, a period when, in one year, the Dominican Republic had eight governments.[2] Civil unrest occurs so frequently that Salomé's family has a hiding place under the house, like a storm cellar, where the women shelter when fighting breaks out. Salomé's father, her husband, and friends enjoy periods of power that alternate with periods in exile.

Salomé's story begins a dozen years after independence, and during the 118 years the novel covers, the country experiences a return to colonial status under Spain, periods of dictatorship, and occupation by Haiti and the United States, in addition to periods of democracy.[3] The meaning of *patria*, or the homeland, is central to Salomé's life and writing, a theme emphasized by the novel's epigraph, taken from one of her poems: "What is a homeland? Do you know, / my love, what you are asking?"[4] The political drama is more than a backdrop for her and her daughter's stories—it shapes their identities. *In the Name of Salomé* is also a story about memory and the life after death that a writer can achieve with her words: commenting on a period when Salomé's poems have been out of print, her son says, "This is how poets really die."[5] Alvarez brings the poet to life again for a wider audience—a poet who Camila says is "As good as your Emily Dickinson, as good as your Walt Whitman,"[6] Alvarez's touchstone American poets.

As in her other novels, Alvarez splits the narrative voice and, as in *How the García Girls Lost Their Accents*, disrupts chronology. She tells the two stories in alternating chapters: Salomé's story, which unfolds chronologically from 1850 to 1897 in chapters uno through ocho, and Camila's story, which unfolds in reverse chronological order from 1960 to 1897 in chapters one through eight. The forward movement of Salomé's narrative and the reverse chronology of Camila's memories move the novel toward convergence of the mother's and daughter's lives. Each chapter is titled with the name of one of Salomé's poems, in Spanish in her narrative and translated into English in Camila's narrative, and the order of the titles is reversed: the first chapter of Salomé's story is "El ave y el nido," and the last chapter of Camila's is "Bird and Nest." Two reasons may be given: first, the late-blossoming Camila seeks direction for her life through studying her mother's poems and, second, she reflects at the outset that her mother's titles might serve as labels for important episodes in her own life.[7]

A prologue set in 1960 and an epilogue set in 1973 frame the dual narrative. In the prologue, Camila leaves Vassar College, from which she has just retired, to return to Cuba, her adopted homeland, where she will work for Castro's new government, finally able to give her life to a cause she believes in. In the epilogue, she returns to the Dominican Republic after many years' absence, to die among family members and finally claim her full name, Salomé Camila, which she gave up at the centennial of her mother's birth. In the prologue, as she leaves Vassar, her friend and former lover, Marion, asks her to talk about her life, launching the novel into Salomé's story, told in first person in Salomé's voice.

"El ave y el nido" begins in 1856 in Santo Domingo, when Salomé is a child. She links her life story with her country's story: the Dominican Republic achieved independence just six years before she was born. Though she is sickly, she says, she is healthier than the country, which has already had 11 governments.[8] Her mother has left her philandering father to share a house with Salomé's Tía Ana, who runs a small school for girls in the parlor, and Salomé and her older sister Ramona (Mon) have not seen their father for some time because he is in exile. Salomé's earliest memory is of hiding in the frightening dark hole under the house and then, when the gunfire subsides, being lifted up to the roof to discover the color of the flag flying over the capitol. When she reports "red," she is told her father will return. She and Ramona enter into a clandestine verse-making correspondence with him, adopting pen names. Later, when she begins publishing her poems, she uses her childhood pen name, Herminia. Her father teaches the girls poems about their *patria*, inspiring Salomé's patriotic fervor, and she grieves when the Dominican Republic returns to colony status under Spain in 1861. Young as she is, she asks the question that will echo throughout the novel, "What is a patria?"[9] The pattern that shapes her life is set early: she is passionately devoted to her homeland and her father, and both disappoint her idealism. Enchanted by the charming father whose politics take him away for long periods and who cannot remain faithful to his wife, she will marry a man like him.

Salomé's second chapter is "Contestación," or "Reply," chronicling the development of her reputation as a poet in the years 1865–1874. Salomé's first publication is unintentional: she shares some poems with a young man, and after he goes into exile in Haiti, she is surprised to find one of her poems in print in a Santo Domingo newspaper, signed "Herminia." Salomé's poetry is outspoken; she is resolved against politically expedient caution or politeness and has committed herself to writing truthfully. At first shocked by its publication, Salomé discovers that writing in support of her country's freedom liberates her as well. When a frivolous poem by another writer is published as one of Herminia's productions, Salomé must claim her identity to avoid being trivialized and, for the first time, she signs a poem "Salomé Ureña."

"La fe en el porvenir," or "Faith in the Future," covers 1874–1877. Salomé becomes a local celebrity, and her aunt's parlor schoolroom is turned nightly into her salon. Still, she is shy and says little in company, her fervor displayed only in her writing. Her reserve is compounded by grief after her beloved father dies. She dresses in black and refuses all invitations. Then, at age 27, she attends a celebration of her poetry at a social-political club, Friends of the Country, at the invitation of the charming, fiery, young Pancho Henríquez, nine years her junior, who is a passionate admirer of her writing. Hearing the sounds of drum, flute, and trumpet outside her window (used symbolically by her father to describe the functions of poetry), she finally accepts the public calling that her father bequeathed to her.

In "Amor y anhelo," "Love and Yearning," Salomé becomes an increasingly public figure as she attends Friends of the Country events, drawn to Pancho, the club's president, who recites her poems as ardently as if he had written them. Pancho identifies himself as a positivist, a believer in humans' perfectibility through creation of a more progressive society. His friend, Hostos, is dedicated to starting progressive schools, and Pancho offers to educate Salomé in science, previously omitted from her education. Salomé falls in love, and it is her love poem, published during his absence from the city, that brings them together. Viewing the double standard in action, she has declared her love publicly in the belief that a true revolution must include equality for women.

The narrative of hope in "Le fe en el porvenir" ("Faith in the Future") that culminates in her public declaration of love is followed by a period of oppression and deteriorating health, even as she embraces the roles of mother and teacher. In "Sombras," or "Shadows," covering the years 1880–1886, Salomé discovers that Pancho does not understand her wholly, as she had hoped her husband would. Instead, it is Pancho's mentor, Hostos, who sees her for what she is, recognizing her natural aptitude for teaching, and she founds a girls' school based on his progressive ideas. She also bears three sons over a period of five years. Although celebrated as a national public figure, Salomé no longer has the time or energy for writing poetry. In "Sombras," she says a formal farewell to poetry.

"Ruinas" traces the deterioration of her marriage to Pancho in a series of letters to him in France, where he stays from 1887 to 1891, ostensibly for the study of medicine at the outset but also in exile during the Lilís dictatorship. Pancho's involvement with a French woman extends his stay. Paradoxically, his suspicious older brother, Federico, constantly watches Salomé for signs of infidelity. She struggles to raise the money that Pancho's studies require, sometimes borrowing large sums. After she sends their oldest son, Francisco, to Pancho because she cannot handle the child's terrible temper, she learns about Pancho's mistress when she reads a letter to Federico that has been delivered to her because Federico is in prison. Salomé breaks off communication, sending only a final terse letter to inform Pancho of Federico's release.

During his long absence, Salomé ages dramatically, suffering from severe coughing fits at night. To hide her illness as well as to sever marital relations, Salomé refuses to share a bedroom with Pancho after his return, as narrated in "La llegada del invierno," or "The Arrival of Winter," in 1891–1892. Fresh from French medical training, Pancho argues with the doctor over the diagnosis of Salomé's illness, but they agree in prescribing an extended stay at the seaside, and for a time this treatment restores her. Shortly after returning to the capital, in the wake of a violent suppression of political opposition to Lilís's government, Salomé becomes pregnant with her last child, Camila.

The final chapter of Salomé's story, "Luz," or "Light," chronicles Salomé's difficult pregnancy as she suffers from consumption in 1893–1894. Sure that she will bear a daughter and fearful that her physician and husband will try to end the pregnancy, she keeps the pregnancy secret as long as she can. Salomé Camila is born prematurely, and with all efforts concentrated on keeping the mother alive, the infant is saved only by the quick action of the maid Tivisita, the beautiful young woman who will become Pancho's second wife. When Tivisita places the infant on Salomé's chest, Salomé pulls herself back from the brink of death, back from darkness into light, to live for her children. This is the end of Salomé's narrative.

Salomé has only three years left to live, and she is isolated from her children much of the time, since medical opinion is divided on whether consumption is contagious. She completes her poem for her thoughtful second son, Pedro (also known as Pibín), the future intellectual who is wise beyond his years. The early memory that establishes Camila's obsession with her mother's poems, a memory she is not even sure is true, is about this poem: her mother told her the poem was for her as well as Pibín. She also told Camila to stay close to Pedro and trust his judgment. On the strength of this memory, Camila later pencils feminine endings into the poem in the published collection of her mother's works to adapt the poem to herself, earning punishment from her father, who refutes her memory. It is not until many years later that she discovers Pedro shares the memory of being entrusted by their mother with Camila's guidance.

Camila's narrative starts with "Light" and is set in Poughkeepsie, New York, in 1960, when Camila, unable to ask her long-dead mother how to live the rest of her life, reads Salomé's poems for answers. A program marking the first anniversary of the Cuban revolution is on television when she opens the book to "Light," with its lines, "Where shall the uncertain heart attempt its flight? Rumors of another life awaken it."[10] Having renounced her first name, Salomé, because she feels she has not earned it, Camila decides that she can live up to her mother's example by returning to Cuba to support Castro's new society. Before she moves, her brother Max sends her two trunks of family papers for sorting. This task connects her to the past, helping her exorcise ghosts and fill the emptiness caused by her mother's absence. In the future that remains to her at age 66, she wants "to become Salomé Camila."[11] Her renewed sense of union with her mother, symbolized by their shared name, echoes the sense of union she felt before she fully understood her mother's death, in an episode recounted in chapter eight.

Chapter two, "The Arrival of Winter," is set in 1950, at a centennial observance of her mother's birth in Middlebury, Vermont, where her friend Marion teaches. Marion is leaving, she informs Camila, to live with her lover, Lesley, in Florida. Camila is saddened by the news, but Marion exhausts Camila, and Camila has been ambivalent any time Marion suggested the two of them should settle down together, although they were lovers when they were young. She is depressed, too, by Pedro's recent death and the centennial, which "[brings] back, as she knew it would, that hollowed-out feeling of original loss."[12] Camila rises to the occasion by speaking out against Trujillo, claiming her mother's patriotic legacy and, for the first time, allows herself freedom from worrying about "her words' effect on the important roles her father and brothers and uncles and cousins were playing in the world."[13]

Camila's third chapter, "Ruins," marks the end of her hopes of becoming a poet herself, when she visits Pedro in Cambridge, Massachusetts, in 1941 to hear his last lecture as the prestigious Norton Lecturer in Latin American Studies at Harvard. It also marks the beginning of her teaching career at Vassar. Camila reflects that her truly significant relationship with a man is her relationship with Pedro, even though they have been separated for 20 years, at odds over her relationship with Marion. Camila is making a fresh start, leaving behind Batista's dictatorship in Cuba, where she has lived for decades, and breaking off her romance with the sculptor Domingo. Excited about writing poems and hoping to follow in their mother's footsteps, Camila is anxious for Pedro's reaction to her writing. She recalls the conversation in which her mother told her to "Stay close to Pibín. Trust what he tells you"[14]; Pedro dashes Camila's hopes for a career in poetry, which she has envisioned as her way to continue the struggle for their homeland. Perhaps most hurtful is his rationale that he is defending Dominican poetry, their figurative homeland, from "the well-meaning but lacking in talent."[15] She accepts his judgment that she should take the position at Vassar and stop writing poems.

Chapter four, "Shadows," takes place in Havana in 1935, at the time of her father's death, and chronicles the beginning of her involvement with the sculptor commissioned to create a memorial bust of her father, who was president of the Dominican Republic for four months. A teacher at the time, Camila has been increasingly involved in political demonstrations for women's voting rights. When her brother Max, working in Trujillo's government, visits, he plans to take her home to the Dominican Republic and silence her opposition to the government, threatening her with extradition if she refuses. However, she has applied for Cuban citizenship and plans to stay. She flees to Domingo in an effort to break with her past.

"Love and Yearning" is set in Washington, D.C., in 1923, a dozen years before her father's death. Camila has accompanied her father to petition the U.S. government for support of his position as president after American occupation has ended his government. Love and politics collide, and Camila turns down an American major's proposal after she discovers his complicity in keeping her father away from U.S. authorities. Much of this chapter is related through letters to Marion, from whom Camila is separated when Marion spends a summer back home in North Dakota. (The following chapter, "Ruinas," also telling of ruined romance, is also related through letters—Salomé's letters to Pancho in France.)

Before Pancho and Camila left for the United States, Pedro visited them to introduce his new wife and warned Camila not to "let Papancho's [their father's] politics take over [her] personal life."[16] He also asked whether Major Andrews knew of her mixed racial heritage on their mother's side; Pedro is one of the darker members of the family and was denied entry to Minneapolis clubs when they were both in graduate school there.

During that earlier period of "Faith in the Future," in 1918, Camila and Pedro are separated by her defiance of her family to pursue her own goals. She plans to spend a summer at Marion's home and then teach in Minnesota, living with several other young women. Despite a clear sense of duty to her *patria* that derives from studying her mother's poems, Camila wants to shape her own future. For Pedro, keeping his promise to take care of Camila means leaving the United States, with its racism and post–World War I xenophobia. But U.S. interventions in several Latin American countries are making it difficult for Pedro to figure out where he can live outside of U.S. occupation. Camila defies patriarchal control and the limited options available to her in Latin America by accepting the teaching post, and her relationship with Pedro ruptures when he discovers her romance with Marion.

"Reply" is set in Santiago de Cuba in 1909, where Camila lives with her father, her stepmother Tivisita, and her half-brothers. Reunited with Salomé's sister, her Tía Ramona, after a five-year separation, Camila tries to recapture her few memories to construct a picture of her mother. The idealized portrait of Salomé that her father commissioned reshapes Salomé's nose, lightens her skin, and removes the kink from her hair, eliminating signs of her mixed racial heritage. He has edited Salomé's poems, too, fitting her verse as well as her memory to his own standards. Pancho has denied Camila contact with her aunt or grandmother and also denied Pedro's request that Camila be sent to live with him in Mexico. She suffers from asthma, and her father claims to be avoiding "another lung tragedy"[17] like her mother's illness, but Camila believes this is just an excuse to keep her from doing what she wants to do.

Ramona gives Camila her copies of Salomé's poems, made from the manuscripts, as well as Salomé's elegant black dress and silver comb. Ramona has also brought many of Pancho's books from the Dominican Republic, and in them Camila finds her mother's letters to Pancho in France, thus discovering her father's betrayal. Ramona reminds Camila how attached she was to Tivisita, who kept her alive when she was born, inspiring Salomé to live for three more years. Although Camila does not want to admit this, Tivisita is the only mother she truly remembers.

Chapter eight, "Bird and Nest," is about "Departing Santo Domingo, 1897." Camila is already forgetting her mother, remembering only her coughing, so her Tía Ramona teaches her to say, "In the name of the Father, the Son, and the holy spirit of Salomé, my mother,"[18] every time she makes the sign of the cross. When Tivisita reports this sacrilege to Pancho, in exile in Cuba, he sends for his children. His orders spark a loud argument between Tivisita and Ramona, and Camila hides in the hole under the house. When the adults find her, someone says, "You'll be the death of us."[19] She denies responsibility for her mother's death, and, for the first time, she feels the pinch of breathlessness in her chest, the onset of asthma. The adults assure her that she was not responsible for Salomé's death. But on the boat, Camila entertains another illusion, that her mother has returned from heaven with a new baby and will be waiting for her with her father in Cuba. Distressed when this fantasy is dismissed as "stupid" by one of her brothers, Camila hides again.[20]

In the hold of the boat, she remembers the day of her mother's death, when she was called into the room to recite Salomé's poem, "El ave y el nido," telling how a mother bird flies from the nest when it is disturbed. Her dying mother struggles to speak, and her father pushes Camila away, reporting Salomé's last words as "I see more light,"[21] but Camila struggles to recall something else she thinks her mother said. As the boat arrives in Cuba, and Camila hears the cries of family members searching for her, she remembers her mother saying their special name, "Salomé Camila," and she replies, "Here we are."[22] Thus her name unites her with her mother's memory.

The last phase of her life is recounted in the epilogue in Camila's first-person narrative, in contrast with the third-person perspective maintained throughout the rest of her story. Camila reflects on the fulfillment she found working in Cuba's Ministry of Education, although she was poor, her pension blocked by U.S. policy toward Cuba. Now nearly blinded by cataracts, on the eve of her death she chooses her place in the family cemetery plot and insists that her headstone include her full name, reclaiming her relationship to Salomé.

Throughout her life, Camila has kept her mother's memory close with her prayer, "In the name of the Father, the Son, and of my mother, Salomé."[23] The emptiness at her emotional core caused by her mother's death is never really filled with another love. Her relationship with Marion fades into friendship, and her relationships with men are short-lived and unsatisfactory. Her father's concerns take over her life, and her brothers are absent in her teenage years, while later their reputations overshadow her own achievements. She refuses "to be buried . . . among the great dead" members of her family, telling her half-brother Rodolfo that she does not need to be reunited with her mother in death: "I learned how to be with her as an absence all my life."[24] At the same time, sharing her mother's name, intimately acquainted with her mother's poems, she feels connected to Salomé. Her early memory of calling out, "Here we are," when she emerged from her hiding place on the boat is the first indication that Camila has internalized Salomé. She is too young to understand Pibín's explanation that, instead of being "in heaven," their mother lives in their hearts, and she is too young to understand his statement, "We're going to keep Mama alive, you and I,"[25] but in fact, she lives a life shaped by her mother's presence. Her final insistence on having her complete name on her headstone emphasizes Salomé's continued life in Camila.

Salomé's example shapes Camila's ideals, but Salomé sometimes suffers as much from disappointed idealism as from the illness that kills her. Her farewell to poetry, "Sombras," is written when, she says, "I had lost heart in the ability of words to transform us into a patria of brothers and sisters"[26]; her poems are quoted by the dictator, Lilís, whose claim to power is the opposite of what she stands for. Her husband briefly serves in the usurpers' government, believing he can do more good by serving the government than resisting it, as her son Max later will in Trujillo's government. Pedro identifies Salomé's disease as "moral asphyxiation" and says he must choose exile in Mexico for the same reason: he simply refuses to live in a corrupt atmosphere.[27] In her 20s, with high hopes for her future, Camila chooses to stay in Minneapolis partly from a desire to avoid the heartbreak her mother experienced, thinking, "She would not throw herself away on a country that could not keep faith with the dreams in her heart."[28]

Salomé is self-sacrificing. She gives up her poetry first as a patriotic duty, and second to devote her life to children—the girls she teaches and her own children. Losing faith in poetry's power, she thinks, "The last thing our country needed was more poems. We needed schools. We needed to bring up a generation of young people who would think in new ways and stop the cycle of suffering on our island."[29] She tells Pancho, "My children are the only immortality I want."[30] Nonetheless, she writes two poems for the anniversary of Columbus's arrival, "¡Tierra!" and "Fe," the first a rousing patriotic poem, the second a "quieter" poem set "mid-ocean" when the sailors "need[ed] the faith to continue with no sign of land ahead."[31]

Camila's name comes from a poem by Florian, which Salomé loves, about a woman who walks lightly through the world, even over the ocean. Salomé seems to have accurately foreseen her daughter's life, alternating between Cuba and the United States. Castro's patriotic call to duty motivates Camila's final return to Cuba, where she teaches at the university and in factories and writes teaching materials. When her half-brother

Complete texts of Salomé Ureña's poems on the Web (Spanish only) include "A la patria," "El ave y el nido," "La llegada del invierno," "Mi Pedro," and "Ruinas."[32]

The United States occupied the Dominican Republic from 1916–1924 and occupied neighboring Haiti from 1915–1934.[33]

Rodolfo questions the value of Castro's revolution, Camila says: "The real revolution could only be won by the imagination. When one of my newly literate students picked up a book and read with hungry pleasure, I knew we were one step closer to the patria we all wanted."[34] Both mother and daughter devote their lives to teaching, and the novel ends with Camila teaching a boy to read the letters on her headstone. Moreover, both women have worked to breathe freely, in free countries.

As Salomé's death approaches, she lacks the breath to speak, able only to move her lips, and she feels the loss of language as death itself: "This must be the beginning of death, I thought, the tendrils of language unable to reach beyond the self and catch the attention of others."[35] Camila's many efforts to recapture her mother in memory, losing her mother's face and remembering only her coughing, lead her to reflect, "This is how people can really die."[36] But ultimately, the words live.

DISCUSSION QUESTIONS

- What does poetry accomplish, if anything, in Salomé's lifetime? What is her more lasting achievement—her poems or the school she founds?
- The reader is privy to Salomé's account of herself and understands the significance of some of the items in the trunk that Camila sorts, such as the broken flag. Can Camila really know her mother, basing her knowledge on the poems, family members' memories, and this small store of artifacts? Does she succeed in living up to her mother, at last?
- What elements of Camila's adult personality can be traced to the early trauma of her mother's death? To what extent is Camila's sexuality a factor in her personality?

7

SAVING THE WORLD
(2004)

In *Saving the World*,[1] Alvarez again explores a historical subject: the small-pox vaccination expedition led by the Spanish royal physician Francisco Xavier Balmis in the early 1800s. The historical story is framed in the contemporary story of a novelist who researches and writes about Dr. Balmis's expedition. In a note at the end of the novel, Alvarez explains that the novel originated in a footnote she read in a history of the Dominican Republic: there was a smallpox epidemic in 1804, the same year that, sadly, the vaccinating expedition visited other Spanish colonies in the Caribbean but bypassed the island of Hispaniola because of unsettled conditions.[2] The vaccination project used the milder cowpox virus to inoculate against the virulent smallpox. To keep the vaccine fresh during the long ocean voyage to the western hemisphere, Dr. Balmis requisitioned orphaned boys to act as living carriers of the cowpox virus. The novelist protagonist of the contemporary story, Alma Rodriguez, becomes intrigued by references to a woman who accompanied Dr. Balmis, Isabel Sendales y Gómez, rectoress of the Spanish orphanage where Dr. Balmis recruited his boy carriers.

Like *In the Name of Salomé*, this novel intertwines the two stories in alternating chapters. Alma's story begins in a period of midlife depression that echoes the 13th-century poet Dante Alighieri's spiritual crisis, with which *The Divine Comedy* begins, and ends like Dante's, with a mountaintop experience of release and faith in the future. Isabel's story begins with Dr. Balmis's initial visit to the orphanage and ends with her death.

Portions of both narratives are told through letters or diary entries. Both revolve around dangerous trips, deaths of loved ones, idealistic projects in which the means to a noble end are sometimes questionable, the difficulties of maintaining faith in a fallen world, the sacrifice of the lives of the poor to the projects of the privileged for sometimes dubious benefit, the infections people carry and the maladies they survive, the power of stories to sustain hope, and ultimately the meaning of salvation, of "saving the world."

At the outset, Alma is living through a dark period in the fall of her 50th year. Struggling with writer's block, she has lost faith in herself. She is painfully aware of the mortality of people dear to her: her husband of 10 years, Richard; her best friend, Tera; her elderly neighbor, Helen, who is a mother figure to Alma. Alma fears living a long life and spending her declining years in loneliness. She resolves to stop seeing her psychiatrist, Dr. Payne, and buries her medications, rejecting a medical approach to her crisis of the soul. Her reflection that she is at the midpoint of her life evokes Dante. Also similar to the opening of *Inferno*, threats cross her path before she finds her spiritual guide: first, one evening when Richard works late, a strange man roams through her rural Vermont yard; then, the same evening, a woman whom Alma has never heard of calls to inform her that she has AIDS and is contacting the wives of men with whom she has been intimate.

Richard is in a state of suppressed excitement when he arrives. He has been offered the responsibility for starting a "green project" in the mountains of Alma's native Dominican Republic. He anticipates that she will accompany him for his five-month stay, since she periodically visits family members there. But with her own emotional balance disturbed and her direction as a writer to resolve, Alma balks at accompanying Richard to a remote mountain village without electricity or running water. It will take too much energy to reinvent herself in a different environment, energy that she needs for dealing with her personal crisis.

It is not until Richard arrives in the Dominican Republic that he discovers the village is also the site of a new AIDS clinic built by a drug company to test experimental medications—the same drug company that is funding the green project. The villagers fear and resent the clinic. About the same time, Alma learns that her elderly mentor, Helen, is in the late stages of cancer. Helen's son, Mickey, has returned to the neighborhood to care for his mother after decades of separation. He is the disturbing stranger who appeared suddenly in Alma's yard. A former Marine nurse, Mickey has other caretaking responsibilities as well: his wife is the disturbed woman who has been making the false calls about AIDS to randomly selected married women.

These elements suddenly erupt into a dual crisis on Thanksgiving, when Helen suffers a stroke and Richard is taken hostage in the AIDS clinic. Alma is suspicious of Mickey, so when she sees him about to administer an injection to Helen, Alma fears it will harm her friend, so she calls 911, bringing not only the paramedics but also the police, who arrest Mickey. By calling in authorities, Alma has interfered with Helen's previously expressed wishes: Helen wants reconciliation with her son, and she does not want hospitalization. Alma is deeply distressed, questioning whether she misinterpreted what she saw—making it into a dramatic but unfounded story. Still reeling from the night's drama, Alma returns home from the hospital to find a phone message from Richard's boss, who informs her that Richard is a hostage in the AIDS clinic, seized by a group of angry young men from the village and surrounding area. Alma heads to the Dominican Republic, where the hostage drama plays out inexorably into explosive violence, despite Alma's warnings to officials on the scene. The unimaginable happens: Richard dies in the military assault on the hostage-takers. Then, in paradoxical anticlimax, after being freed from the hostage situation, Alma is quarantined because, back in Vermont, Mickey claims to have infected her with monkey pox. His claim proves false: with Hannah, Mickey is staging "ethical terrorist" events. A few weeks after Richard's death, Helen dies. Alma is in the position she most feared—nearly alone (she still has Tera) and grieving for her loved ones.

Yet as events unfold, Alma finds a new path through the dark wood of midlife depression and trauma in the story that preoccupies her: Isabel's story of the Royal Spanish Expedition's voyage halfway around the globe, "saving the world" from smallpox. Throughout Alma's story, her interest in Isabel and Dr. Balmis forms the basis for transitions into the chapters of Isabel's story as Isabel's story becomes Alma's current writing project. Isabel's story also proves to be Alma's salvation, confirming her belief in the saving power of stories. Faced with her own crisis, she draws parallels between her challenges and Isabel's challenges, imagining her way into the other woman's thoughts and motives. She writes Isabel's story as a way of affirming the larger scale of history within which individual stories play out, and thus she puts private trials into a larger human perspective.

Isabel is in her mid-30s when she meets the physician who will give her the opportunity to reinvent herself. As a teenager, she lost her parents and sister to smallpox. Though she survived, she was severely scarred, and in public she wears a heavy veil to conceal her face. Having acquired immunity to the disease, she began nursing almost immediately after recovering. At the beginning of her story, Isabel has spent six years as a nurse and 12 years as rectoress of an orphanage in La Coruña. Like Alma, she has arrived at a dark place in her life. Feeling trapped, she needs a new sense of purpose when Dr. Balmis, the royal physician, arrives to claim 22 of her orphans as vaccine carriers. He will expose the boys two at a time to cowpox and each time will harvest the fluid from the blister that results from inoculation, using this fluid to infect two more boys, thus keeping the virus fresh throughout the voyage across the Atlantic. He plans to visit Spain's Caribbean colonies, South America, and Central America, and then continue to the Philippines and China, circling the globe. He is a visionary, and his project fires Isabel's imagination.

Isabel sees the potential for a new life for herself as well as the boys, who are promised a special upbringing after their service to the Crown, and she insists that she be allowed to accompany and care for them. Ready to help Dr. Balmis "save the world" from smallpox, she is prepared for some but not all of the challenges of the voyage. More surprising than the problems of the ocean voyage are the challenges that await the mission in various ports, where they are sometimes welcomed, sometimes ignored. As she gets to know Dr. Balmis (also known as Don Francisco), she finds him irascible, capable of pettiness as well as impolitic anger when he receives less respect than he anticipates, but nonetheless capable of kindness. Whenever her faith flags, his noble vision recalls her to continued effort. Her abilities moderate the difficulties his temper causes: she tells stories, at first to the boys, then to a larger shipboard audience. With her stories, she takes people's minds off the annoyances and discomforts of day-to-day travel in difficult conditions—stormy weather, stifling heat, food of poor quality, cramped sleeping quarters, and illnesses other than the pox they carry. She aids in the vaccinating process by reducing fear with her soothing voice and compelling eye contact.

As she travels, Isabel grows more confident. Having discarded the impractical veil at Dr. Balmis's insistence, she discovers that the sun and sea air improve her scarred complexion. Actually, she is less disfigured than she has imagined, and she is otherwise an attractive woman. Her good qualities win the love of the ship's first mate, but their duties take them in different directions, preventing a reunion and marriage. Separated by her travels from little Benito, the boy she has planned to raise as her own son, as well, she has a happier outcome in her reunion with him in Mexico and a new life there after her parting from Dr. Balmis.

Though Dr. Balmis sets up a network of administrative centers to provide a store of fresh vaccine to continue the inoculation program, political upheaval in Spain's colonies eventually disrupts his centers. Inevitably, another smallpox epidemic strikes, but Isabel is able to set the program in motion once more as an old woman, and when she dies, she feels that her life has had meaning, even though her story may be lost.

The theme of "saving the world" is embodied by characters in both stories. Richard's idealism takes him to the Dominican Republic, working for a nonprofit organization that spreads the knowledge that can solve the problems of communities where poverty, ill health, and illiteracy are widespread. Alma's friend Tera wants to save the world with political activism, attending protest rallies and rousing people to action on a range of issues. Alma sometimes finds her friend's constant commitment intrusive. She does not want to hear about injustices and dangers in the Dominican Republic when Richard is there, and she discourages Tera from giving Helen a pile of brochures about hospice care as soon as she learns of Helen's cancer.

Helen turns to her Christian God for salvation, and her optimism comes from her faith that human lives are in God's hands. She is not a proselytizer, but she quietly shares her insights. Helen tells Alma that not everyone has to save the world, and it is all right to write stories instead of undertaking larger projects. The small network of neighbors and hospice workers who form Helen's support system bring their own brand of salvation to Helen, saving her from the discomforts and indignities of a lingering death in the hospital. The women's model for maintaining the social fabric is sharply contrasted with actions taken by the men managing the hostage crisis in the Dominican Republic. Arguably, those men, military and diplomatic representatives of the United States and the Dominican Republic, are acting on their principles to save their world from terrorist incursions, but their actions result in needless violence and the death of the innocent Richard. The hostage-takers, simple village boys who are transformed into terrorists by the reactions of their society, also claim an ethical stance. Instead of an AIDS clinic that will benefit affluent customers for expensive drugs that have been tested on the poor, these young men want, at first, a clinic that will save their families and neighbors from the easily treatable ailments that result in death for those too poor to pay for medical treatment. They also seek fair economic opportunities in the short term, impatient with the longer-term benefits of the farm that Richard has just started. Even Helen's son, Mickey, and his deranged wife, Hannah, are trying to save the world: with their threats of infection by AIDS or monkey pox, they see themselves as engaging in ethical terrorism to spark public awareness. In the 19th-century narrative, Isabel, who has begun to question her faith, is captured by the vision of saving the world through science that Dr. Balmis's project represents. Dr. Balmis is a zealot, often blinded by his own mission to save the world, so that he misinterprets others' motivations and ignores their legitimate interests.

In contrast to these characters, each of whom acts with the assurance that his or her vision is the right one for everyone, Alma is troubled by the impact her stories may have. She questions her own commercial success and the means by which it is achieved in the professional world of publishing. She has used the pseudonym Fulana du Tal, meaning "nobody"—claiming nonidentity for herself—and maintained her privacy by refusing to be photographed fully lit. This has caused her to come under attack by a Hispanic critic who accuses her of falsely presenting herself as a writer of color. Alma's agent rejoices in this "negative publicity,"[3] which will likely pay off in increased book sales. The agent's reaction is as distasteful to Alma as the ferocity with which she has been attacked, and she has decided to begin writing under her own name.

This is the point when Alma's malaise strikes. She cannot write the multigenerational novel for which she is under contract. Because it is long overdue, she has been hiding her writer's block from everyone except Helen. She also conceals her decision to give up therapy and antidepressants. Alma is conscious of a splitting of her identity, a condition that is intensified when she plays out a role with Richard after the AIDS call, acting like a "magazine wife." However, the magazine wife is not the person she is developing into: she feels a new self "splintering off, . . . a woman from some other story."[4] She sends Richard to the Dominican Republic without her because she needs solitude to redefine herself as a woman separate from him, although, despite her forebodings, she does not seriously expect that she will need to develop an identity as a solitary woman.

Similarly, Isabel's name and identity change in the course of the novel. Alma finds that records are inconsistent: variations of Isabel's last name appear in different historical sources. Alma, or Alvarez, builds the variant names into Isabel's narrative, a practice that suggests the new fluidity of Isabel's identity as she travels. Even to little Benito, her identity changes—from Mama to Doña Isabel during their long separation, and eventually back to Mama.

The depth of Alma's spiritual crisis is suggested with allusions to *The Divine Comedy*. Dante identifies himself as wandering into a dark wood midway through life; Alma "finds herself lost in a dark mood she can't seem to shake."[5] She considers herself to be near the middle of her life, since all indications are that she will live into her 90s. The first part of *The Divine Comedy* is *Inferno*, or Hell, and Dante's life journey, at this point, is a descent into Hell, for which the great classical poet Virgil is his spirit-guide. Alma finds a spirit-guide on her journey: imagining Isabel's brave endurance of severe challenges, Alma's own courage, hope, and faith are restored. Alma apparently considers Tera as a guide when she refers to her friend's consignment of wasteful people to a "circle of consumer hell,"[6] but she rejects her as a mentor. Alma removes herself from the 21st-century conflicts that beset her by "fleeing" to the 19th century,[7] seeking help from a long-dead mentor.

Alma describes her spiritual state with other allusions throughout the novel. One example is Alfred Hitchcock's film *The Birds*. Alma tells her psychiatrist she feels that "whirling darkness" is enveloping her, which she explicitly links to the film.[8] Isabel, too, describes her state at the beginning of her narrative in terms of a flock of black birds that extinguish her will.[9] For Isabel, this sense of darkness contrasts strongly with the orphanage's gold-embellished tapestry of the Annunciation, the angel Gabriel's announcement of pregnancy to the Virgin Mary. As darkness descends on Dr. Balmis's first visit to the orphanage, a narrow shaft of light strikes the gilding, and Isabel momentarily envisions the smallpox vaccine as a small glowing element, lit by human reason, in the painting.[10]

Alvarez makes substantial use of allusions in *Saving the World*. Tera reaches out to her unhappy friend as God reaches to touch Adam's extended hand in Michelangelo's painting on the ceiling of the Sistine Chapel.[11] Alma fends off her doubts about Richard by holding up her faith in him like a crucifix wielded against Dracula.[12] She misses the "independent warrior woman" she used to be, alluding to Maxine Hong Kingston's *The Woman Warrior*.[13] When Richard flies to the Dominican Republic, Alma waits anxiously to hear he has arrived safely, that he has passed unscathed between "the Scylla of mechanical failure and the Charybdis of terrorists,"[14] in a reference to Greek mythology that is most familiar from Homer's *Odyssey*. Richard's company redistributes wealth like Robin Hood did.[15] She and Helen's other neighborhood helper, Claudine, are like two kids lost in the woods, Hansel and Gretel, with no way back from Helen's illness.[16] Alma feels like Malinche, Cortés's mistress, a betrayer of her own people.[17] Later, she offers the kidnappers "a narrative of hope" that she likens to Ariadne's thread, by which Theseus found his way out of the labyrinth after his encounter with the Minotaur.[18] After the clinic is stormed and almost all of the hostage-takers are killed, the families of the slain set up a wailing that reminds Alma of a Greek chorus.[19] Both Alma and Isabel refer to paintings by Goya.[20] The combined effect of these and other allusions is to embed Alma's and Isabel's personal narratives in the long tradition of human storytelling, to lend universality to their suffering and their aspirations.

Religion is largely dismissed by both women as a means of "saving the world." Isabel's religious doubts are conveyed early in her narrative when she speculates that the Virgin Mary may not have felt joy when she learned that she would bear a child out of wedlock.[21] Alma refers several times to the Fall of Man, beginning with her reading to the blind Helen from the blind poet Milton's epic *Paradise Lost*. Helen's deep sighs lead Alma to abandon it after the first two books, in which Satan awakes to his defeat after being expelled from heaven and calls his minions to a meeting to plot against God by leading Adam and Eve into sin. Helen says the arguments among the demons sound like the congressional debates on C-SPAN.[22] When Alma learns that Helen is dying of cancer, she tries to convince herself that it is okay because Helen's life has been long, with many good moments, but she "feels like one of those devils in *Paradise Lost*, full of logical reasons why it's okay that somebody else is going to die."[23] Traveling to the site of a hostage standoff, Alma reflects that she cannot trust all of the men who are planning how to handle the situation, but she has no one else to turn to, concluding, "This is what it means to live in a fallen world."[24] The theme is underscored by one of the epigraphs to the novel, a quotation from T. S. Eliot.

The novel's epigraphs come from two poems and an article: Eliot's "Gerontion," Seamus Heaney's "Voices from Lemnos," and Sherbourne F. Cook's "Francisco Xavier Balmis and the Introduction of Vaccination in Latin America." The quotations from the poems focus on history but in significantly different ways. Eliot emphasizes human sinfulness after the Fall, when Adam and Eve ate forbidden fruit from "the wrath-bearing tree," and humans' quest for forgiveness in the twisting paths of history, where individuals may be misled by ambition or vanity and cannot find salvation through fear or bravery.[25] In this fallen world, heroism itself can lead a person into crimes, but virtues can grow out of those crimes. Heaney's line about the outcome of the quest for justice—that when it periodically manifests itself as a "tidal wave," then "hope and history rhyme"—is quoted several times in the novel.[26] It is given the most emphasis when Alma converses with the mayor of the Dominican village before making her desperate gamble to mediate the hostage situation. It is "only by violence or sheer accident" that hope and history rhyme,[27] when idealists' efforts to spread justice are corrupted by the conviction that the end justifies the means—in Richard's company's project, in the village boys' seizing the clinic, and in Dr. Balmis's infecting orphan boys. As the mayor walks away, Alma makes her decision to join the hostages in an effort to assist the process of rhyming hope with history.[28] Another poem quoted in the novel is Emily Dickinson's "After Great Pain, a Formal Feeling Comes," which comes to Alma as she waits for news of Richard after the violent end of the hostage situation, views his body, and grieves.[29]

The third epigraph, from Sherbourne F. Cook's article, makes the point that ordinary people's efforts in the struggle to save the world must be remembered: "The child carriers are all but forgotten, but their humble if wholly unrewarded efforts deserve a place in human recollection."[30] One question that arises for both Alma and Isabel is whether individual stories will be remembered, and if not, whether individual lives—with their sufferings and their aspirations—have ultimate meaning. Both Isabel and Alma show more faith in stories, reason, and science than in conventional religious precepts. Isabel says of Mary's response to the angel Gabriel that it is "One of those scriptures that, the more I lived, the harder I found to believe. There were many such doubts these days, . . . I was discovering,"[31] and when she sees the smallpox vaccine instead of an angel in the tapestry of the Annunciation, she finds herself thinking sacrilegiously, "We had been looking to God, but salvation had issued from our own reasoning minds."[32] Whenever Helen alludes to her Christian faith, Alma substitutes her own agnosticism through "an instantaneous translation" of "God as a metaphor for the stunning, baffling, painful, beautiful spirit of the universe."[33] She needs to believe in a more personal God when she tries to bargain. Waiting for Richard to call from the Dominican Republic, she makes a promise to "Helen's God—since she knows that the baffling, painful spirit of the Universe doesn't make deals."[34] She bargains again, unsuccessfully, after she learns Richard is a hostage, promising not to pursue her suspicions of Mickey, hoping to win her husband back in exchange. After the hostages are rescued in a hail of gunfire and Alma fears Richard is dead, she once again tries to bargain with God.

Alma moves on from temporary belief in this God who is impervious to her pleas. The following summer, when she takes Richard's and Helen's ashes up Snake Mountain for the memorial service, months after Helen's church funeral, she believes that "Helen's God is with Helen now" but Alma "will miss him."[35] She recalls how Richard liked to call out on the mountaintop, "Are you there, God?" and inform Alma, "He's out. . . . Busy with the trouble spots."[36] Now, waking in the night, Alma listens for spiritual communication from Richard and whispers, "Hello? Are you there, Richard?" but hears nothing.[37] The world is baffling, but she has stories. She must keep faith by telling them, rather than seek spiritual solace from another being, and she concludes, "So this is how the dead live on."[38] She has answered the question she asked herself immediately after Richard's death—"What does it mean not to lose faith with what is grand?"—when she resumed Isabel's story as "a thread of hope."[39]

Alma is a "carrier" of stories, and she is "infected" with questions—an association first made by the hostage-takers, who want to "infect the

The complete text of Emily Dickinson's poem is available on the Poetry
Foundation's Web page.[40]

world with [their] questions."[41] Isabel's story—her life—ends in the recognition that she is "a carrier, . . . carrying this story, which would surely
die, unless it took hold in a future life."[42] The infections that threaten
multitudes in this novel—smallpox, AIDS—can be neutralized with vac-
cines, but the important questions generated by the narrative remain.
What can be done about the injustice of unequal distribution of the
world's resources and technologies? Why do men react with violence to
disruptions of the social order, causing more deaths with their cure than
are caused by those who disrupt it?

When all of the events have been set in motion in the first part of the
novel—Helen's hospitalization, Mickey's arrest, Richard's being taken
hostage—Alma sees their lives as "hurtling over the edge, floating on
faith, floating on love."[43] At the end of the novel, she sees the scattered
ashes as "floating on faith, floating on love—blessing the ground."[44]
All that endures—the lives of loved ones, ultimately their memories—is
preserved through love and the faith that individual stories are part of
something grand.

DISCUSSION QUESTIONS

- What motivates people to take up a cause, trying to save the world? Can a
  humanitarian project that aims to give material aid to people be compared
  with the goal of winning souls to salvation?
- Others' stories often inspire us and may seem to afford a kind of guidance.
  Can stories save us? Does fiction matter?
- Is the title, *Saving the World*, meant literally or ironically?

8

BOOKS FOR YOUNG READERS

Starting with *The Secret Footprints* in 2000, Julia Alvarez has published eight books for young readers, with a ninth scheduled for release in 2010: three picture books, one book for eight- to ten-year-olds (with a sequel in press at this writing), one book for intermediate readers (ages 10 to 12), two books for young adults, and a book listed on Alvarez's Web site among her "Books for Young Readers of All Ages," *A Cafecito Story*. Two novels, *Before We Were Free* (2002) and *Return to Sender* (2009), received the Pura Belpré Award, annually given by the American Library Association for a book that "best portrays, affirms, and celebrates the Latino cultural experience in an outstanding work of literature for children and youth."[1]

Like her fiction for adults, Alvarez's fiction for intermediate and teen readers mixes perspectives and settings, using first-person and third-person narrative, and sometimes mixing genres by incorporating diary entries or letters. Issues include life in a dictatorship, transition to democracy, intercultural adoption, and illegal immigration, along with the usual concerns of this age group, especially fitting in with peers and coping with the death of older relatives.

BEFORE WE WERE FREE

Before We Were Free[2] adds to the story of the Torre family (of *How the García Girls Lost Their Accents* and *¡Yo!*), depicting the dangers to family members who stayed in the Dominican Republic to oppose Trujillo after the García family's escape. It is told from 12-year-old Anita's perspective and covers a little over a year, from the day in 1960 when the Garcías leave the Dominican Republic to Thanksgiving Day in 1961, when Anita's family is with the Garcías in the United States.

Following the Garcías' departure, the secret police (SIM) search the family compound and maintain surveillance for two weeks, until the American Washburn family moves from the U.S. embassy into the compound, giving the family some degree of international protection. Anita's questions go unanswered by adults, so she observes carefully: her Tío Toni returns secretly to his house and Anita must not mention him; her mother warns visitors to watch what they say in front of the new maid; and her parents are distressed about an accident involving "butterflies." Even before her mother asks Anita to stop writing in her new diary, she practices self-censorship, writing daily and then erasing her entries with the Dominican Republic–shaped eraser her cousin Carla left behind.

Trujillo's surprise appearance at Susie Washburn's birthday party leads to disillusionment about the leader Anita always viewed as a hero. Her parents send Lucinda to the United States with Susie Washburn on a hastily arranged visa, fearing Trujillo will demand Lucinda as his mistress. Subsequently, Anita becomes more aware of her family's involvement in antiregime activities: when Mr. Washburn's car is rear-ended, she sees that the trunk is full of rifles. Overhearing her father's late-evening conversations with friends, she learns that they plan to kill Trujillo. All that she witnesses transforms Anita from a carefree "little parrot," a chatterbox, to a girl who is afraid to speak and begins to forget words. Only her classmate, Oscar Mancini, whose Italian-born father works in the Italian embassy, still treats her normally. As tension mounts, Mrs. Washburn and Sam leave the Dominican Republic and Mr. Washburn is ordered to move back to the embassy.

One morning in May, after a restless night of dreams, overhearing her father's end of frantic phone calls, Anita wakes to the SIM's invasion of her bedroom. Trujillo's body is found in the trunk of her family's car, and Anita witnesses the arrest of her father and uncle. Trujillo's son is bent on bloody vengeance, and Oscar's father takes Anita and her mother to a hiding place in the Mancinis' master bedroom suite. Her brother, Mundín, is hidden in the Italian embassy until he can be smuggled out of the country in July. Anita's diary entries chronicle two months of hiding, until she escapes the Dominican Republic with her mother. Her father's and uncle's fates remain unknown until autumn, when Mr. Washburn learns that Trujillo's son has had them killed in one of his last actions before being forced out of the country.

The remaining family members observe an American Thanksgiving in the Garcías' home in New York, starting with a prayer of remembrance for their loved ones who sacrificed their lives in the cause of freedom. The day ends with Anita's first experience of snow, and her cousins show her how to make snow angels.

Throughout the novel, freedom is associated with spreading one's wings and flying. Their trusted servant, Chucha, dreams that Lucinda, Mundín, and then Anita and her mother will sprout wings and fly, but when Anita asks about her father, Chucha responds, "Not everyone can be a butterfly."[3] As each member of the family leaves for the United States, Anita sees Chucha's prophecy fulfilled. In hiding, Anita's mother explains Anita's father's commitment to the work that the Mirabal sisters, the Butterflies, were unable to complete. Shortly before their escape, Anita receives a reminder from Chucha to prepare to spread her wings. Anita thinks about Chucha as she flies—in a plane—from the island. Later, Oscar sends her another message from Chucha, reminding her of her wings, and Anita realizes that the wings are inside her: the ability to be free comes from within. The snow angels she makes with her cousins look like butterflies from the second-story bedroom window, and Anita thinks of them as a message from her father to appreciate her freedom.

The snow seems magical, making the world fresh and new, unmarred by human actions, and it restores Anita's sullied sense of purity. Her first menstrual period arrives on the night before Lucinda leaves the Dominican Republic, timing that associates her menstrual blood with the dictator's lechery and, later, his blood that stains their driveway. Having looked forward to boyfriends and eventual marriage, Anita is temporarily repelled by the prospect of maturation. She is numb after her father's death until Oscar's letter reminds her of her butterfly wings, and her interest in Oscar reawakens as she comes to terms with her father's death. The snow restores her innocence and brings a feeling of lightheartedness that Anita associates with waking from a bad dream.

Anita has troubling dreams the night of Trujillo's death: she sees the García sisters in snowy Central Park and Carla's Dominican Republic–shaped eraser; Sam Washburn on his trampoline, turning into an astronaut; Oscar's sisters hanging out their window to watch Trujillo pass; the transfer of ex-U.S. Marine Wimpy's eagle tattoo to Anita's face; and her menstrual blood turning into Trujillo's blood. She enters a trance-like depression in her grief over her father's death, feeling buried alive, "a substitute because no one can find Papi's body."[4] She wakes from depression when she realizes her father wanted her to fly free from the nightmare of the dictatorship.

Anita initially wants to be like Joan of Arc, with the maiden saint's courage to fight oppression and a boy's appearance, after she learns about Trujillo's abuse of young women. Caught between childhood and young adulthood, burdened with adult knowledge, Anita wishes that she could age backward to 11 instead of turning 13 on her birthday. It is her womanhood that is most vulnerable. Her fear of arrest and murder, veiling a fear of rape, leads her to resolve that she will take pills to commit suicide if she is arrested. Wishing for death rather than torture, she reflects that her brave desire to be like Joan of Arc did not last long. Yet her menstrual blood is a weapon, used by Chucha in a ruse to drive the spying maid out of the house, which she reinforces with prayers to San Miguel (Saint Michael). Anita also plays her small part as a woman warrior by bearing witness in her diary. While in hiding, Anita realizes that her mother has been involved in the underground and is a Joan of Arc mother. Her message from Chucha comes on a card that shows "San Miguel lifting his huge wings above the slain dragon"[5] in a link between flying and defending the good.

After fear has silenced Anita, writing in her diary restores her ability to talk. Listening to two contrasting radio broadcasts in the Mancinis' bedroom—one the official state version of events, the other the forbidden outside radio station's version—Anita needs to create a "third radio, tuned to [her] heart."[6] Words return, and she begins to regain control over her life. Reading *The Arabian Nights*, Anita wonders whether a beautiful storyteller could have countered Trujillo's violence as Scheherazade did the evil sultan's. Or, by extension, how powerful are stories? Alvarez asks the reader to consider the importance of stories in keeping people free. Anita is silenced by political oppression (rubbing out her words with a Dominican Republic–shaped eraser) and her fear of betraying her

In addition to receiving the Pura Belpré Award, *Before We Were Free* was listed as a Best Book for Young Adults and Notable Children's Book by the American Library Association (ALA); a Best Book of the Year by the *Miami Herald*; a Notable Children's Trade Book in the Field of Social Studies by the National Council for the Social Studies (NCSS) and Children's Book Council (CBC); and one of 100 Titles for Reading and Sharing by the New York Public Library. It won the Américas Award for Children's and Young Adult Literature, which is sponsored by the Consortium of Latin American Studies Programs (CLASP).[7]

> In the Dominican Republic, Trujillo's death is known as the *ajusticiamento*, or "bringing to justice," rather than as an assassination, or murder.[8]

loved ones, but she writes her way back into speech and makes her diary a *testimonio*, an eyewitness account of significant events, claiming her right to challenge the master narrative of the dictatorship.

DISCUSSION QUESTIONS

- What does it mean to be free? Can people be free in their minds when living in a totalitarian society? Is violence a justifiable means for bringing freedom to oppressed people?
- The adults in Anita's life try to protect her from knowledge of their political activity and the dangers in their society. Does this keep her safe? Does it keep her parents' secrets safe?

Anita's mother sometimes treats Anita as a child, sometimes as if she were older than she is. Does Anita feel like a child or a young adult?

FINDING MIRACLES

In *Finding Miracles*,[9] Milly Kaufman's ordinary, all-American life is transformed when she comes to terms with her adoption and learns about the country where she was born. Nothing is known about her background; even her "birthday" is the date she was left outside the orphanage. The only clue to her identity is the paper that was pinned to her clothing, bearing the word Milagros—Spanish for "miracles." In the orphanage she was known as Milagros, but her parents, who adopted her while they served in the Peace Corps, named her Mildred, a family name, keeping Milagros as her middle name.

Milly has a learning disability, and when it was diagnosed several years earlier, she overheard a tutor say that many Third World children who survive trauma have learning disabilities; just surviving is a "miracle."[10] She doesn't think about her life as a miracle of survival, though. She has her family—her parents, her sister Kate, and eight-year-old Nate, along with a grandmother and cousins that she likes; she has friends, who identify themselves as "border-liners,"[11] neither popular nor outsiders in their school. Milly is happy with the normality of her life.

Milly's only problem is a chronic rash that breaks out as a reaction to stress. The rash is set off when Pablo Bolívar, from her birth country, arrives in school. Then her rich grandmother writes a will that treats her differently from her siblings and cousins. These two irritants push Milly to confront her mysterious origin. Pablo's questions as well as his mere presence remind her that she is different from her siblings and classmates. Her grandmother's will makes her feel like an outsider in her family.

Milly initially pretends she does not understand Pablo's Spanish because he makes her uncomfortable, and she makes excuses to avoid him. Then, she learns of his family's plight due to their opposition to the dictator: Mr. Bolívar's older brother, a journalist, was murdered; one of Pablo's brothers is imprisoned, and his other brother is in hiding. Milly's resistance melts away, and the two families become close.

Milly decides to reopen "The Box" that came with her from the orphanage, but it holds only her adoption papers and pictures from the orphanage. A stronger clue to her identity comes from Pablo, who says her eyes are like his aunt's, who comes from a mountain village that suffered severely in the civil war. Milly begins to feel like Pandora in Greek myth, who opened a mysterious box and loosed a host of evils on the world. Milly's secrets were safely put away in The Box; now she fears that bad things will come of opening it.

Elections in the Bolívars' home country will determine the family's fate. If their Liberation Party loses, a bloodbath is likely. Watching television coverage, the Bolívars hope that the vote will be fairly counted, and Pablo reminds his mother that "miracles happen."[12] Milly reflects that her own miracles are occurring—she is more comfortable acknowledging her adoption, and her lonely grandmother wants to restore their relationship—but miracles sometimes have to be found.

The Liberation Party's victory means that the Bolívars can return home for a summer visit. Seeking miracles, Milly convinces her parents to let her accompany the Bolivars. But her need for independent exploration causes tension: her parents are concerned about her safety and emotional well-being, and her sister is angry because she thinks Milly is rejecting her family, What Milly has not admitted is that her interest in Pablo is as compelling as her curiosity about their shared homeland.

Even before she arrives in "*el paisito*" ("the little country"), Milly finds some relief in Mrs. Bolívar's herbal salve for her rash. She feels welcomed by the country as well as the Bolívars' large family. But she also sees firsthand the sorrows caused by the dictatorship. A truth commission is holding televised hearings for citizens' stories of human rights abuses. Milly learns of Pablo's other dead uncle, a general who committed suicide rather than face consequences for his role in carrying out the dictator's orders.

Pablo says the country is "a cradle and a grave"[13]; democracy is newly born, but many have died to bring it to birth. Even Milly's romance with Pablo is "born" on a beach where eight members of the resistance were murdered. On a personal level, Milly's most important visits are to a nearby orphanage—the cradle—and the memorial service for Pablo's journalist uncle at the graveyard when his remains are reburied.

In the mountain village Milly is thought to be from, she meets an elderly blind woman who knows the village's stories, many of them heart-wrenching tales of victimization under the dictatorship. Doña Gloria lives with her mute great-granddaughter, whose tongue was cut out after she witnessed her mother's rape and murder. Doña Gloria's stories suggest three possibilities for Milly's parentage, all of them with sad endings and each containing some detail that Milly can associate with the slim facts she has about her birth; there is no decisive clue. Emotionally drained, Milly is ready to see her family. They have made travel arrangement, her grandmother planning to marry her lawyer in Milly's homeland. Milly has learned many sad and terrible things, but her life is enriched by knowledge. Pablo identifies them both as border-liners between their two cultures: they can connect people from their two cultures.

The last two chapters list the miracles Milly, known as "Milagritos" ("Little Miracles") in Pablo's family, has found: the blending of the two families; Milly's grandmother's donation to the local orphanage; and Milly's romance with Pablo. Milly and Pablo pledge their wish for a future together by offering *milagritos*—little medals they pin to the Virgin Mary's statue as emblems of prayers.

Milly has become stronger by listening to the harrowing stories told to the truth commission, and she responds by considering what she can do to help others. Doña Gloria admonished her to bring light to the world—the light of knowledge, the light of commitment to justice and peace. Milly resolves to write the stories, although for the moment she is storing them away as memories, as though putting them away in a box. Her willingness to write true stories shows how she has changed since the beginning of the novel, when she avoided writing about real experiences in her creative writing class. The Box has changed from Pandora's box of evils to a strongbox of memories, both dark and light.

The emphasis on truthful stories with which the novel ends reinforces the truth commission's goal. *Testimonio* brings healing. Remembering individual lives, telling painful stories, is an important part of connecting the past and the present. Milly embodies the dual identity typical of Alvarez's

> Truth commissions have been created in a number of countries after violent civil conflict as an instrument of restorative justice—justice aimed at creating closure and reconciliation for victims rather than exacting punishment for perpetrators of crimes.

protagonists and claims their borderline identity as a privileged place from which the clearest insights into human connections come.

DISCUSSION QUESTIONS

- What challenges are involved in international adoption? How does the adopted child's experience differ from the immigrant child's experience?
- What makes it important to tell or write painful stories of torture and massacre? What do the tellers of such stories gain? What role do the listeners or readers play?

RETURN TO SENDER

In *Return to Sender*,[14] written for intermediate readers, Alvarez explores complex questions raised by the presence of undocumented Mexican workers in the United States. The Paquette family's Vermont dairy farm is saved by the hard work of three migrant workers when Tyler's father is badly injured in a tractor accident. The Cruz brothers arrive on the farm with three young daughters, the oldest of whom becomes Tyler's friend. The story unfolds in nine chapters, each telling their story first from Tyler's point of view in third person, present tense, and then from Mari Cruz's in first person, told through letters. The dual perspective shows Tyler's and Mari's growing understanding of each other as their families' fortunes intertwine.

When Tyler returns home from a summer visit in Boston and finds the Cruzes installed on the farm, he suspects that they are illegally in the United States and anticipates his parents will report them to the authorities. However, his father states their dilemma starkly, asking Tyler if he wants to lose the farm. Mrs. Paquette calls the Cruz brothers "angels" who have saved them. The occasional phone calls to the Paquettes' home that end abruptly when the caller hangs up soon convince her that someone is trying to reach the Cruzes. From Mari's letter, the reader learns that the Cruzes are waiting to hear from her mother, who disappeared months earlier after flying home to be with her dying mother and reentering the United States illegally. Because of their status, Mr. Cruz cannot report her disappearance; all he could do was to leave the phone number with friends before leaving North Carolina. Both his limited English and his illegal status prevent him from explaining this family situation to his new employers.

Mari's letters reveal the compelling financial argument for working in the United States, even illegally: her grandfather cannot get a fair price for his crops from North American buyers, but her father and uncles earn enough to send $120 a week home, later $180 a week when Mari's grandmother needs expensive medication. Mari calls attention to the increased globalization of the economy, arguing that borders and laws are barriers that prevent honest, hard-working farmers from supporting families in both the United States and Mexico.

Tyler's relationship with Mari is complicated. At first, he sees her as an interloper in his special place in the hayloft, but he then discovers that she loves the swallows that nest there as much as he does. When he allows her to look through the telescope that his grandfather gave him, he finds that she is as excited about the stars as he is. However, friendship with a girl is problematic at school, where Tyler is teased, and bullying classmates tell Mari to return to her own country. Feeling ambivalent, Tyler pulls away.

Mari's younger sisters are like family members after Mrs. Paquette hires the girls to help Tyler's grandmother, who also lives on the farm and has been lonely since her husband died. The girls call her "Grandma," and together they plan a Day of the Dead celebration that helps her mourn her husband. His grandma helps Tyler conclude that his grandfather, whom Tyler idolized, would have approved of his family's silence about the Mexicans' status. As a result, Tyler finally becomes their ally, planning ways to hide the girls if the authorities should raid the farm.

However, the first arrest comes unexpectedly; their young uncle is caught after bolting from Tyler's brother Ben's car when Ben is stopped for speeding. The Paquettes become involved, first trying to establish just where Felipe is being held and then hiring a lawyer and a translator to help him. Tyler did not at first understand how the Cruzes could have lost touch with Mrs. Cruz, but when Felipe's location in the U.S. justice system is difficult to establish, Tyler glimpses the complicated web of secrecy woven around illegal border crossing. Felipe is released from jail but deported.

A town meeting, a Vermont tradition, brings crusty old Mr. Rossetti into their family circle and eventually into the secret. Initially, he proposes that any illegals in the community be rounded up and deported, but the resolution is voted down. At the meeting, Tyler finds and returns Mr. Rossetti's lost $800, and Mr. Rossetti hires him for odd jobs, enabling him to earn money for a trip to Washington. Not only does Mr. Rossetti fill a grandfatherly role in Tyler's life, but he becomes fond of the Cruz girls, who accompany Grandma when she takes food to him.

Word finally comes that Mrs. Cruz is being held for ransom by "coyotes," guides for illegal border crossers. Tyler's Washington trip has been canceled due to demonstrations opposing stricter measures against illegal residents, so he is happy to loan his earnings to Mr. Cruz for the ransom. Tyler takes advantage of his aunt and uncle's belated birthday gift of a trip to pick up Mrs. Cruz in North Carolina. After the ransom has been paid and Mrs. Cruz pushed rudely out of the coyotes' van, she tells her story, making it clear that she narrowly escaped death after a year of enslavement and beatings. Her horrible experience makes Mr. Cruz curt and angry with everyone. Their relief over the reunion is short-lived. The adult Cruzes are picked up by Immigration and Customs Enforcement agents, who arrested Mrs. Cruz's kidnappers and were led to the Paquette farm by information in her bag. This is only one raid in a big Memorial Day roundup of illegal workers, known as "Return to Sender." Grandma takes the girls to hide out with Mr. Rossetti, until Mari decides that she can best help her parents by turning herself in and telling the whole story of her mother's imprisonment and release, a story that helps excuse Mr. Cruz's aggressive defense of his wife and clears Mrs. Cruz of suspicion that she was one of the coyotes. The whole family is released and deported.

Contact with the Cruzes continues when Tyler's grandmother and Mr. Rossetti take a previously planned trip to Mexico with her church youth group, which ends in a bittersweet leave-taking. Tyler's family has a happy ending: they arrange to lease the farm to Tyler's prosperous Uncle Larry for his organic dairy farm and fertilizer business. This arrangement allows them to stay on the farm.

A theme that runs throughout the novel is naming the Paquette farm. In a letter to Mari, Tyler enlists the Cruz family's help in choosing a name before the lease is drawn up. Grandma and Mr. Rossetti join in a brainstorming session in Mexico, where the suggestions for names identify some of the important ideas and images of the novel. One important motif is the swallows, who summer in Vermont and winter in Mexico. The swallows' arrival in each area is a glad sign of spring. One of the songs that Tío Felipe sings is *"La Golondrina"* ("The Swallow"), a mournful ballad about a swallow who is lost in the migration, which is sung at the funerals of Mexicans who die far from home. Another important element is Tyler and Mari's interest in stars. Tyler has a star named for Mari as a birthday gift, he gives her his telescope when she leaves, and both associate the stars with their dead grandparents. The telescope, enabling the user to see something distant with more clarity and detail, symbolizes their opportunity to know each other. In Mexico, Grandma, Mr. Rossetti, and the Cruzes settle on the name of "Stars and Swallows Farm" (*Estrellas y Golondrinas* in Spanish). This name, Mari says, includes the things that connect them—the stars that can be seen from both places, the swallows that move between the two places. Naming is an important idea in this novel that mingles Spanish with English.

Each chapter of Tyler's story suggests an identity for the farm in its title, while each of Mari's chapters is identified by the recipient of her letter. In Chapter One (*Uno*), the farm is "Bad-Luck Farm"; Mari writes a letter to her mother that she cannot mail. It is "Nameless Farm" in Chapter Two (*Dos*), when Mari writes anonymously to the president of the United States to explain illegal workers' dilemma. In Chapter Three (*Tres*), when Tyler feels his grandfather's presence and his grandmother sets up an altar, it becomes "Watched-Over Farm," and Mari writes to her deceased grandmother. In Chapter Four (*Cuatro*), it is the "Farm of Many Plots," and Mari addresses her letter to the Virgin of Guadalupe as a form of prayer. In Chapter Five (*Cinco*), when Tío Felipe is imprisoned, the farm is "Christmas Tears Farm"; Mari writes to Tío Felipe. Chapter Six (*Seis*) focuses on the town meeting and is titled "Farm for the Lost & Found"; Mari writes a letter to her whole family in Mexico, including Tío Felipe. Chapter Seven (*Siete*) chronicles Mrs. Cruz's dramatic deliverance. In school, Mari and Tyler have learned about the "interrobang," which combines the question mark and exclamation point, and this is a month of surprises. The title of this chapter is "Interrobang Farm"; Mari writes to the family in Vermont as she travels. Chapter Eight (*Ocho*) relates the raid by immigration officers, and it is titled "Return-to-Sender Farm"; Mari records events in her diary. The final chapter, Nine (*Nueve*), consists of two letters: Tyler sends his to Mari just before she is deported, and Mari finishes her letter to Tyler the last night of his grandmother's visit.

The new name for the farm creates a positive feeling at the end of a novel that could, instead, leave a sad impression; friends are separated, and the younger girls, especially, find it difficult to fit into Mexican village life. The novel's title is the name of the Immigration and Customs Enforcement roundup, derived from the phrase stamped on unwanted mail. This title emphasizes the implications of the widespread deportations: referring to people as though they were inanimate objects dehumanizes them and overlooks the devastating impact their deportation

> The most frequently cited current estimate of the number of illegal immigrants in the United States is about 11 million,[15] although one study in 2006 suggested a number as high as 20 million.[16]

would have not only on their lives, but also on the lives of U.S. farmers who depended on them. Alvarez does not oversimplify the issues involved: she is clear about what is legal, what is not, and about the moral dilemma facing each person who breaks the law. By telling this story, though, she enlists the readers' compassion for everyone involved.

DISCUSSION QUESTIONS

• The swallows' migration is a metaphor for workers' migration, with its seasonal cycle of planting and harvesting crops. Is there a difference between animal migration and human movements across borders? Why or why not?
• To what extent should the Paquettes be considered lawbreakers, since they only suspect that the Cruzes are in the United States illegally? Whose responsibility is it to ensure that everyone is legally in the United States—only the authorities' or employers' or everyone's?

A CAFECITO STORY

A Cafecito Story[17] is a beautiful little book, illustrated with woodcuts by Dominican artist Belkis Ramírez. Is it fiction for adults? Is it an educational story for young readers? Alvarez's husband, Bill Eichner, refers to it as a "parable" in his afterword to the book.[18] On her Web site, Alvarez calls it a "green fable."

The story is told in four parts. In part A, a Nebraska schoolteacher, Joe, schedules a Christmas trip to the Dominican Republic. He misses his boyhood farm life, which has lost out to big agricultural corporations, seeing many former fields buried under parking lots, malls, and houses that have destroyed bird habitat. In part B, Joe buys dark, rich coffee at a Dominican *barra*, where his fortune is told from the stains in his cup. Foreseeing his new life, the *barra* owner's wife directs him to a small coffee farm in the mountains. In his travels, Joe sees pesticides in use and the effects of deforestation—trees have been stripped to grow the coffee faster in full sun, resulting in erosion. In contrast, Miguel grows coffee organically on shady terraces, and the air is full of birdsong. Although this way of life nourishes the spirit as well as the palate, small farmers leave their farms for the big plantations because they cannot earn enough with their own crops. Joe tells Miguel he should write his story for consumers outside his country, but Miguel and his family are illiterate, unable to communicate their dilemma.

Joe stays to help Miguel farm, reading in the evening—stories that he says convey meanings about human life. The story that Miguel has to tell explains the time-consuming, labor-intensive traditional methods of growing coffee, harvesting the first crop after three years. Having lost his Nebraska farm life, Joe buys land himself and stays to help the Dominican farmers keep to traditional ways. In exchange for their lessons in growing coffee, he teaches literacy. Miguel's family's progress in reading is correlated with the farm: they can read a whole book by the date of Joe's first harvest. Reading stories is natural, just like the birds' singing while the coffee plants grow. Joe and Miguel start a cooperative to obtain better prices for small farmers. This enables them to add livestock, diversifying what they produce for their own consumption, and as they offer more services to the community, literacy spreads, and everyone has more leisure time.

When Joe returns to Nebraska for a visit, described in part C, he orders a "cafecito" in a local coffee shop but is disappointed in its flavor. He tells the owner, who was reading when he arrived, that the difference in coffees is like the difference between a book that holds the reader's interest and a book that may as well be used as a doorstop. The woman smiles, thinking of the book she has always wanted to write. Joe returns with coffee from his farm and tells her fortune from the stains in her cup—seeing her writing a book about coffee after doing research in the island mountains.

The single page of text in part ABC is by the woman, now married to Joe and living on the coffee farm. The *campesinos* read; the woman writes. She makes the book's lesson explicit: that change starts when one individual plants a seed, literally or figuratively, with a story. She invites the reader to drink coffee grown like this, listen for his or her "own song," and then pass along the story.

The illustrations that introduce each section build a picture of the birds' habitat, showing its importance for migratory birds. Part A begins with a solitary bird on a branch. At the beginning of part B, the same bird has been joined by another, smaller bird, on a second branch. Part C opens with three birds: the original thrush, a sparrow, and a wild parrot. The fourth section, part ABC, opens with the wild parrot alone, suggesting that the other birds have returned north.

> Belkis Ramirez is a Dominican artist known for her installations. She makes her strong political art with a combination of woodcuts, the actual woodblocks with which she produces the prints, and other objects, both natural and man-made.[19]

Another story told by the illustrations contrasts locations. Part A opens with a view of Nebraska fields and a flock of birds and ends with the view through Joe's window of rows of identical buildings that replaced the fields. On his desk, the scene from the Dominican Republic on his computer contrasts with the view that his window frames. The *barra* owner's wife's fortune-telling is illustrated with a vision of the mountain village. An image of Miguel's small cabin, surrounded by trees and bushes with a songbird in the foreground, accompanies Joe's arrival. Progress of the coffee crop is shown with a small illustration of seedlings and a four-part illustration of their nurture, plants growing on the shaded terrace, and hands working the picked beans. The Nebraska coffee shop's diner-style interior is shown with the owner's book lying open on the counter. When the woman tastes Joe's coffee, she is depicted inhaling the steam, her eyes closed, a slight smile curving her lips, with the steam opening up a vision of tree-covered mountains under an open sky.

Several illustrations show Joe's intervention in the mountain community: the illiterate children gathered around Joe, Miguel, and his family seated before an open book. After the cooperative is established, a gathering under the shade trees in front of Miguel's cabin is depicted, showing adults dancing, children playing, and a goat and several chickens in the clearing, underscoring the theme that community develops and there is more leisure time to enjoy it when the work load is shared. Bill Eichner's afterword, relating the story to their real-life coffee-growing venture and urging readers to consider the economic and ecological impact of their day-to-day choices, is illustrated with a man and a woman standing side by side, the fields visible between them.

DISCUSSION QUESTIONS

• Are there ways to build housing and convenient shopping and business areas that minimize destruction of habitat for birds and other animals?

• What does literacy mean to Joe? What does it mean to Miguel and his family? What does it mean to the woman who leaves her coffee shop to marry Joe and live in the Dominican mountains?

How Tía Lola Came to ~~Visit~~ Stay

In her Tía Lola stories for eight- to ten-year-olds, the first of which was *How Tía Lola Came to ~~Visit~~ Stay*,[20] Alvarez shows the importance of the *familia* and Dominican culture in sustaining immigrants and their children through life changes. After his parents' divorce and a move to Vermont with his mother and little sister Juanita, nine-year-old Miguel Guzmán is depressed and lonely. When his mother invites her Tía Lola to come from the Dominican Republic to stay with them, Miguel is ambivalent. He appreciates Tía Lola's affection, spicy food, and storytelling, but he is embarrassed by her colorful clothing, bright red lipstick, and lack of English. Tía Lola is difficult to keep under wraps as the cold Vermont winter gives way to spring. She makes friends everywhere, teaching dancing as well as cooking to a local restaurant owner, Rudy. Teaching her English is a near-disaster, and Miguel's and Juanita's Spanish lessons end in arguments over the gender of nouns. Their great-aunt is less conspicuous in New York, when they visit their artist father there, but she keeps wandering off. She is happiest in the Miguel's grandparents' Spanish-speaking neighborhood.

In the summer, the Little League team plays in the pasture behind their house. Rudy coaches, Miguel is elected captain, and Tía Lola is manager because she makes *frio-frios* (smoothies) for the team. She also sews their purple-and-white Little League uniforms and paints the house purple. The summer ends with a rainy-day birthday party for their mother, entertaining over 70 guests. Tía Lola's birthday story makes their mother homesick, so at Christmas, they all visit the *familia* in the Dominican Republic, where Miguel discovers a baseball-playing cousin his own age. Tía Lola is obviously happy here, but, no longer ambivalent, Miguel wants her to return to Vermont with them.

Baseball is widespread in the Dominican Republic. Introduced in the 1880s, it was sufficiently established by the 1920s that Dominican teams played against U.S. teams and teams from other Caribbean countries.[21] Today, there are more Dominican players in the U.S. major leagues than players from any other Caribbean nation.[22]

This light-hearted episodic book introduces young readers to Dominican culture, including a sprinkling of Dominican Spanish words. Alvarez revisits topics that appear in other works: adjusting to a new home, coping with dual identities, belonging to a minority culture in the United States, and using storytelling to tie the individual to her or his history. One of Miguel's favorite stories is the legend of the *ciguapas*, told in the picture book *The Secret Footprints*.

DISCUSSION QUESTIONS

- Have you ever had mixed feelings about a relative, feeling love and embarrassment at the same time? How do you let your love outshine your embarrassment?
- What special traditions does your family have? Any special foods, or special dances, or special stories?

THE SECRET FOOTPRINTS

The Secret Footprints (illustrated by Fabian Negrin)[23] tells a story about the legendary *ciguapa* tribe that lives underwater and comes onto land only at night to find food. Their feet are attached to their legs backward, so no one can track them. In this story, one brave young *ciguapa* makes friends with a human boy in the daytime, even though she has been warned to distrust humans' scientific curiosity about creatures unlike them. She slips away after making friends but leaves a seashell in exchange for the food the boy's family has given her, thinking she has injured her feet in a fall. She has no further contact with the family, but she folds their laundry when she finds it hanging on their clothesline, and the boy leaves *pastelitos* in his pants pockets for her.

In her author's note, Alvarez says the common elements in versions of the *ciguapa* legend are the backward feet, their life in the water, and nighttime forays for food. It is associated with the Taino Indians, either as one of their legends or a description of their secrecy after the Spaniards arrived.

A GIFT OF GRACIAS

In *A Gift of Gracias* (illustrated by Beatriz Vidal),[24] the *Virgencita*, or Virgin Mary, appears in a dream to María, the daughter of a poor olive farmer, and tells her to plant the seeds of the oranges her father brought from the city. Acting on the dream message, they plant a grove

Alvarez's given name is Julia Altagracia. She visited the chapel on the site of the appearance of the *Virgencita* to Maria to ask her help in writing the story.[25] Alvarez thanks the *Virgencita* in the acknowledgments section of each of her books.

that miraculously bears fruit within months. When her father takes the oranges to market, she asks for a picture of *Nuestra Señora de la Altagracia* (Our Lady of High Grace) from the city. Their Indian friend, Quisqueya, sees the stars move to outline the face of the lady late one night, and a shower of stars falls on his blanket, creating her portrait. The blanket portrait sheds radiance in the orange grove that enables them to pick the new crop of oranges at night.

In a note, Alvarez explains that Our Lady of High Grace is the Virgin as she appears in the Dominican Republic. A chapel to the *Virgencita* was built in María's family orange grove. Quisqueya's name is the Taino name for the island, "Mother of the Earth." Alvarez links the Mother to whom Catholics give thanks with Mother Earth, saying that both belong to everyone.

El major regalo del mundo: La leyenda de la Vieja Belén/ The Best Gift of All: The Legend of La Vieja Belén

In 49 rhymed couplets in English, accompanied by the Spanish translation, *The Best Gift of All* (illustrated by Ruddy Núñez; translated into Spanish by Rhina P. Espaillat)[26] tells the story of the busy old woman *La Vieja Belén*, who brings small gifts to poor children after Christmas. Always hard-working, she never took time to sit down with her family or guests. The three kings came to her home in their search for Jesus, "a king born for the poor."[27] They insisted that she eat with them and invited her to go with them, an invitation she turned down because she had so much work to do. A week later, she decided to follow them. Not knowing what to give a king, she packed a sack of treats and toys and followed the star. Still seeking, she leaves a treat or toy at every poor child's door, but more important, having learned that the best gift is the gift of time, she stops to listen to each child as she continues to wander.

Alvarez's note explains the three occasions when a child received gifts in the Dominican Republic: Christmas Day, when the Baby Jesus left gifts (since replaced by Santa Claus); the Feast of the Three Kings, or Magi, on Epiphany, January 5; and a week later, when La Vieja Belén left gifts for poor children. Italy's La Befana may have inspired the Dominican story, but some believe that the story came from the *cocloos*, immigrant workers from the English Caribbean, who had a legend of an old black woman who rode a mule to give Christmas gifts to poor children. The book is dedicated to Alvarez's mother, whom she calls her dear Vieja Belén.

Beatriz Vidal, born in Argentina, has been illustrating children's books since 1981, after establishing her career with illustrations in major U.S. periodicals and designing cards for UNICEF. She divides her time between New York City and Buenos Aires.[28]

Rhina P. Espaillat was born in the Dominican Republic but moved to the United States as a child. She is a poet, essayist, and translator, who writes mostly in English but also in Spanish.[29]

9

NONFICTION

Alvarez is as good a storyteller in nonfiction as she is in fiction. Her nonfiction consists of a 1998 collection of essays, *Something to Declare*, and a 2007 study of Latina girls' 15th birthday celebrations, *Once Upon a Quinceañera: Coming of Age in the USA*. Alvarez establishes a sense of intimacy with the reader on the first page; throughout each book, she treats the reader as the recipient of personal confidences. The essays are prefaced with "Something to Declare to My Readers," and *Once Upon a Quinceañera* begins with an "Invitation" to imaginatively enter the book. Both books portray coming of age in the United States—as a Latina, as an immigrant, and as a writer.

SOMETHING TO DECLARE

About half of the 24 essays published in *Something to Declare*[1] appeared originally in periodicals or anthologies between 1992 and 1998, a history that indicates the degree of public interest that Alvarez generated with her first three novels. The title alludes to the requirement that international travelers "declare," or identify, to customs officials any goods they take across a border. As a bicultural immigrant, with family members in both the United States and the Dominican Republic, Alvarez is a border crosser. What she declares is political history with which many U.S. readers are unfamiliar, as well as a personal history previously unknown to readers. To declare something also means to take a firm position or make an official statement. By sharing her answers to readers' typical questions, Alvarez makes public statements about her life and work to a wide audience.

In her preface, Alvarez explains that her essays originated as responses to questions asked by readers. At first, she wanted to refer them to her novels and poems for answers, but she realized that people wanted "straight answer[s]."[2] When an answer turns into an essay, she says, the essay is an acknowledgment that "we have something to declare."[3] Most questions focused on immigration, language, writing, teaching, and family life. The book is divided into two parts, each with 12 essays. "Customs" focuses on family and personal history. The word "customs" puns on her border-crossing family history and the alternative meaning of ways of life in another culture. "Declarations" focuses on her career as a writer.

Part One begins in the Dominican Republic with "Grandfather's Blessing" and "Our Papers." The first essay tells how her poetry-quoting grandfather approved her aspiration to be a poet after discouraging her ambitions to be a bullfighter or a cowboy. Those paths, she was told, were closed to girls. The second essay relates her confusion at the time of her family's escape from the Dominican Republic, when the children were misled as to their destination when they left their home and emigrated to the United States. The next essays treat the early days of transition to U.S. life. "My English" chronicles stages in Alvarez's relationship with the English language. In her early years, English was the language of adults' secrets. When she started learning English, she could become fascinated with a single word, not noticing that she was injecting it into a sentence in Spanish. Once in the United States, she soon "learned . . . to hear it as sense" rather than a foreign language.[4] Finally, her sixth-grade teacher's creative writing assignments helped her feel at home in English, borne on the "waves" of language to the "shores of [her] new homeland"[5]; English had become *her* language. In "My Second Opera," Alvarez points out the parallels between the opera at Lincoln Center and a voodoo ritual that she attended in the Dominican Republic, each involving dancing, singing, and spectacle.

The next essays show how adjusting to a new culture sometimes put Alvarez and her sisters at odds with their parents. "I Want to Be Miss America" contrasts the "American" style of beauty with their Dominican looks and the bright clothes their mother bought them that marked them as foreigners before "ethnic" looks came into fashion in the late 1960s. "El Doctor" is a touching portrait of her father, who worked long hours and built a solid fortune with his medical practice but lived like a poor man, scrimping on electricity. He liked his daughters' company in the evenings, though he shied away from intimate conversations, and kept them with him by doling out facts from the history books he read until he finally doled out their nightly mints, one apiece. He once told Alvarez he would have liked to be a poet, admiring those whose words could make other people think.

In "La Gringuita: On Losing a Native Language," Alvarez explains the limits on her bilingualism: after becoming an English speaker, she retained only "childhood Spanish."[6] By her teenage years, her limited Spanish made having a serious romance with any nice boy back "home" impossible: "as English became my dominant tongue, too many parts of me were left out in Spanish for me to be able to be intimate with a potential life partner in only that language."[7]

Several essays deal with Alvarez's married life. "Picky Eater" describes her gradual transformation into a person who savors food and enjoys preparing certain dishes for family meals. In "Briefly, a Gardener," she tells how she tried to share her husband's interest with a brief foray into gardening. She planted an herb garden, only to discover that her favorite flower was a weed, whose name she never learned. The best part of her gardening experience, ultimately, was learning the names of all the plants.

In "Imagining Motherhood," Alvarez discusses her decision not to have children, coming from a home culture where "being a woman and a mother are practically synonymous."[8] When all three of her sisters became mothers, she felt left out, and she worried about missing out on a life experience that she would want to write about in her fiction. She learned to treat it as a loss, one of the many things, like reading Dante in Italian, that she would not do in her life, but she realized that it would not limit her as a writer because she can imagine many life situations without having to live them.

One life experience she imagines is her parents' life in the Trujillo regime in "A Genetics of Justice." Her father first left the Dominican Republic in 1937 to avoid imprisonment for plotting against Trujillo. He returned in 1950, with the wife he had married in the North and two daughters, because Trujillo promised liberalization. In exile for the second time, both of Alvarez's parents kept silent about politics, remembering that a prominent opponent of the dictator had disappeared in New York City only five years earlier. Her parents had internalized their oppression. When Alvarez's fiction was published, her mother's nervousness about her speaking out was exacerbated by some friends' assumption that Mrs. Alvarez was the author because mother and daughter share the first name, Julia. Her mother was so distressed by the exposure of family matters in *How the García Girls Lost Their Accents* that she did not speak to Julia for a month. Alvarez's decision to write about the Mirabal sisters caused even more anxiety; her mother feared its publication would literally endanger the lives of those in her family. Alvarez identifies this decision as "one of the hardest challenges [she] had ever had to face as a writer,"[9] but she went ahead. She sent her parents a copy of *In the Time of the Butterflies* with a note that read "Thank you for having instilled in me through your sufferings a desire for freedom and justice," and her mother thanked her, in tears. Alvarez had achieved a moment of "genetic justice" for the earlier generation's oppression.[10]

Similarly, the next essay, "Family Matters," discusses the barriers to Dominican women's speaking out: women were expected to keep family secrets, and they did not have public voices. Like her parents, who had internalized their oppression with self-censorship, Alvarez internalized patriarchal prohibitions. It took Maxine Hong Kingston's words, "My mother told me never ever to repeat this story," to free her.[11] Discovering that not all of her family members disapproved of her writing, she exchanged her sense of the "monolithic" family for a more complex view of them as individuals,[12] and this enhanced her ability to write about people as complex individuals. Shifting her primary loyalty from the family to her writing has allowed her to fulfill her duty to the human family. This sentiment serves as a bridge to the essays about her writing in Part Two, "Declarations."

In several essays, she discusses the wellsprings of her writing. "First Muse" and "Of Maids and Other Muses" describe childhood influences. Her first muse was Scheherazade, the storyteller of *The Arabian Nights*. Scheherazade's life as a storyteller provided an alternative to the marriage in which fairy tales typically end. From her "first muse," she learned to put the stories first. Other muses included the maids, especially Gladys, the singer. Alvarez's writing voice came alive in her "Housekeeping Poems" when she began hearing the voices of the women who dominated her childhood. Alvarez found models for writing about bicultural experience in William Carlos Williams and Maxine Hong Kingston, as described in the essay, "So Much Depends," an allusion to Williams's well-known poem. Son of a Spanish-speaking Puerto Rican mother, Williams (1883–1963)[13] is known simply as an American poet. Alvarez, in contrast, became part of a movement when Latina writing became visible in the early 1980s. Yet, like any serious writer, she does not want to be pigeonholed as an ethnic writer; she speaks from her particular background and experiences to a wide audience of readers. In "Doña Aída, with Your Permission," Alvarez claims her hyphenated Dominican-American identity in response to the argument made by

Dominican poet, novelist, and essayist Aída Cartagena Portalatín that she should write in Spanish, as a Dominican. Like other writers with dual cultural identities, such as Salman Rushdie and Edwidge Danticat, she is a new kind of writer, with "a pan-American, a gringa-dominicana, a synthesizing consciousness."[14]

The rest of the essays focus on the years when she practiced, rather than served apreenticeship in, her profession. "Have Typewriter, Will Travel" describes her nomadic life before finding success in conventional American terms: a tenure-line teaching position, publication, a husband, a house on 11 acres. Twenty years of temporary circumstances made her cautious but also compassionate: she has learned "the lesson of immigration," that life is uncertain and circumstances can change suddenly.[15] She analyzes her status in "A Vermont Writer from the Dominican Republic," concluding that what really makes her a Vermont writer is the fact that she has written most of her books there.

"Chasing the Butterflies" is the story of the inspiration and research for her novel about the Mirabal sisters, whose memory haunted her, as it did other Dominicans. In 1986, she met Patria Mirabal's daughter, Noris, who accompanied her to the Mirabal home, now a museum. Noris introduced Alvarez to others she should interview, including Minerva Mirabal's daughter, Minou. The story of the Butterflies seemed "too perfect, too tragic, too awful" to write about.[16] Then, in 1992, she met Dedé, the surviving Mirabal sister, and heard the Butterflies' story from her. Afterward, she traveled around the island with Eichner, "chasing the Butterflies," the novel gradually taking shape in her mind because she "didn't want them to be dead."[17]

After achieving success as a writer, Alvarez gave up her tenured position at Middlebury College, as she explains in "Goodbye, Ms. Chips." She enjoyed being in school, both as a student and as a teacher, but her intense involvement in teaching creative writing classes kept her from concentrating fully on her own writing. "In the Name of the Novel" describes her research for a story that she thought might make a novel, about a Wisconsin woman who saw visions of the Virgin Mary in the 1950s. This long essay is followed by "Ten of My Writing Commandments," a list of quotations from a wide range of sources, including her mother. One of the "commandments" that she quotes frequently is Anton Chekhov's statement, "The obligation of the artist is not to solve the problem but to state the problem correctly."[18]

Alvarez's last two essays focus entirely on writing. In "Grounds for Fiction," she explains how she gathers material for fiction and poems. Poems begin in a fascination with words, but her fiction is woven out of many elements—interesting news stories, gossip, and bits of overheard conversation. "Writing Matters" is a punning title: she begins by discussing the curiosity that readers express about how she writes—various "writing matters"—and ends by making the statement that "Writing matters." For Alvarez, writing is a way to find things out, not a way to communicate answers.

DISCUSSION QUESTIONS

- Alvarez's essays retell a number of the stories told in her fiction and poetry. How does her nonfictional retelling illuminate her creative work? Do her essays change your interpretation of her fiction or poetry?
- Learning the English language and losing fluency in Spanish is a topic that Alvarez addresses in a number of her works. What does today's immigrant child gain from learning English? What does he or she lose in the process? What are the implications of Alvarez's experience for today's immigrants?

ONCE UPON A QUINCEAÑERA: COMING OF AGE IN THE USA

Once Upon a Quinceañera: Coming of Age in the USA[19] is the only book that Alvarez has written on assignment. When an editor approached her about the project, she was surprised.[20] Her writing is not about "girly" girls; she is a feminist, critical of cultural fairy tales that limit young women's ideas about life choices—those tales of the princess who needs only to find the right prince to live happily ever after. The *quinceañera*, which crowns a 15-year-old as princess for a day, resplendent in a ball gown and attended by her court, intrigued Alvarez after she watched a documentary her editor had sent her. She spent a year in research, interviewing teenage girls, their family members, and others involved in *quinceañera* celebrations, also attending a number of *quinceañeras*.[21]

The resulting book, a blend of narrative, analysis, and autobiography, was a finalist for the National Book Critics Circle Award in criticism.[22] The book is organized around one typical *quinceañera* (the term can be used to refer to the ritual or the girl, and is often shortened to *quince*). Alvarez dedicates the book to "all the girls and . . . the wise women who raise them"[23] and the epigraph is from Plato: "Education is teaching our children to desire the right things."[24] The quotation anchors her discussion: What are Latina girls being taught to desire?

Alvarez opens with an "Invitation" to the reader to put herself into the picture, wearing the long pink gown, surveying a court of 14 couples, about to walk to a swing, carrying a doll; she will be crowned with a tiara and exchange her flat shoes for high heels, then start the evening's dancing with her father. Alvarez continues to address the reader throughout the book, as "you" or as "reader," sometimes "dear reader," and, in the conclusion, as "wise reader."

Alvarez identifies the purpose of the ritual in the same way as the young women she has interviewed—to celebrate transition into womanhood. In many Caribbean and Latin American countries, the legal age for marriage is 15 for girls, or was until recently.[25] The *quinceañera* announced her readiness for marriage, sometimes with a simple party including a cake and dancing, but in upper-class families with an elaborate formal celebration. The ritualistic elements—the court, the last doll, and so forth—became standardized, and this was the tradition poorer immigrants to the United States had in mind when their increased affluence made possible the lavish parties that only the rich could afford in their home countries. This association with success ensured its survival in the United States.

Today's 15-year-old Latina thinks of the *quinceañera* as a "right of passage" (one of Alvarez's informants identifies it as a "right" rather than a "rite"),[26] whereas many older Latina women did not have *quinceañeras* either because of the expense or their desire to be as American as possible. Subsequently, an atmosphere of paradoxical nostalgia sprang up around it: people believe that today's teenagers should have the ritual to connect them with the past, at the same time that today's teenagers are having the ritual their mothers did not have.

Alvarez was initially "skeptical about the tradition,"[27] seeing the gulf between the ritual and the futures that young Latinas can look forward to, based on their disproportionate statistical representation in at-risk behaviors and the financial burden on families. At the same time, she was moved by older Latinos' obvious "desire to empower our young women."[28] She suggests that the *quinceañeara* can be a valuable ritual that aids girls in reconciling split identities in today's globalized culture. Alternatively, its ubiquity may be attributable to profit-driven marketing. Alvarez invites the reader to consider these and other questions and to reflect on the need for meaningful rites of passage that hold out hope for young people. Her invitation is also to a specific *quinceañera*, around which the book is organized.

The subject, "Monica," lives within blocks of Alvarez's home as a teenager in the 1960s. Returning to her old neighborhood reminds Alvarez of her first months in the United States, when she encountered prejudice against "spics" and then felt her pride restored when the family ate in a Spanish restaurant and she was given a Barbie doll dressed like the flamenco dancer in the floor show. That doll had symbolic value, just as the "last doll" has, representing the "life-sized doll" that the 15-year-old is on her special day. Alvarez collected three dolls linked with the meanings she explored as she researched and wrote the book: a princess like the *quinceañera*, a fairy godmother, and a woman warrior. She ends her invitation with a wish that today's young women may feel "as special as princesses, as empowered as fairy godmothers, and as fiercely committed to the struggle for equality of all people as women warriors."[29]

The story of Monica's *quinceañera* begins with Alvarez's arrival in New York hours before it begins. Finally reaching the family by phone, she learns that Monica and her sister Silvia need a ride home from the hairdresser. Alvarez rescues the girls and hears about their first round of disasters: the limousine company that burned down a few days earlier, the cake that wasn't ready on time (because Monica's father has gone to get it, they've been stranded at the hairdresser's), the photographer who is double-booked for the evening. Monica dresses in her sparkly white gown, then paces as she waits for the limousine with her court.

Integrated with this narrative are chapters on Hispanic girls' life prospects, the literature about *quinces*, the costs of *quinceañeras* (Alvarez notes that Monica's father is not working), and the justifications offered in defense of excessive spending, based on cultural traditions. Alvarez includes autobiographical details of adjustment to the United States. Realizing that her parents lacked the knowledge to guide her in their new culture, she struggled to map a future when she lacked a "story in [her] head of who [she] might become."[30] She found a role model in her English teacher at the expensive boarding school she began attending at age 14.

Monica's *quinceañera* has a Disney theme. In an earlier interview, she told Alvarez that each of the 14 members of her court (one for each year of her life) would be costumed as a Disney fairy-tale heroine. Alvarez is surprised to see "Snow White" putting on a purple dress; the girls couldn't afford authentic Disney costumes. Initially disappointed, Alvarez warmed to the girls' efforts to pretend, remembering "another fairy tale, *The Emperor's New Clothes*."[31] In the absence of other adults, she becomes "the designated fairy godmother," escorting the girls to the limousine with her umbrella when they go to church for the priest's blessing.[32] From there, Alvarez goes to the club to watch for the photographer, while Monica and her court spend an hour riding around in the limousine.

The priest's blessing launches a discussion of the church's role in preparing young people for adulthood. Alvarez also discusses the secular rite of shopping for the *quinceañera*, which often brings mothers and daughters together. She investigates the nebulous origin of the *quinceañera*, concluding that elements of today's celebration are inspired by European courts and debutante balls. Photographs are an important modern element. Among some Latinas in Miami, the photographs are substituted for the whole *quinceañera*; gowns can be rented and hotels offer two-hour rental rates for photograph shoots.

Following her discussion of shopping as a rite of passage, Alvarez segues from Plato's statement, "Education is teaching our children to desire the right things," to a reflection on the summer when she was 15, in a chapter titled with a quotation from Zadie Smith's *On Beauty*: "Time is how you spend your love."[33] The "true lesson" she learned from working for her father in his Brooklyn clinic, where nearly all of his patients and staff were Hispanic, was that she needed periodic opportunities "to drink at the springs of [her] culture."[34]

Monica arrives at the hall with a headache, writes out a script for the emcee, and collapses on a couch before throwing up. She has not eaten all day and is under stress. Noting the attention Monica receives from the older women, each of whom lovingly offers a palliative, Alvarez discusses the generational factor in this "tradition"—the immigrant narrative of parents and grandparents, whose lavish spending on their girls demonstrates their success in the United States. Teens want the trappings of success as well, and they want to be celebrities. At Monica's *quinceañera*, the program begins with an introduction of family members and friends, who comprise her court. "[R]adiant and lovely" as she is announced, Monica is welcomed by the applause of her guests, and Alvarez finds herself teary-eyed, wishing her success as "the queen of her own life."[35]

As a teenager, Alvarez, too, wanted success: she wanted to be a successful writer, but she "was deeply conflicted and confused about achieving [her] dream."[36] She suffered from test anxiety and repeatedly walked out of examinations. In retrospect, she believes that she was as terrified of success as of failure, split between the desire to make her family proud and the desire to obey the family's prohibition on public identities for girls. This kind of pressure, Alvarez believes, is what made Monica ill and leads other girls to drop out of school or become pregnant.

For the older woman, at "the other end of the Cinderella story," the daughter's *quinceañera* represents her achievement, the product of her life's work. Mothers experience "nostalgia for the fairy-tale life the mothers themselves never had" and blame themselves for their failures.[37] Alvarez is concerned that the fairy tale they offer as a template for their daughters' ambitions is inadequate, returning to the quotation, "Education is teaching our children to desire the right things." Beyond the fairy tale, two opposing models for womanhood are deeply embedded in Hispanic culture: Malinche, the betrayer of her people, the Indian mistress of the conquistador, Cortés; and the self-sacrificing Virgin Mother.

Monica has scripted a Cinderella story, playing on the ritual of the father's gift of high heels. Alvarez kept returning to the Cinderella story as a script for her life, seeking a happy ending in a story that didn't fit her life. First, she looked for a prince in the Dominican Republic the summer after she graduated from high school, unsure about her college future. Then, during her senior year in college, she married a 17-year-old musician and a year later got a quick divorce in the Dominican Republic. She married again, despite last-minute misgivings, during her years as a poet in the schools in Kentucky when she met an impressive Englishman whom her mother liked. This marriage foundered as well, because she wanted a life as a writer, while he wanted her to be a wife and mother, as most men did at the time.

At Monica's party, the candle-lighting ceremony begins, each candle dedicated to an important person in her life. The ceremony goes well, and Alvarez says she is "convinced that Monica will take wing, achieve her dreams."[38] It gives Alvarez the opportunity to consider how more "light" can be shed on women's futures. When her own fairy tale failed, she found a strong woman counselor who gave her "a small but significant light."[39] Later, she joined a Women's Way workshop, where she discovered the power of sharing stories, which freed her to reenvision her life, abandoning paradigms passed on by mothers and grandmothers that were no longer relevant to the life choices open to her generation. The *quinceañera*, she says, can help today's Latina girls develop new stories by which to live their lives. Looking to Latina scholars, as well as the creators of *quince* alternatives, for new stories, she identifies herself as an "elder" and asks what the elders of the Hispanic community, now "coming of age" as a group in the U.S. population, can contribute to their youths.

When Alvarez says good-bye to Monica and her family, she gives her a ceramic winged girl who holds a heart in her hands, along with one of her books. Alvarez established her own identity by writing "[her] way through all the contradictions, to make a new narrative out of the weaving of these old threads,"[40] instead of waiting for a knight in shining armor, and she found a true companion, her third husband.

The last section of the book is "La Bendición." What she felt toward the girls she spoke with was, above all, a maternal feeling, so she offers her blessing as parent to child. Girls want *quinceañeras* because they need to connect Hispanic culture—community—with their contemporary

> Between 2000 and 2006, the Hispanic population of the United States grew from 35.6 million to 44.3 million, according to the U.S. Census Bureau.[41]

> U.S. Census Bureau projections anticipate that in 2050, Latinos will represent 24.4 percent of the U.S. population; currently, they represent about 15 percent.[42]

identities. The Latino community that has taken root in the United States needs to educate itself in "right things," rather than reproduce the patriarchal paradigm in its rituals, in order to do a better job of teaching young people. So Alvarez contacts her own circle of "wise women" to ask them what they would say to young women. She has concluded that "Wisdom happens in relationship, in a context of the back-and-forth."[43] Contacting these women has proven to be Alvarez's *quinceañera*. Having received their *bendición*, Alvarez passes it on.

Significantly, Alvarez uses the same pattern here that she uses in novels, that of alternating stories. Here, the pattern works to establish a reflective attitude toward the material that has emerged in her research. She also reaffirms the importance of stories in shaping lives, particularly those of young people.

DISCUSSION QUESTIONS

- What rituals do you think of as rites of passage for young people within your community or faith tradition or family? How do rituals and rites of passage bring communities together? What do young people learn from them? What do older people, the "elders of the tribe," gain from them?
- Throughout her book, Alvarez discusses the impact of narratives, especially fairy tales, on young women. Are there powerful stories other than the Disney movie versions of fairy tales that shape young women's lives? What are the stories that shape young men's lives?

10

POETRY

Poetry was Alvarez's first love as a writer. Devoted to her craft from an early age, she recalled, "I overcompensated for my feelings of literary and linguistic insecurity by making myself learn and master everything I could about the tradition."[1] Her poetry is deceptively simple, almost conversational in tone, but close reading shows how carefully her poems are crafted and how the structure of her books builds her themes. Her poems are collected in *Homecoming: New and Selected Poems*,[2] *The Other Side/El Otro Lado*,[3] and *The Woman I Kept to Myself*.[4]

"HOMECOMING"

The title poem, "Homecoming," is a narrative about returning to the Dominican Republic at age 17 for a cousin's wedding. In retrospect, Alvarez sees the fragility of the class system that supported her uncle's wealth, showcased in the lavish wedding. His life was built on the under-paid labor of others: a servant class invisible to the wealthy and a cadre of cane-field laborers. The society is racist as well as classist: the men marry light-skinned women. They spoil their children, raising them to be masters who will take inequities for granted. At the wedding, Alvarez envisioned the cane fields ablaze at sunrise, an indicator of the tensions sparked by inequality. The wedding cake, an image that duplicates the family house, starts to melt in the heat, and one aunt devotes her evening to "housekeeping," refurbishing it. The cake is the visible symbol of systemic unfairness that threatens to dissolve in the heat—held in place by the subjugation of women as well as the lower class by the wealthy landowners.

The poems of the first section, "Housekeeping," depict women's work, which Alvarez learned from her mother and maids along with lessons on women's place in Dominican society. Men's bad "housekeeping"—their military operations that tear up the world—plays a dark counterpoint to her efficient sweeping.[5] In "Dusting," she is taught her part in a patriarchal society: to remove evidence of her self-expression, the writing she has done in the dust. Learning to make the beds with her mother, she learns about superstitions, her mother's fear that her father will remarry after her death, and the responsibility of caring for elderly relatives. But the ordinary evidence of her parents' bodies in their bedroom—the glass of water, the crumpled tissue—gives no hint of the mysterious knowledge she seeks about her conception in the parental bed ("Making the Beds"). Denied knowledge, she is similarly denied the exciting opportunity to climb high in "Storm Windows," where she might escape into the sky—escape the mother. "Hairwashing" is a punishment, but the mother cannot wash away her daughter's nature as she matures sexually and experiences desire. Family relationships and intimacies are revealed in the clothes pinned to the clothesline. Alvarez reveals the inherent tenderness involved in folding clean clothes, the substitute for expressions of intimacy in family interactions. Similarly, ironing her parents' clothes, she can linger as if touching them in an affection that is often denied expression.[6] Rolling pastry dough is a skill prized by a prospective suitor, in the mother's lore—the ideal crust so thin that he could read through it. The text was the Bible, according to the mother; for the daughter, the text was the world.[7] In "What Could It Be?," Alvarez describes the women in her life tasting a stew to decide which ingredient it needs, working together like a coven of witches; the satiated men go off to nap, under the women's spell. The mother requires good posture but sends her daughters back to housework that hunches shoulders and bends them double, subjecting them to patriarchal expectations ("Posture Lessons").

The poems about sewing originated in a fascination with names, according to Alvarez's essay, "Grounds for Fiction."[8] One, "New Clothes," lists garments and their parts, colors, tools, and tasks. The rhythm echoes the fast-paced whirr of the sewing machine. "Naming the Fabrics" is a long poem that lists fabrics, associating them with a range of knowledge and relationships, one section spoken by the mother, one by the daughter. Women's knowledge and skills, as well as the young girl's initiation, are acknowledged in another long poem, "Orchids," about an aunt who chose gardening, where she could be in charge, over marriage and impressed the men of the Orchid Society by growing 22 varieties. When Alvarez slipped into the off-limits shack where the orchids grew, she was awed by the orchids' sexual suggestiveness in their resemblance to human reproductive organs.

The sonnet sequence, "33," was intended to be a 33-poem sequence marking Alvarez's 33 birthday, but she ended up with over 40 sonnets as she just "kept writing them and writing them."[9] Like Renaissance sonnet cycles, Alvarez's tells a love story, but hers is the story of a woman still seeking a happy romantic ending, feeling the pressure of mortality and pouring her soul out onto paper. Ultimately, she aligns herself with Walt Whitman, who expressed his love for humanity in his poems instead of relationships. Recurring topics include magic, loneliness, Platonic idealism, mortality, and failed love. Near the end of the cycle, she experiences despair, from which she recovers by claiming her identity as a poet. The sequence combines narrative with reflection.

Alvarez begins with an emphasis on danger—the gamble of love and mortality—in the realm of imagination. Aging without a partner, she is aware of losing her sexual advantage. Dating is fraught with failure: she does not know what kind of man is a match for the kind of woman she is. Her age makes her think about Jesus, who accomplished his life work by age 33. Having sought a minister's consolation for her sense of failure, she reflects that humans chronically suffer loneliness (sonnet XV[10]). Considering what it means to be human, she catalogs sites of violence, from Auschwitz through Zaire, and asks whether humans' artistic creations outweigh the horrors they cause. Traveling to Germany, her parents have left instructions for their daughters in case of their death. Her 33rd birthday reminds her of her own mortality. She flirts with the delivery man who delivers a birthday package, only to discover she is 10 years older than he is, and thus far more aware of mortality (sonnet XXIV).

Analyzing why she has so far failed at love, Alvarez attributes it to accepting a stereotypical romantic movie as the standard for relationships (sonnet XXVIII). It plays in Plato's cave, an allusion to the allegory in which Plato argues that people live their lives seeing only shadows, not reality. Sonnet XXX links this idea of the film as shadows in the cave with elements of sorcery; they project emotional needs onto others in a failure to see others truly. She associates her desire for relationship with writing, the only place she seems to be able to love. She ends sonnet XXX with an allusion to *The Tempest* by Shakespeare, "Lie there, my art," which is Prospero's line as he sets down the cape he wears to wield magic and turns to his daughter to confide in her, that is, to enter into a real relationship with her.

In the next poems, Alvarez comments on lovers, one of whom carved her a set of Plato's forms. She embraced another lover in London's Tate Gallery before a painting by Turner, known for his use of light in paintings of ships on the ocean. An influx of light into her heart suggests Plato's light of understanding (sonnet XXXII), but lust rather than understanding was at the heart of their romance (sonnet XXXIII). She climbed back into the light in the plane, flying home. Alvarez turns to a more general love for humanity in sonnet XXXVI, where she alludes to Whitman in her love of multitudes. This celebratory sonnet is followed by a darker narrative.

Returning from a writers' workshop, Alvarez is tempted by suicide on a winding mountain road, imagining she could take off toward the sky. A workshop speaker has warned against writing too autobiographically, and at the summit of the mountain, Alvarez questions what she can write about if not her life experiences (sonnet XXXIX). A critic was severe in responding to her work as she gazed out at a meadow that reminded her of Robert Frost; its many blades of grass, with voices out of Babel, again allude to Whitman (sonnet XL). Close to madness, she pulls herself back by listing names—towns, friends, family members, streets, and wildflowers, making madness nothing more than a word (sonnet XLII).

Concluding in the present moment, Alvarez explains that she uses her writing to reach for the reader's heart, and her true identity is in writing (sonnet XLVI). She addresses readers as those who seek freedom, echoing the poem on the Statue of Liberty and thus reminding readers of her immigrant identity. She encourages them with her own history of rewriting her own identity, as though it were a series of drafts of her writing. She ends with an allusion to Whitman, claiming her identity in her poems in a line that echoes Whitman's lines, near the end of *Leaves of Grass*: "This is no book, / Who touches this touches a man."[11]

The sonnet "33" is followed with a 10-sonnet cycle, "Redwing Sonnets." These further develop the themes of mortality and naming the world: knowledge of the names of things is knowledge of the world, which must be acquired before dying. The opening of the sequence is sparked by a redwing blackbird's song, followed by a silence that reminds Alvarez how girls have been taught to fill awkward silences with small talk. In recent social situations that called for empty talk, she risked meaningful conversation (sonnet IV). Human voices are not really different from birdsong, she concludes, as she listens to a recording of birdcalls. The insight brings a sense of humility, which she illustrates by presenting the beginning of Chaucer's *Canterbury Tales* as a birdcall (sonnet VI). There are many words for kinds of talk (like Babel, like birdsongs) because talk is so important to humans: when talk fails, relationships fail. She concludes the ninth sonnet by commenting that she revises past failures through writing. When the bird returns, singing, his red-barred wings remind her of epauletted uniforms in the Dominican Republic under Trujillo, when any expression of a real opinion could result in execution (sonnet X). She concludes with a belief that humans must speak about what the world means to them because speech is their purpose, as singing is the birds' purpose.

In "Last Night at Tía's," Alvarez concludes the volume in the present, on an occasion in the Dominican Republic when family members have been sharing memories. Together, they mourn their scattering and the older generation's passing. They are now the grown-ups, mortal and separated, no longer joined by their shared past.

DISCUSSION QUESTION

• This book begins and ends in the Dominican Republic. Where is the "home" of "homecoming" for Alvarez?

THE OTHER SIDE/EL OTRO LADO

The two-part title of *The Other Side/El Otro Lado* announces the book's theme of dual cultural identity. The opening "Bilingual Sestina" states the linguistic problem, that Alvarez has things to say that she cannot say in English, and invokes the Spanish influences on her linguistic development. Her successful use of the complex sestina form undermines her argument that English limits what she can say. In each section about her past, she discusses an important influence on her use of language and says good-bye to that period. "The Gladys Poems" present a maid who taught her popular songs in the Dominican Republic; "Making Up the Past" describes Alvarez's transition into English and love of poetry; "The Joe Poems" link love with words; and "The Other Side/El Otro Lado" narrates her residency at an artist's colony in the Dominican Republic when she suffered from writer's block and considered moving back to her homeland. The single poem of the concluding section, "Estel," is addressed to a deaf-mute Dominican child, whose language learning has been delayed. In this book, Alvarez analyzes the division at the core of her identity, ultimately bidding farewell to the person she imagines she might have been in the Dominican Republic.

"The Gladys Poems" attest the importance of the maid's brief influence on Alvarez's life. The poems focus on Gladys's love of singing and her reactions to the family's possessions: the Gauguin painting of bare-breasted island girls and a snow globe and a spotted dog that bore evidence to the wonders of the United States. In "Abandoned," Alvarez concludes, sadly, with Gladys's sudden disappearance one Sunday, fired for a mysterious reason—either stealing or catching the eye of one of the uncles.

The next section, "Making Up the Past," mourns the loss of her childhood world, covering about three years. It starts with "Exile," about the family's flight from the Dominican Republic and Alvarez's bewilderment during her first week in New York, and ends with the elegiac "Making Up the Past." The poems' narrative of arrival and acclimatization begins with her father's practice in a Spanish-speaking clinic, where he attracted homesick patients needing to hear the doctor's verdict in their native language. "Queens, 1963" describes the reception of a black family in their neighborhood: on the child's face, Alvarez recognizes her own expression on arrival in the United States, the closed expression that acknowledges one's outsider status. In the six-part prose poem "New World," Alvarez contrasts her assimilation into American culture with her old-fashioned great-aunts' Old World ways.

The seven-part poem "Sound Bites" traces Alvarez's acquisition of English in a series of moments, each poem including some Spanish words. In "First Days," she learns words for new experiences in New York. "First Year Anniversary" comments indirectly on the source of prejudice against Hispanics, the timing of their immigration, which coincided with Cold War tensions in the Caribbean. In "Mami's Advice," Alvarez depicts her mother's mangling of English clichés, along with her dismissal of the name calling the girls endured. "I size up *la situación*" is a poem in Spanglish that addresses the difficulty of fitting in with American classmates because she looked and acted foreign and spoke English with an accent. Becoming acculturated means deviating from her mother's conduct rules, as she explains in "Talking Back to Mami (Years Later)." In "The Word Made Flesh," Alvarez recalls the difficulty of learning about sexuality and the body in her second language during a time when such knowledge was withheld from girls. She had no way of talking about desire or setting limits with English-speaking boys. "*El Round Up*" comments on contemporary attitudes toward bilingualism, remembering the period of Babel that she and her sisters experienced in their transition.

"On Not Shoplifting Louise Bogan's *The Blue Estuaries*," identified as a 1968 experience, correlates Alvarez's development of her writing voice with her acquisition of English: the swans the poet describes come alive on the page in a moment that makes a clear connection between reading and writing, the latter a visualization of a scene from the printed word. In "Beginning Again," she mourns the loss of language as the most difficult part of moving, but she asserts that it is compensated by renaming the world in poems written in a new language. "Making Up the Past" recalls the fear she felt setting off alone on an errand for her mother, who watched through the window as Alvarez left childhood behind with this independent act. She relives this moment when she writes, still fearful but determined not to look at what she must leave behind.

"The Joe Poems" are 11 poems about language and intimacy, beginning with "First Love Letter" and ending with her last day with Joe. Leaving for the Dominican Republic, she loses an English word—the title of the poem, "Touchstone"—and the loss makes her anxious until she remembers the word in a telephone call to Joe. "Bookmaking" is Joe's craft; in this poem, Alvarez compares knowing another person to knowing a book. Her "Anatomy Lesson," about the way the body fits together and the seven-year cycle of cell replacement, leads to reflection about the selves she has been. The effects of past love affairs are illustrated in "The Last Love Story" when bars of light created by the window blinds show how Joe is caged. "Missing Missives" reveals how closely she reads his words and interprets his silences. In "You Remember the Definitions, Not the Words," reflecting on the way love cools into friendship, she asks Joe for definitions of words, seeing them as seeds of comfort that bring hope when they sprout. In contrast, trees are felled in the concluding poem, "Home Fires." It bears an epigraph from Rumi that points out that light is let in when the roof is destroyed. Their lives are represented in their homes: Joe's new house on the solid foundation of a stable life; Alvarez's homes a string of temporary residences. She associates the remnants of a house that burned down with the destruction of trees cleared for Joe's new house. Both kinds of destruction are emblems of the end of their romance. On another level, the poem alludes to the difficulties she has in finding a home when she is caught between two cultures.

The Other Side/*El Otro Lado* is a long account, in 21 poems,[12] of Alvarez's exploration of the small Dominican fishing village of Boca during her artist's residency, when she tries to break through two years of writer's block. She considers staying in the Dominican Republic because she cannot settle, lacking a guiding narrative for her life—either the fairy-tale love story or a cause she could commit to (poem IV). Her first poem in English showed her how to establish a sense of home that she could carry with her, but now, after years of writing, she is living on paper, and that is not enough to sustain her writing or her selfhood.

With her lover, Mike, she visits the nearby village, where children follow them, begging. In conversations with residents, they avoid awkward personal questions by passing as a married couple, but they learn they are not alone: many village couples cannot afford to marry nor can the men afford to support all the children they sire, in many cases with several different women. Boca's mayor wants them to marry and stay, seeing Mike as the potential father of light-skinned babies. Village women are trapped, barred by government regulations from selling the only products they can make; and they are victimized by the tourists who leave them to support fatherless babies instead of taking them away to new lives. The school is closed for repairs that no one can afford, and the teacher meets with children in the church to school them in the mathematics of poverty.

Alvarez consults a Haitian *bougan*, or voodoo priest, seeking inspiration for writing and resolution of her bifurcated identity, and shops at the *bodega*, whose owner has a product for nearly every emotional need—but he cannot help a woman whose insatiable longings resist resolution (poem XIII). Alvarez joins their ranks; her need is spiritual. In conversations about love, she and Mike observe that they are too mismatched to be Plato's two halves of the same self. Rilke's model—lovers as two solitudes that protect each other—suits Alvarez but threatens imprisonment in Mike's view (poem XIV). He suggests love like Odysseus and Penelope's, which would allow him to roam. Whatever love is, he wants to meet her family, but they argue on their way to Santo Domingo, never visit the family, and on the way back discuss the end of their romance.

Alone, she still seeks answers, like the village's crazy homeless stranger. Looking for peace and solitude, she is pursued by a five-year-old beggar. He pleads and she returns a request for peace until both fall silent, but still he follows her, making her feel deficient (poem XVIII). Ultimately, she cannot envision a life for herself in this village. She laughs when she remembers her Illinois psychiatrist's diagnosis of her as an unrealistic dreamer (poem XIX). Here, in the Dominican Republic, she sees that she cannot pursue the new plotline she envisioned for herself because money has divided her from the villagers even more deeply than her American life. Unlike them, she has safety nets—the best is the one she has woven out of narrative, of language. The only poverty she has experienced is writer's block. Alluding to William Carlos Williams's claim that people die daily because they lack what they could gain from reading poetry, she sees clearly that poetry is a luxury for those who daily experience literal hunger. Ashamed, she initiates a fund-raising campaign to give the village a school, a medical facility, and a better road.

On her last day in Boca, she has her fortune told. When Alvarez tries to explain her dilemma in her limited Spanish, Luis's wife says her *santos* is homesick. She encourages Alvarez to return "home," but Alvarez realizes that she will never again live in the Dominican Republic; her choice has been made (poem XX). She sees her life doubled by the life she could have led if she had stayed in the Dominican Republic. As she leaves the village by boat, she sees a ghost figure, the self that looked for a happy ending there but went on to pursue a writer's life in another country (poem XXI). She heads toward the shore of "the other side."

"The Other Side," the final section, consists of the single poem, "Estel." Alvarez began to teach words to the eight-year-old deaf-mute in Boca and subsequently sent her to a special school, where she would have a new life with language. She has remedied her silence vicariously with Estel, who embodies the acceptance that Alvarez has reached through these poems.

DISCUSSION QUESTION

• What is "the other side" for Alvarez, in the final analysis?

THE WOMAN I KEPT TO MYSELF: POEMS

This collection bears an epigraph from the Polish poet, Czeslaw Milosz, asking whom we can tell our stories to. The book opens with the "Seven Trees" poems, which comprise a brief autobiography that is developed in more detail in the rest of the book. The theme is mortality, announced in "Intimations of Mortality from a Recollection in Early Childhood," moving through meditations on turmoil of the soul and the meaning of writing—and reading—in Alvarez's life, and ending by equating her work with her identity and her life, addressing the reader in a final summation of her achievements.

The first of the "Seven Trees" is "Family Tree," in which she fits herself into her extended family. Despite the efforts she and her sisters made to break away, they reconnect to the family by spotting family traits in their children. Though they moved away, they were not completely changed. Her efforts to write stylish American fiction get lost as she keeps writing about where she is from. The last poem in the group is "Last Trees," a reflection on the story told in the tree poems, with a glimpse of her future, associating death with Dante's "dark wood." The intervening poems are set in 1957, 1960–1961, 1973–1975, 1985–1987, and 1998, each associated with a particular place: Ciudad Trujillo, New York, Syracuse, Champaign, and Weybridge, Vermont, respectively. "Samán," the second poem, connects learning about the way women's bodies work with Trujillo's tyranny, as she sat with her sister in the tree and watched the military planes that disposed of "imprisoned" citizens by dropping them into the sea. Having glimpsed this evil, Alvarez associates Trujillo with Joseph Conrad's tyrant in *Heart of Darkness*, who is worshiped by his subjects. "Weeping Willow" tells of her father's struggle during their first winter in New York City. In graduate school in Syracuse, she could not distinguish the North American trees, "Maple, Oak, or Elm?," nor did she know where she was headed. "Arborvitae," set in Illinois in the mid-1980s, recalls her despair after a divorce. In "Locust," she tells the reader of her midlife happiness that came with a job, publication, love, and a home. Here, she says that she has learned from trees that we must live as unique individuals, our identities determined from the "seed," or soul.

The next part of the book begins again in childhood and announces her theme of mortality. Alvarez discovered her mortality while she played outdoors at dusk, she says in "Intimations of Mortality from a Recollection in Early Childhood," when she looked closely at her arm and associated her selfhood with the body. The title alludes to Wordsworth's ode, "Intimations of Immortality." "Anger & Art" echoes this theme but finds an alternative to accepting death in creative work. "The Red Pickup" that she wished for on her birthday symbolized the future she envisioned, full of exciting, forceful possibilities that adults told her were reserved for boys.

"Spic" and "All-American Girl" revisit prejudice she encountered in the United States and her response to it: identification of herself as "all-American." "Bellevue" retells another story from Alvarez's fiction: predicting that the willful girls will drive her to the mental hospital, her mother leaves home to drive around for an hour. At "Abbot Academy," Alvarez escaped from the family into English literature, where her English teacher demonstrated a way to channel wild adolescent energy into a force appropriate for leadership. In "Vain Doubts," Alvarez describes being accused of vanity by a disgusted male passerby when she checked her appearance in a store window, destroying her pleasure in her youth; consequently, she wants to reassure young women that they are beautiful.

Holding her first job after college, Alvarez spent her "Lunch Hour, 1971" in the library, nourishing her need to write with the words she read. An important factor in surviving uncertainty and nomadic living was her relationships, for which she shows appreciation in "Bad Weather Friends" and "Reunion." Calling her husband "My Bottom Line," she celebrates the solid, everyday quality of the love that comes in middle age, and examples of this kind of love are illustrated in several poems. A number of poems focus on the political nature of reading and writing. She humorously questions how "Canons" are formed when she has to decide between two volumes of poetry to take on a climb of the Dominican Republic's highest peak—she chose Elizabeth Bishop over Robert Frost on the basis of weight. Commenting on women's place in religion and history in "My Kind of Woman," she praises the curiosity, calmness in the face of shock, and willingness to save the world she sees in exemplary strong women in the Bible. "Ars Politica," her political art, is anchored in storytelling that helped her create the world in accordance with a model she could accept.

Another theme is psychological distress, and Alvarez refers explicitly to psychotherapy and loss. In "Disappearing," she says that she wasted away to a condition like a single line of print, bent on disappearing, and was hospitalized for anorexia until she could regain enough weight to qualify as human. Her experience is like that of the astronauts when they pass behind the moon, losing contact with Earth, with loved people and places, as she says in "That Moment." She has survived losses, finding new strength and a new home. She suggests two maxims for living— holding on and letting go. It is letting go that frees the hand for holding on. Writing aids her in making whole what has been broken.

Mortality is directly addressed in the next group of poems. She commemorates "Deathdays," like birthdays, and celebrates all the days, knowing that one of them will be her own deathday in some future year. The "All Clear" after cancer treatment gives her new insight into the vulnerability of bodies, as she says in "Now, When I Look at Women" and "At the Gyn." Images of spring create hope in these poems. With spring comes the birth of her "Grand Baby," Naomi, but Alvarez asserts that a baby's perfect selfhood precludes any need for commemorative writing; babies themselves are poems. After coping with partings, including deaths, and the attacks on 9/11, she appreciates "Spring, At Last!" as a second chance to write about whatever she has overlooked.

Several poems deal with language, aging, and depression. "Regreso" describes how her father speaks more Spanish as he ages. Spanish phrases help her check the sound of her English by distancing her so that she can see the truth in her writing more clearly, as she says in "In Spanish." Still, this does not indicate a preference: she notes that she talks and talks in English when she is "Leaving English" for a visit home. In "Touching Bottom," she comments on the advice that comes through random ordinary comments, like the answering machine admonition that she takes as a maxim for handling writer's block; a friend's words form a thread like Ariadne's that can recall her from a labyrinth; and her father's comment on finances enabled her to "touch bottom" and recover.

Focusing specifically on poetry, Alvarez says in "Cleaning Ladies" that her work is the same kind of work as the cleaning lady's, though it is language that she cleans up. She mentions a dream about Allen Ginsberg, she describes her creative writing students' desire to write free from constraints of form, and she lists poets she reads. "Small Portions" explains poetry's appeal: looking at a single detail, she sees the beauty of the world in a manageable portion, and like Jane Austen, she works on a small scale. W. H. Auden's poem of tribute to William Butler Yeats suggests that poetry has little effect on events in the world[13] in the line Alvarez quotes to title a poem, "'Poetry makes nothing happen'?" in which she lists people who were saved from some bad event when they were delayed by reading a poem, but were changed so slightly that they claim poetry had no material effect. Yet it is the smallness of poetry's effect, Alvarez concludes, that makes poems trustworthy.

Even more significant than poetry's impact, poetry is actually the medium through which Alvarez lives—and will continue to live after bodily death—echoing an idea expressed in the Renaissance by some of the greatest poets who wrote in English. Alvarez begins to address the reader directly, ending "Reading for Pleasure" with an invitation to intimacy, and in "Direct Address," she celebrates Whitman's way of drawing the reader into relationship and imagines her impact on readers even after her death.

The "Keeping Watch" poems address the soul's desire to overcome loneliness and come to terms with mortality. She remembers the night watchman of her childhood in "El Sereno." "Looking Up" and "What We Ask For" enjoin mindfulness, living fully in the moment by giving our attention to the details of the world. Insomnia—hinted at in "El Sereno"—presents her insight into the loneliness of those who keep vigil through the night, identified with the world's great religious traditions. In "What Was It That I Wanted?" Alvarez sums up her life in terms of her desires. "Keeping Watch" links watching with the dying and caring for infants; in the eyes of each she sees a simple human need, to know that someone is with them.

The next-to-last poem in the book is "Why I Write," in which Alvarez presents writing as a means of reaching understanding. Without writing, she does not know what she thinks or feels: even her desires emerge as she writes, her prayers are more meaningful in written form. She equates writing with focusing binoculars. Moreover, writing tells her she is alive;

"Why I Write" is the title of an essay by George Orwell, in which he identifies his primary motivation as political. Following in Orwell's footsteps, Joan Didion titled an essay "Why I Write," in which she claims, "I write entirely to find out what I'm thinking, what I'm looking at, what I see and what it means."[14] Both purposes are relevant to Alvarez's writing.

once she is reduced to an epitaph on a headstone, she will be silent. The final words, "the rest is silence," Hamlet's last words, are as ambiguous in Alvarez's poem as in the play, suggesting at least two meanings: the remainder of what she has to say will go unspoken, or death brings a rest from writing.

The final poem is a series of questions, titled with the question "Did I Redeem Myself?," which is addressed to her parents, sisters, lovers, friends, her two countries, and finally, readers, whom she questions about their final judgment of her accomplishment in the last lines of the book.

DISCUSSION QUESTION

• Given the strong autobiographical foundation of Alvarez's writing, some readers might say that the book's title is misleading because she has exposed so much of her life in other books. What does her title imply?

11

JULIA ALVAREZ AND CONTEMPORARY ISSUES

Julia Alvarez's writing—fiction, poems, and nonfiction alike—revolves around a core group of interrelated topics: immigration and assimilation; bicultural identity, especially Latino(a) culture in the United States; language; literacy; women's roles; patriarchy; resistance to political tyranny and economic injustice; sustainability; and storytelling as a means of achieving shared understanding. In fiction, her protagonists face ethical dilemmas about their roles in the world as well as in their families. They make political choices when they speak out against oppressive governments, take action to spread literacy, defend other women against abuse, and act to dismantle hierarchical class structures and economic inequities. Her most overtly political protagonists are historical figures: the Mirabal sisters commit to armed resistance to Trujillo in *In the Time of the Butterflies*, and Minerva ensures that her father's illegitimate daughters receive schooling; Salomé Ureña commits her poetic talent to a patriotic cause and starts a school for women out of the same conviction, and her daughter Camila demonstrates for women's suffrage and returns to Cuba to teach as a patriotic duty in *In the Name of Salomé*. Her protagonists are committed to countering inequities in private life as well as public life, at the same time as they seek personal fulfillment. In *¡Yo!*, the contemporary protagonist is relentlessly democratic, treating Dominican servants as equals as well as initiating literacy instruction when she discovers a need and supporting poor women's efforts to separate from abusive men. Alma Rodriguez, in a misguided attempt to rescue her husband, tries to negotiate the hostage situation in *Saving the World*, simply listening to the hostage takers, while her 19th-century heroine Isabel negotiates for her orphan boys' futures and actively aids Dr. Balmis in the inoculation process. Alma's husband, Richard Huebner, heads up a green project to teach sustainable agriculture to impoverished Dominican farmers; Joe, in *A Cafecito Story*, successfully brings such a project to fruition and starts a community education center; Yolanda's husband, Doug, plans to buy land in the Dominican Republic and employ the importunate José. The poem "Homecoming" calls attention to the underpaid labor on which the Dominican class structure is built: the cane-field workers and domestic servants are taken for granted by the aristocrats whose wealth they sustain. *The Other Side/ El Otro Lado* ends in activism: fund-raising for the poor fishing village and, on an individual level, placing a deaf-mute child in a private school. In *Finding Miracles*, Milly campaigns for school office on the principle that teens are practicing real democracy, and she helps channel some of the family's U.S. wealth directly where it is needed—to an orphanage and the education of a mute teen. The Paquette family in *Return to Sender* becomes involved in obtaining legal aid and a translator for their Mexican employees, and Tyler loans money for Mrs. Cruz's ransom and arranges for her transfer. Alvarez's characters are sensitized to inequities because of their perspective, which is shaped by divided, bicultural identities.

Some form of *testimonio* appears in several of Alvarez's books, and thus storytelling itself becomes a political act. In an address presented at the National Book Festival in 2009, Alvarez pointed out that dictators suppress voices: they ban books; they control the press; they silence opposition through imprisonment and violence, controlling others through fear; and they impose a single narrative, the official one.[1] Simply speaking out, telling the stories of human rights abuses, is a means of taking action.

Alvarez's characters, divided at the core by early uprooting from their homeland, seek a secure place in the world. The episode with which *How the García Girls Lost Their Accents* opens illustrates Yolanda García's restlessness and rootlessness. Several characters in *¡Yo!* comment directly on her foreignness: to Dominican servants, she is a North American; to her New England landlady, she is "foreign"; her relationship with Dexter founders on the split. Her transition is difficult every time she returns to the United States from the Dominican Republic. *In the Name of Salomé* focuses on the nature of the homeland from the outset, with its epigraph, "What is a homeland?" Camila and her brothers live with this question throughout their lives, deciding where to live and how to serve their homeland and taking dramatically different paths. In *Finding Miracles*, after Pablo has developed a North American identity and Milly has discovered her home culture, Pablo explains their function as "border-liners": "We hold the worlds together. Without us . . . everything falls apart."[2]

In her essay, "Doña Aida, with Your Permission," Alvarez discusses the advantage, as well as the challenge, of this position in terms of "a country that's not on the map, . . . a world formed of contradictions, clashes, comminglings—the gringa and the Dominican."[3] She says that the person so situated is always "looking at one side from the other side," and this division creates "a new consciousness, a new place on the map, a synthesizing way of looking of the world."[4] This is what globalization ultimately implies; mobility in this era of fast travel and communication means that "nationalities are on the move," so she concludes that "A multicultural perspective is more and more the way to understand the world."[5] The writer Gloria Anzaldúa defined this perspective as *mestiza* consciousness, and Alvarez quotes her analysis in *Once Upon a Quinceañera*, saying that it is "hybridity as a state of mind" that "inspires" her.[6] Although her focus is on Hispanic culture in *Once Upon a Quinceañera*, noting the prediction that by 2050, approximately one-quarter of the U.S. population will be Hispanic, Alvarez points out that "Globalization brings the 'immigration experience' beyond our borders and makes the collision of cultures a reality everywhere."[7] As a result, we must all "evolve a new kind of world consciousness that is transformative and synthesizing."[8] Alvarez and other new immigrant writers, with their dual cultural identities, demonstrate the complexity of American identity in the 21st century.

The complexity of the issues surrounding illegal immigration, specifically, is clear in the dilemmas Alvarez portrays in *Return to Sender*. Two families are supported through the efforts of the migrant Mexican workers, but the seemingly straightforward economic benefits involve everyone in breaking the law, posing a series of ethical dilemmas. The compassion with which all the characters are drawn challenges the distressing implications of the "Return to Sender" operation, whose name suggests that human lives can be treated like unwanted inanimate objects. Whatever the reader's position on immigration, he or she is confronted with the thorny individual human dilemmas involved in the immigration debate.

The economic inequities that prompt illegal immigration as well as generate anger about it are most directly addressed in *A Cafecito*

Story, Alvarez's most didactic book, in which the plight of the small farmer is clearly presented: he can earn more working for others on big plantations that strip the land of trees and use chemical pesticides and fertilizers. The solution that Alvarez and Eichner offer is the collective, which enables small farmers using labor-intensive but environmentally friendly methods to negotiate better prices. The Café Alta Gracia Web site identifies the goals of the couple's project in the Dominican Republic as "environmental sustainability through organic agriculture, economic sustainability through fair trade, social sustainability through education and health care, [and] political sustainability through transparency."[9] The "green project" that takes Richard Huebner, in *Saving the World*, to the Dominican Republic is similar to Alvarez and Eichner's. However, the corporation that funds Richard's project conducts trials on AIDS drugs in the same village; Alma suspects the project is "only a front for some clinical-testing sweatshop,"[10] and once the drugs are approved, the villagers will no longer be able to afford them; it is just another version of exploitation. Even if that is not the case, the villagers see it that way. This kind of exploitation of the "Third World" by the "First World" leads to terrorist acts. Posing as a journalist, Alma interviews the chief hostage-taker, who tells her, "we are sick of being utilized."[11] The drug company builds the clinic and makes "empty promises," while "our children die because they cannot get medicina for a little fever that would cost us una fortuna to buy!"[12] Access to medical care is a fundamental human need. As the United States works out its own system for providing it, it is important to remember the wider gulf between income and the cost of medical treatment in neighboring countries.

In a shrinking world, brought closer together by high-speed transportation and communication, the inequities between rich and poor are made visible to the poor, while the rich continue to take their labor for granted. Explosive anger is the result. After 40 years in the United States, Alma reflects, she still feels "homeland rage," believing that "her own luckiness was off the backs of other people."[13] In *The Other Side/El Otro Lado*, when Alvarez comes to the realization that she cannot live in the poor fishing village, she says, "I was a foreigner in Boca from a country even further / than the USA they could get to with a green card or on a *yola*; / I came from the monied class—and although I rejected the label, / I knew in the back of my mind, there were safety nets below me."[14] Alvarez's characters and situations remind U.S. readers of their "luck" and comfort through her protagonists' awareness of the wide gulf in economic conditions between ordinary North American lives and the majority of lives in the Dominican Republic and Mexico. In *A Cafecito Story*, the reader is explicitly asked to consider the choices he or she makes in buying a cup of coffee and other products and to choose fairness to others as well as preservation of the environment.

Although economic exploitation is an ongoing problem, the injustices of totalitarian rule are the backdrop in most of Alvarez's novels, showing how governments that maintain their power through violence affect citizens' daily lives. The alignment of U.S. economic interests with dictatorships is an underlying cause of the injustices made explicit in the texts. U.S. intervention in the Dominican Republic contributed to Trujillo's ability to take control, initiating three decades of totalitarian rule. The dictatorship's effects are most fully delineated in *In the Time of the Butterflies*, where the Mirabal sisters' radicalization develops over a period of years as Trujillo's injustices become more and more apparent. The historical sweep of *In the Name of Salomé* is broader. Camila's father's presidency lasted only four months; thereafter, the U.S. occupation that would ultimately put Trujillo in power kept Francisco Henríquez in limbo. In the same period, the United States occupied Mexico, making Camila's brother Pedro reflect that it was difficult to find a place to live that was not under U.S. domination. The dictatorship of Fulgencio Batista, in neighboring Cuba, was similarly backed by the United States. Camila's imagination is fired by the opportunities Castro's revolution affords for serving the people's interests, rather than the interests of the elite few. In the novels featuring the Torre family (the García girls' mother's family), as well as *In the Time of the Butterflies*, the reader sees the end of Trujillo's rule and his son's retaliation for the *ajustiamento*. In *Finding Miracles*, Milly learns how a violent dictatorship can leave its mark on every family in a nation, a legacy that can be addressed through a truth commission. The consistent theme of these works is that totalitarianism must be resisted and justice restored. The only question is how best to resist it. Some take up arms, some tell the stories suppressed by official censorship, some flee, and some leave written records. Many die for their convictions, without seeing the impact of their actions.

The irony for the immigrants in Alvarez's fiction is that the United States offers freedom—free speech, freedom from imprisonment and rape and torture—but it bears responsibility for creating the totalitarian conditions from which the immigrants fled. U.S. citizens need to pay attention to this history of intervention that continues to have ramifications for international relations today, especially with Cuba. When U.S. economic interests override a commitment to democratic institutions in neighboring societies, the outcome is political oppression as well as economic inequities. This is why the fourth pillar of sustainability, which is the goal of Café Alta Gracia, is "political sustainability through transparency": communities and the environment must be preserved, not depleted through exploitation.[15] Nonetheless, readers of Alvarez's works will also find reminders of the promise of freedom the United States holds out to immigrants.

Immigration transformed Alvarez's life, even as it brought significant challenges. In *How the García Girls Lost Their Accents* and in essays and poems like "Spic" in *The Woman I Kept to Myself*, she describes the prejudice encountered by Hispanic immigrants in the 1960s. Her fiction and poetry also bear witness to the impact of her U.S. education. She discusses this most fully and explicitly in *Once Upon a Quinceañera* and *Something to Declare*, describing her acquisition of English, her transformation into a reader, and the influence of teachers who encouraged her to write and served as role models for life choices that were alternatives to the possibilities held out to girls in the conservative, patriarchal Dominican culture her family brought with them.

The patriarchal family reproduces the oppression of the dictatorship, as Yolanda makes clear in *How the García Girls Lost Their Accents* when she accuses her father of being a dictator, like Trujillo. Women are trapped or caged by patriarchy, and they internalize their oppression, just as the citizens living under Trujillo's government internalized self-censorship. Minerva Mirabal attempts to free a caged rabbit, only to discover that the rabbit will not flee, in a symbol for Dominicans; a similar reference to monkey experiments, in which caged monkeys refused to leave the security of the cage even to find food, occurs in *Before We Were Free*. Yolanda García's cousin, Lucinda, feels "trapped" in her world.[16] The machismo element of Lucinda's world, the world that Yo and her sisters have largely escaped, is shown in Mundín's attitude toward his sister's virtue and Sofía's boyfriend's restrictions on her actions in *How the García Girls Lost Their Accents*, as well as in the second families fathered by Enrique Mirabal and Salomé's father and husband.

In *Once Upon a Quinceañera*, Alvarez points out that the impact of machismo on male behavior has been thoroughly discussed, but there is a "reverse side of that gender coin"—Marianismo, the ideal womanhood represented by the Virgin Mary: "She is submissive, self-sacrificing, long-suffering, putting up with her husband's infidelities, devoted to her *familia*, and most especially to her children."[17] Writing about her choice not to have children, Alvarez says that in her culture, "Being childless—by choice—is tantamount to being wicked and selfish."[18] This cultural mandate, combined with the fairy tales that hold up a happily-ever-after marriage as the goal for U.S. girls, limits Latina girls' models for fulfilling lives. In *Once Upon a Quinceañera*, Alvarez attests to the frustrations she felt as she tried to find a pattern to fit her life to—new narrative possibilities. The epigraph from Plato, "Education is teaching our children to desire the right things," emphasizes the importance of establishing good models for young people. Alvarez points to the contrast between risky and self-destructive behaviors that young Latinas engage in at higher rates than other U.S. teenagers with the promise of the *quinceañera*—that the 15-year-old girl is a princess with a successful future. Furthermore, Alvarez notes the disturbing trend toward violence at *quinceañeras*, a circumstance that one of her informants, a police chief, attributes to "wholesale systemic racism down the line in our institutions."[19] A Latina activist points out the impact of major crises and challenges that the world is facing today, arguing for "creating and affirming a consciousness in our young women about the sacredness of the feminine, the connection between their bodies and the natural world and the body politic."[20] Alvarez concludes, "Our young Latinas should feel free to reimagine the old stories so that they do not feel divided by their dual cultures, as many in my generation did."[21]

In her portrayal of the Mirabal sisters, Alvarez rewrites their mythical identities and shows their courage—Minerva holding to her goal to study law despite family and government resistance, later refusing a pardon and inspiring solidarity in prison, and overcoming a crisis in courage during a period of exhaustion and illness after her release; María Teresa overcoming her fear, pain, and grief in prison; Patria coming late to the struggle but accepting it as her duty to her children and other women's children. These women combined political activism with family life and, in Alvarez's depiction, achieved a measure of equality with their husbands that reflected the political beliefs that underpinned their actions. "Speaking the same language" is essential for fulfilling romantic relationships, as Yolanda's experiences with failed romances show in *How the García Girls Lost Their Accents* and *¡Yo!*, as well as in the poems that deal with romantic relationships, especially the sonnet sequence "33" in "Homecoming" and "The Joe Poems" in *The Other Side/El Otro Lado*. Men's expectations of wives, as well as family expectations of daughters, limit their growth, as Alvarez explains in *Once Upon a Quinceañera*, commenting on her failed second marriage: "My husband wanted what most men wanted back then, a devoted wife, not without her own interests and hobby-jobs, which it was understood she would soon set aside to start a family. . . . My old-world culture and familia had taught me to want that as well."[22] She needed "just the right measure of support and autonomy,"[23] which comes, finally, in the companionate marriage she describes in fiction in *¡Yo!*, in essays in *Something to Declare*, and in poems in *The Woman I Kept to Myself*.

Education that liberates the imagination and instills compassion is essential for women, especially, but for youth in general. Minerva

Mirabal pays for her illegitimate stepsisters' education; the Garcías' maid's daughter asks her employer for financial assistance to attend the academically challenging Catholic school that the García girls attended, with the result that she ultimately attends medical school. Alvarez's liberating experiences with literacy in the United States grew partly out of love for the English language, partly out of the good teaching she encountered throughout her schooling, and partly out of the loneliness imposed by being an outsider and victim of prejudice. These experiences are reflected in almost all of her writing: in her poems and essays about reading and writing, in Yolanda García's devotion to writing, and in Mari's letter-writing in *Return to Sender*. In all of her semiautobiographical fiction and poetry, the protagonist persists and finds fulfillment in a writing career. Writing as a form of bearing witness, or *testimonio*, as well as expressing oneself, appears in María Teresa Mirabal's diaries, Anita's diary in *Before We Were Free*, Isabel's diary in *Saving the World*, and Milly's intention to write the true stories she has heard in *Finding Miracles*. The subject of *In the Name of Salomé* is a highly visible, public poet. Having a public voice, as a writer, means overcoming cultural prohibitions against women's speaking out. Alvarez found inspiration in Maxine Hong Kingston's *The Woman Warrior*, a memoir about Chinese American girls' experience, which begins, "'You must not tell anyone,' my mother said, 'what I am about to tell you.'"[24]

In the United States, Alvarez writes in *Something to Declare*, the parental prohibitions on "the independence we needed in order to survive in this new country"[25] caused substantial conflicts over speaking out. In creating protagonists that find a public voice, and nonetheless are loved, Alvarez creates a model for other women, the kind of model she calls for from "elders" of the Latina community in *Once Upon a Quinceañera*. Overcoming her fears of breaking with her *familia*, a situation dramatized in *¡Yo!*, Alvarez discovered that, just as her perspective is enriched by her dual cultural heritage, she reached "a new attitude towards familia, not unquestioning worship, but a desire to see and celebrate human beings in their full complexity rather than as icons."[26]

Alvarez sees similar potential in reading, as she explained at the National Book Festival: reading stories fosters compassion and develops the imagination.[27] Hence, literacy is of paramount importance. In Alvarez's fiction, Yo, Salomé, and Camila and Joe (*A Cafecito Story*) start young people and adults on the path to literacy. Near the end of her life, summing up her contribution to Cuba, Camila declares that "The real revolution" occurs in "the imagination" when people read.[28] Storytelling and literacy have political implications; they empower people. This is why "social sustainability" involves education.[29]

Compassion is essential to overcoming racism, a topic that recurs throughout Alvarez's work, although it does not play an important role in the plots. Frequent references to color in the Dominican Republic are reminders of how mixed race is in the Caribbean. The preference for light-skinned women and babies recurs in Alvarez's fiction and poetry. *In the Name of Salomé* shows the significance of race when Pancho commissions a touched-up portrait of Salomé after her death that lightens her skin and remodels the features that reveal her African ancestry. In an interview, when asked about her interest in Salomé's Ureña's story, Alvarez responded that the person who gave the new Dominican Republic its voice was "A woman of humble origins, a woman of color, a woman who would become the national poet!"[30] Alvarez was the target of racist epithets in the United States, and some of Yo's failed relationships are founded on stereotypes of the "hot-blooded" or "exotic" Latina. One of the texts that Alvarez identifies as meaningful in her development as a young writer is Langston Hughes's poem, "I, Too, Sing America," which spoke the electrifying message that one can be a person of color and also be American.[31] In a period of our history when national security issues threaten to further institutionalize racism in the form of racial profiling, Alvarez's writing conveys the same message about what it means to be American: she, too, sings America.

DISCUSSION QUESTIONS

- Alvarez came to the United States at a time when immigrants were discouraged from continuing study of their first language in school. She was advised to take French in high school. With a well-established and still-growing Latino(a) population, should children from Spanish-speaking households be encouraged by schools to develop literacy in that language?

- Are there advantages to Third World countries that host clinical trials of experimental medications? Do drug companies have an obligation to continue providing medications, free or at an affordable price, once their clinical trials have been completed, when they can make substantially more profits by selling the medications at high prices in First World countries?

- *In the Time of the Butterflies* and *Before We Were Free* link girls' first menstruation with the acquisition of adult knowledge about human rights violations perpetrated by the Trujillo regime. These fictional episodes seem symbolic of the education described by the Latina activist who wanted young women to see "the connection between their bodies and the natural world and the body politic." What other connections can be made?

12

JULIA ALVAREZ AND THE INTERNET

The most important source of information about Julia Alvarez on the Web, and an excellent starting point for learning more about her, is her own Web site. On her home page, she writes that she was hesitant about having a Web site but concluded that it was the best venue for posting routine news about her books and appearances. Asked by an interviewer about the Internet's impact on writers, she said in 2000, "still a writer becomes a writer word by word and . . . contact with a mentoring spirit. You pick up a book you love and read it sentence by sentence to figure out how the writer did it. Those tiny increments make a writer."[1] Despite Alvarez's reservations about the Web, her site is another manifestation of her intimate relationship with readers. The image that identifies each page on the site is Dominican artist Belkis Ramirez's *Pensamientos de Julia*, or "Julia's Thoughts." The "Julia" of the engraving is the Puerto Rican poet, Julia de Burgos,[2] but in addition to the shared name, the image's appropriateness for Alvarez's site derives from the woodcut illustrations Ramirez made for *A Cafecito Story*. Alvarez's stated purpose on her "Welcome!" page is to "keep it simple, informative," a place where her appearances and newest publications are announced.

Alvarez's autobiographical statement highlights what she feels is most important about her as a public person. Information linked to her statement—her résumé, a list of publications, and a list of interviews and articles about her—gives the reader an authoritative overview of her work. Alvarez's "La Ñapa" page—"a little bit more," a phrase explained in *How Tía Lola Came to* ~~Visit~~ *Stay*—includes more poetry by Alvarez, 31 haikus about March in Vermont. Pages devoted to her books reflect her career as a teacher: these pages add information about her interest in the topic of each book, as well as links to discussion questions and useful items such as news stories related to issues raised in her books.

Alvarez's Web site provides a link to the Café Alta Gracia Organic Coffee Web site, the coffee produced on the farm she owns with her husband, Bill Eichner, in the Dominican Republic. The site explains their commitment to sustainability and to modeling mutually beneficial economic relations between U.S. consumers and Dominican farmers. There is also a link to an article about their venture, "Hill of Beans" by Emily Brady, which appeared in 2007 in *Smithsonian*'s online magazine. In addition to supplementing information about coffee growing in *A Cafecito Story*, the article explains how the farm's purpose and scope were extended when the nonprofit Dominican Institute for Agricultural and Forestry Research took over management and used it as a training and research center.[3]

One page of Alvarez's Web site is devoted to images, including a couple of recent photographs of herself, but mostly featuring Dominican artists and the art that illustrates some of her works. Her interest in images is underscored by the comment on her "News" page that she does not know which of two cover images for the Spanish translation of *How the García Girls Lost Their Accents* she prefers.

Appearances in the fall of 2009 for honors or awards are available as videos on the Internet. Alvarez spoke at the National Book Festival in Washington, D.C., on September 30 and October 1.[4] Her formal evening speech and talk the following day both focus on the importance of literacy. She describes censorship in the Dominican Republic under Trujillo, linking it with attacks on books used in U.S. schools, especially her own *How the García Girls Lost Their Accents*. She describes her immersion in reading as a new immigrant, the joy of discovering the library, and, especially, Langston Hughes's poem, "I, Too, Sing America," which attests to the rightful place of people of color in the United States. She also promotes reading stories as a means of developing compassion. On October 27, 2009, she was interviewed on Montgomery College's television station on the occasion of receiving the F. Scott Fitzgerald Award for Outstanding Achievement in American Literature.[5] In this interview, she speaks about the way that writing starts for her in an in-between place, where something unsettles her, impelling her to write in order to make sense of it. Asked for advice to Latino(a) students, Alvarez says that they should look deep within themselves to find the combination of their two cultures that feels right for them as individuals, and they should seek careers that excite them rather than careers that offer monetary incentives.

Alvarez's first two novels, which are read as part of many high school and college courses, have been targeted by parents' groups as objectionable. Grounds for attacks on *How the García Girls Lost Their Accents* are the passages with sexual content. In the case of *In the Time of the Butterflies*, the rationale was security risk, due to some content about the resistance movement. The National Coalition Against Censorship interviewed Alvarez in 2008 when *García Girls* was under attack at one school. Though brief, the interview illuminates the significance Alvarez attaches to freedom of expression in the United States.[6]

One of the best resources on a specific book, the book that makes the most impassioned case for freedom of expression, comes from The Big Read, sponsored by the National Endowment for the Humanities, which selected *In the Time of the Butterflies* as one of its titles. The Big Read promotes community sharing of books and provides resources for discussion of its selections. Resources for *In the Time of the Butterflies* are available at its Web site, including a substantial Reader's Guide and Teacher's Guide, in addition to information about Alvarez.[7] Readers interested in learning more about the Mirabal sisters will find substantial information on the Web. A sequence of photographs of the museum and the Mirabal sisters is at *El Bohío Dominicano: A Visual Archive of the Dominican Republics* Mirabal Sisters site.[8] Several brief clips of the elderly Dedé Mirabal, telling her sisters' story in Spanish, with English subtitles, can be found on YouTube.[9] Spanish speakers can also view an interview on YouTube.[10] The Organization of American States (OAS) observes the International Day for the Elimination of Violence Against Women on the anniversary of the Mirabal sisters' deaths, November 25; their Web site for this observance includes links to information about the sisters.[11]

A brief biography with overviews of Alvarez's books and a brief bibliography of useful critical studies is available on the Salem Press Web site.[12] Other useful Web resources are the interviews with Alvarez that coincide with the release of her books. A noteworthy interview was conducted by Robert Birnbaum when *Saving the World* was published.[13] The conversation was wide ranging, covering topics like poetry, Alvarez's recent reading, Mario Vargas Llosa's novel about Trujillo's assassination, the ways that readers use fiction to emotionally integrate information about their world, and her research for *Once Upon a Quinceañera*. Much of their conversation illuminates *Saving the World*: the impact of technology on the contemporary world, the ways that the publishing business can distance a writer from the real work of writing books, some of the facts that reporters get wrong, and the ways that the "First World" interacts with the "Third World," and, of course, the footnote Alvarez read that sparked her research on the Balmis expedition and the questions she had about Isabel.

Another 2006 interview was conducted by Powell's Books. Following Alvarez's comments on *Saving the World*, the Powell's Web site includes a light-hearted Q&A (questions and answers) session that includes questions about her favorite pair of shoes, her favorite breakfast, and favorite characters in history, as well as about her reading and views on more serious topics.[14] A Minnesota Public Radio interview by Kerri Miller, conducted in 2006,[15] includes brief but insightful comments on Alvarez's stature as a Latina author. In a brief 2007 video interview by LatinaLista,[16] Alvarez summarizes the concerns she writes about in *Once Upon a Quinceañera*, commenting on the importance to the Latino community of critical thinking about the celebration. Alvarez was interviewed in 2000 by Bookreporter.com on the occasion of publication of *In the Name of Salomé*. In this interview, she explains how she became interested in Salomé Ureña and in her daughter, Camila, about whom little was known, and describes her research in Cuba, with the gift she received from the city historian of Santiago, Cuba, a 1920 edition of Salomé's poems.[17]

For the most part, Alvarez's presence on the Web, with the exception of her own Web site, is a reflection of her contact with readers through other, formal venues: transcripts of interviews and footage of formal speaking occasions. The printed word takes precedence in Alvarez's world.

DISCUSSION QUESTIONS

• On Alvarez's "La Ñapa" Web page, she introduces her 31 (plus two) haikus for the month of March, a linked group known as a *renga*, with comments on adjusting to Vermont winters. What new insights into Alvarez's writing life, and her recent fiction that stresses the Vermont environment (*Saving the World, How Tía Lola Came to Visit Stay*), does the reader gain from these poems?

• In Alvarez's appearance at the National Book Festival, she names the primary news channel as "Radio Bigmouth" during Trujillo's years as dictator. What new light does this shed on her characterization of the Dominican Republic as "an oral culture" in essays and other interviews?

13

JULIA ALVAREZ AND THE MEDIA

Contemporary media usually seem far removed from the world of Alvarez's fiction. In interviews, she repeatedly refers to the importance of the oral storytelling tradition in her home culture,[1] and she claims that much of the inspiration for her poetry comes from the women's voices in her childhood, the rhythms of women's talk about domestic matters.[2] Yet the popular songs that the maids sang came directly from radio broadcasts. The radio plays a more important role in Alvarez's fiction than other media, but the value she sets on literacy results in numerous allusions to writers, books, and newspapers. The high culture of literature and art is more prominent in her fiction than popular culture. With Milton- and Shakespeare-quoting elders,[3] and Alvarez's own entrance into true literacy coinciding with her immersion in the English language,[4] it is not surprising that her characters exhibit her own love for *The Arabian Nights* and poems by Walt Whitman and Emily Dickinson. Art, too, plays a role: the painting by Gauguin that hangs in the dining room in their home in the Dominican Republic,[5] the paintings that frame Isabel's and Alma's experiences in *Saving the World*.[6]

News, though, is important in several novels: the newspaper and radio in *In the Time of the Butterflies* and *Before We Were Free*, and the television in *How the García Girls Lost Their Accents*, *In the Name of Salomé*, *Return to Sender*, and *Finding Miracles*. Yet for many years, the main source of information in the Dominican Republic was "Radio Bigmouth," or rumor.[7] The news media can pose problems, too: Yo's radio interviews bring her into conflict with her family, and newspaper coverage brings her into danger when her stalker tracks her down in Chicago.[8] Media news affects people's decisions: Tyler's trip to Washington is canceled because of demonstrations over immigration issues in *Return to Sender.*[9] In *Finding Miracles*, Milly's family joins the Bolívar family to watch news coverage of the election in their home country; the election outcome prompts the Bolívars' decision to visit their country during the summer; Milly's father worries about her safety while she is there, due to the news he hears.[10]

In *Saving the World*, Alvarez's most recent adult novel, the media and technology shape characters' lives. Alma is dissatisfied with the publicity machine of contemporary publishing, with its need for creating "buzz" by publicizing the writer, whose life story is expected to be as interesting as her characters' stories. She avoids being photographed fully lit, to protect her privacy and her family's privacy, and is attacked by a critic for falsely posing as a writer of color.[11] The telephone, answering machine, cell phone, and fax bring threats into Alma's home as well as reconnect her with Richard when he is in the Dominican Republic. Cell phone reception is an explicit concern, first in her ability to stay in touch with Richard, and later in maintaining lines of communication during the hostage situation. The contemporary world impinges on the retreat that Alma has constructed for her writing and, as the novel begins, for her Danteesque crisis of the soul. On a societal scale, the globalized economy impinges on mountain village life, with mostly negative effects.

Several of Alvarez's works have been dramatized. Given her use of multiple points of view and gaps in time, her novels pose challenges to dramatization. Asked in 2000 whether a movie version of *How the García Girls Lost Their Accents* was in the works, Alvarez replied that the book had been optioned, but the screenplays she saw were disappointing, and when the term of the contract expired, it was not renewed.[12] Alvarez was enthusiastic about the stage version, written by Karen Zacarias, which debuted in September 2008 at Round House Theatre in Bethesda, Maryland.[13] One of the stories in *¡Yo!*, "The Suitor," has been filmed; the one-hour made-for-television production aired on PBS in 2001.[14] To date, only one of her novels—*In the Time of the Butterflies*—has been presented in its entirety on the screen. The 90-minute made-for-television movie starring Salma Hayek as Minerva Mirabal aired on Showtime in 2001.[15] The production, directed by Mariano Barosso and featuring Marc Anthony as Lio Morales and Edward James Olmos as Rafael Trujillo, won two ALMA Awards: Outstanding Made-for-Television Movie or Miniseries and Outstanding Actor/Actress in a Made-for-Television Movie or Miniseries for Salma

Hayek's portrayal of Minerva Mirabal. Marc Anthony was also nominated for Outstanding Actor/Actress in a Made-for-Television Movie or Miniseries.[16] Hayek was nominated for a Critics Choice Award for Best Actress in a Picture Made for Television.[17]

In the Time of the Butterflies[18] is a successful dramatic production, even if it necessarily simplifies a complex text. Given Alvarez's experimentation with multiple points of view and a 22-year span of events, compression of events and characters was necessary, as Alvarez found in writing the novel, "collapsing characters or incidents."[19] Although this compression is carried further in the movie, many of the novel's major scenes are presented. The perspective is Minerva's, most of the story told as memories relived in her prison cell while in solitary confinement. Several scenes convey a good deal of information in a notably economical fashion: the opening scenes that describe Trujillo's totalitarian rule and show Minerva's barren cell; the confrontation between Minerva and Trujillo at the Discovery Day dinner-dance; the risks taken by the underground; and conditions in the prison.

The film's opening is especially effective. Historical context is developed in a series of black-and-white photographs with text that presents the stark facts of Trujillo's three decades as dictator. The black-and-white stills convey both historical authenticity and the reduction of social issues to simple right-or-wrong terms, presumably the dictator's view—one is either with him or against him. The first photographs show workers in the cane fields, an overseer, unhappy children, and soldiers. Text on the screen explains that Trujillo ruled from 1930 to 1961, his power established through alliances with the church, the aristocracy, intellectuals, and the press. The next images are of bound men, one with a knife to his throat. The text that follows states that Trujillo's formula for maintaining power was to kill anyone who opposed him. This is succeeded by images of torture victims, with one black-and-white image animated: a person screams silently, raising hands to head, as the accompanying text states that more than 30,000 people were executed under Trujillo's regime.

The story of the Mirabal sisters is introduced into this context with a shift to color, and an initial image of the upper part of the walls of a solitary cell, which is lit with sunlight from skylight openings, creating contrast between the natural world and Miranda's confinement as well as contrasting the sunlit trees with the opening black-and-white images documenting Trujillo's brutal rule. Water drips as the camera focuses on the blurred reflection of Miranda's face in a shallow pool of water; she comes into focus, hand over her mouth. Her hair is cropped short, her fingernails are dirty. In a voiceover, Miranda speaks about memories that are put away for "safekeeping" against the times they are needed. The camera moves back to reveal Miranda's position in her cell, huddled against the wall in a shaft of sunlight, wearing a shapeless gray dress and hugging herself. The voice, uttering her thoughts, likens the memories to "soaring" butterflies. The scene quickly fades to black. The memories that Minerva replays in following scenes alternate with views of her in solitary confinement, her face bloodied at one point. The darkness, the dirt, and the wretched conditions of the prison convey the prisoners' despair.

Counterbalancing the prison's darkness and brutality are happy childhood memories, her romance with Lio, and her passionate commitment to justice, love and marriage, and motherhood. After Minerva witnesses the administration of electric shocks to her husband by a torturer, the scene shifts to her solitary cell, with a repetition of the images with which the movie started. This forms the transition from memories into the movie's present time. The things that she remembers most, she says, are her father's eyes, Lio's voice, her children's laughter, Manolo's hands, love, and justice. The widespread support for her and María Teresa becomes apparent from this point forward: a woman guard whispers, "Long live the Butterflies"; a man sits outside the prison holding a butterfly on a pole; after their release, her priest whispers, "Long live the Butterflies" when she takes communion.

Minerva's confrontations with Trujillo are dramatic: as a girl, she intervenes to save him from Sinita's impending attack in a pageant performed at their school, and on the occasion of the Discovery Day Dance, she slaps him in a well-lit ballroom, causing the music and other dancers to stop. Her private moments with Trujillo are the occasions when she gambles with him for her father's release and, later, thanks him for the opportunity to visit her husband in prison, suggesting a strong personal connection. Her anger and rebellion are shown in a scene after her father's arrest, when she smashes the picture of Trujillo that is required by law to be displayed in every household.

Lio Morales is presented as a professor of law, whose dramatic nighttime escape into exile occurs just short of a checkpoint where cars are being stopped and searched. Later, Minerva learns of his death when she sees a newspaper photograph of his bloody body posted on a university bulletin board, shortly after she begins taking law courses. María Teresa's involvement in the underground follows quickly after her discovery of Minerva's involvement when she arrives unexpectedly at Minerva's apartment, breaking up a meeting. Minerva tells her to go home, claiming that her conflict with Trujillo is personal and María Teresa need not be involved. Leandro approaches her on the street, introduces himself, and takes her to put up posters with him the same night. Patria's involvement follows. After a bloodied man fleeing arrest breaks in on a church service she is attending with her children, she is shown talking to a priest with her sisters, urging the church to join the opposition to Trujillo.

Captain Peña is the agent of the sisters' deaths, which follow shortly after a visit to the Mirabal home by Trujillo, a visit that gives Minerva another opportunity to reject him. Trujillo's final comment to her suggests their deaths are near: he says he will do what he can to end her suffering. Peña trails the sisters on their way home from their last visit to their imprisoned husbands, witnessing their forced walk into a cane field. When Patria runs back out to call for help, no one but Peña is there to hear her. Minerva attempts to talk the men out of killing them, but the soldiers are joined by men who emerge from the cane field, holding staves with which they will beat the women. The sisters hold each other inside the ring formed by the men and begin to recite Psalm 23. Instead of seeing the impact of the beating, the viewer sees the slow-motion descent of staves and hears the sound of blows. The scene concludes with an image of one of the murderers stopped in midaction. This shift from motion into stillness mirrors the shift from still photographs into motion at the outset of the movie. The violent scene is followed by a peaceful view of a mountain and a stream, with butterflies in the foreground.

Balancing the opening images and text, the movie ends with text informing the viewer that the Mirabal sisters' deaths were "the final blow" that brought down Trujillo. It is noted that he was assassinated six months later. The viewer also learns that several of the sisters' children became involved in the democratic government of the Dominican Republic and that the anniversary of their death is observed as the International Day for the Elimination of Violence Against Women.

The most significant difference between the book and movie is the substitution of one sister's point of view for the perspectives of all four. The effect of framing the narrative as Minerva's is, primarily, to remove the survivor perspective that the novel shows—the reflective element introduced by three and a half decades of remembering in a home that has become a museum. Also, Dedé's role is reduced, her marriage and children not shown. Some of her husband's role passes to Patria's husband in order to include the element of family opposition to the women's involvement in the movement.

In the movie, the personal element in Minerva's opposition to Trujillo is emphasized, underscored by Minerva's statement to Mate that "this is personal." The story *is* a personal one, but emphasizing this motive at the expense of others tends to reduce the power of the Mirabal sisters' political commitment. Minerva is shocked by Lio's death, seeing his corpse in a newspaper photograph just before she is approached by Manolo to join the underground. When Minerva tells Mate not to join the underground, insisting that her conflict with Trujillo is "personal," she says she is the reason their father died. Perhaps the dictator's personalizing of his opposition was a larger factor in his contest with them, especially when he announced in Salcedo that his two problems were the church and the Mirabal sisters, but that moment is not shown in the movie. Despite the collapsing of characters and incidents, however, the movie is faithful to the novel and successful in its own right.

The Suitor, directed by Julia Solomonoff and starring Rosa Arredondo as Yolanda García and Tim Guinee as Dexter Hays, was produced by Brian Devine, Jason Orans, and Jen Small of the small independent company, Gigantic Pictures, in 2001 and aired on PBS.[20] In the dramatization, Yo lives with Dexter in New York at the time of her trip to the Dominican Republic, and he announces his arrival in the Dominican Republic by telephone, from the airport. Yo is working for her uncle's campaign, instead of gathering research for her own writing, and she comes in conflict with an old friend who opposes her uncle's policies regarding land development for tourist attractions. Her aunts want her to marry him and live in the Dominican Republic. Family scenes and interactions with cousin Lucinda are entertaining, beginning in Spanish, with subtitles, then switching to English. The challenges that the men of the family present to Dexter, who cannot keep pace with their drinking and gambling, are equally entertaining.

How the García Girls Lost Their Accents has been adapted for the stage by Mexican American playwright Karen Zacarias. Since its world premiere at the Round House Theatre in Bethesda, Maryland, in 2008, it has been produced by the Miracle Theatre Group in Portland, Oregon, in March 2010. At the National Book Fair in 2009, Alvarez commented favorably on the Round House production, especially on the four Latina actresses' believability as the García sisters as they grew younger.[21] The episodic structure and reverse chronology of the novel were preserved, the girls' accents growing more pronounced as the play progressed. Newspaper reviews of both productions were favorable.

The challenge of presenting Alvarez's dramatic, complicated characters and plots without stereotypes or melodrama seems daunting. Her own commitment is to the written word, and she has said that she has no interest in being a screenwriter.[22] For the time being, at least, the dramatizations of her work remain limited.

DISCUSSION QUESTIONS

- What are the advantages of presenting the Mirabal sisters' lives and deaths through the immediacy of Minerva's perspective, rather than through the retrospective view of Dedé? What is lost in this approach?
- The novel, *In the Time of the Butterflies*, presents María Teresa entirely through diary entries, and some critics have felt that this approach distances her, making her less interesting to readers than her sister. How does her characterization in the movie version differ from her portrayal in the novel?

14

WHAT DO I READ NEXT?

Julia Alvarez is a reader. In interviews and essays, she refers to books and authors that have had an impact on her, most often poets.[1] Walt Whitman and Emily Dickinson were early and continuing influences on her writing.[2] She was not a reader as a child in the Dominican Republic, but she fell in love with *The Arabian Nights*,[3] a book that she alludes to in several of her works. Later, coming to literature in English with a voracious appetite for reading, she read widely in well-established, canonical literature.[4] One of the writers she loved is the Victorian realist George Eliot.[5] As a writer, Alvarez had to break new ground, given a scarcity of role models.[6]

Alvarez has repeatedly acknowledged her indebtedness to Maxine Hong Kingston, whose 1976 memoir, *The Woman Warrior*, paved the way for writing by other "hyphenated Americans."[7] Once she realized that other ethnic experiences could be the source of rich American fiction, Alvarez explored Latino literature, beginning with authors Piri Thomas, Ernesto Galarza, Rudolfo Anaya, José Antonio Villareal, and Gary Soto.[8] It was not until the 1980s that Latina writers began to find their way into print, with a groundbreaking anthology edited by Alma Gómez, Cherrie Moraga, and Mariana Romo-Carmona, titled *Cuentos: Stories by Latinos,* followed by Sandra Cisneros's critically acclaimed *The House on Mango Street.*[9]

In an essay in *Something to Declare*, Alvarez mentions the "multicultural perspective . . . of some of the most interesting writers of this late twentieth century: Salman Rushdie in London, Michael Ondaatje in Toronto, Maxine Hong Kingston in San Francisco, Seamus Heaney in Boston, Bharati Mukherjee in Berkeley, Marjorie Agosin in Wellesley, and Edwidge Danticat in Brooklyn."[10] She made an important discovery in the poet William Carlos Williams's bicultural identity and linguistic background.[11] But throughout her work, the reader finds references to Dante and Chaucer, and she quotes T. S. Eliot, William Butler Yeats, Theodore Roethke, Gwendolyn Brooks, the Roman playwright Terence, Anton Chekhov, Czeslaw Milosz, Rainer Maria Rilke, and Rumi. Among her "writing commandments" is a quotation from Toni Morrison, whom Alvarez also refers to as an important influence.[12] Her poetry is full of allusions to other poets. In her essay "Writing Matters," she mentions reading poems to start her writing day, listing Jane Kenyon, George Herbert, Rita Dove, Robert Frost, Elizabeth Bishop, Rhina Espaillat, Jane Shore, and Emily Dickinson, but the ellipsis that follows Dickinson's name suggests that the list could be much longer.[13] In a 2006 interview, Alvarez was asked what author she would recommend and answered "J. M. Coetzee" (originally from South Africa, now an Australian citizen), mentioning his novel *Disgrace* as a good starting point.[14]

Given this range of influences and recommendations from Alvarez herself, the reader could choose from a wide spectrum of authors and works to continue reading. This chapter will narrow the focus to, primarily, Caribbean, Latin American, and U.S. Hispanic writers for adults and young readers.

One of the best-known women writers from the Caribbean, writing mostly in the first half of the 20th century, is Jean Rhys, from the English-speaking island of Dominica in the West Indies. She went to England as a young woman and lived most of her life in Europe.[15] Her career had a long hiatus between the 1930s and the 1960s, when she began publishing again. Rhys is best known for *Wide Sargasso Sea* (1966), a novel that responds to Charlotte Brontë's *Jane Eyre* by imagining a life for Edward Rochester's Caribbean first wife, the mad Bertha Mason, who is locked away in the attic in Brontë's novel. Most of her fiction, however, deals with modern women and themes. A strongly autobiographical novel, *Voyage in the Dark* (1934), evokes the Caribbean, in which the protagonist goes to England, where she must cope with being dismissed as a "colonial." A book that exposes British prejudice, it contains some offensive racist language.

Racism is a significant theme in Caribbean literature and plays an important role in the lives of authors and characters living in the United States and Europe. Paule Marshall was born in the United States, but her parents came from Barbados, and her fiction features characters with

Caribbean ties.[16] Her first novel, *Brown Girl, Brownstones* (1959), as well as *Praisesong for the Widow* (1983) and *Daughters* (1991), deals explicitly with their protagonists' need to reconnect with their pasts. She has also published volumes of short stories and, recently, a memoir, *Triangular Road* (2009).

Maryse Condé comes from the French-speaking island of Guadeloupe and writes in French. She was educated in France and spent a number of years in Africa before teaching at several U.S. universities, living in both Guadeloupe and the United States.[17] Ties with Africa are an important element in her fiction. Her historical novel *Segu* (1984–1985) established her reputation, but her novel *I, Tituba, Black Witch of Salem* (1992) makes a good starting point for U.S. American readers. She is a playwright and critic as well as a novelist and short story writer.

Jamaica Kincaid was born on Antigua, which was a British colony until the mid-1960s.[18] She is best known for *Annie John* (1985), a poetic novel composed of related short stories about a young girl's maturation on Antigua. Her 1990 novel, *Lucy*, addresses the challenges faced by a young woman who leaves her island life to work as an au pair in a U.S. city and must come to terms with a very different life. Kincaid is an essayist and memoirist as well as a writer of fiction.

Haitian American novelist Edwidge Danticat, who came to the United States at age 12, has written several novels and memoirs about life in the Dominican Republic's neighboring country, Haiti, as well as her experience of immigrating to the United States.[19] Her 1994 novel, *Breath, Eyes, Memory*, established her reputation and was an Oprah's Book Club selection. Her subsequent books have been equally, if not more, popular with readers: *Krik? Krak!: Stories* (1995); *The Farming of Bones* (1999); *The Dew Breaker* (2004); and the memoir, *Brother, I'm Dying* (2007). Danticat has also written for young readers: *Behind the Mountains* (2002) is a novel in the form of diary entries for readers age 10 and older.

Cuban American Cristina García's first novel, *Dreaming in Cuban* (1992), was nominated for a National Book Award, and *The Agüero Sisters* was also critically acclaimed.[20] Divided identity and family relationships form significant themes in her work. She has written four other novels for adults, as well as two books for young readers and a volume of poetry. Additionally, she has edited the anthologies *Cubanismo!* (2003), a collection of Cuban writing, and *Bordering Fires* (2006), a collection of Mexican and chicano(a) works. García's family came to the United States when she was only two years old; she did not revisit Cuba until the 1980s.[21]

Puerto Rican author Rosario Ferré writes essays, poetry, and biographies as well as the fiction for which she is best known. Her novel *The*

House on the Lagoon (1995) was the first book she wrote originally in English, though earlier novels were translated from Spanish.[22] Like Alvarez's fiction, this novel features a writer as protagonist and combines narrative voices.

Another Puerto Rican writer, Judith Ortiz Cofer, lived her childhood partly in New Jersey and partly in Puerto Rico, then moved to Georgia in her teenage years.[23] Her poetry, fiction, essays, and memoirs evoke both Puerto Rico and Puerto Rican immigrant life in the United States. Her 1989 novel, *The Line of the Sun*, was nominated for the Pulitzer Prize. *The Latin Deli: Telling the Lives of Barrio Women* (1995; originally published as *The Latin Deli: Prose and Poetry*, 1993) portrays Puerto Rican women's lives in New York in essays, stories, and poems. Like Alvarez, Ortiz Cofer values her heritage of storytelling in an oral culture and captures it in *Silent Dancing: A Partial Remembrance of a Puerto Rican Childhood* (1991). She has written several books for young adults as well, and her 1995 book, *An Island Like You: Stories of the Barrio*, received the Pura Belpré Award.[24]

The English writer Andrea Levy is the child of Jamaican parents. She began writing fiction because she wanted to write the kind of novels she would have liked to read as a young woman but could not find. Investigating her roots, she visited Jamaica for the first time in the 1980s.[25] Her early semiautobiographical novels like *Every Light in the House Burnin'* (1994) reflect this voyage of self-discovery. Her historical novel *Small Island* (2004), which earned her critical acclaim, incorporates multiple perspectives and chapters that alternate between the past and the present.

Male writers from the Caribbean of particular interest include Dominican American fiction writer Junot Diaz, who immigrated as a child[26]; the 1992 Nobel laureate poet Derek Walcott, from St. Lucia[27]; and the 2001 Nobel laureate V. S. Naipaul, from Trinidad.[28] Junot Diaz's 2007 novel, *The Brief Wondrous Life of Oscar Wao*, which won the Pulitzer Prize, divides narrative perspective, is nonchronological, and is set in both the Dominican Republic and the United States. Like Alvarez's work, *Oscar Wao* shows Trujillo's long reach in his impact on families and a continuing legacy of violence. Diaz's 1996 book of short stories, *Drown*, was also well received, and his short stories have appeared in several volumes of *Best American Short Stories*.

The Nobel laureate Derek Walcott is from Saint Lucia in the Lesser Antilles. Best known as a poet, he is also a playwright and essayist. His most recent book of poems, *White Egrets* (2010), addresses themes of love, mortality, and the relationship of his beautiful island home to Europe with a personal, autobiographical perspective. His *Collected Poems,*

1948–1984 (1986) and *Selected Poems* (2007) are good introductions to his poetry. Nobel laureate V. S. Naipaul is from Trinidad. Naipaul's post-colonial novels evoke a distinctly darker vision than Alvarez's. His 1961 novel, *A House for Mr. Biswas*, is regarded as his masterpiece by some writers. His semiautobiographical 1987 novel, *The Enigma of Arrival*, reflects on finding a sense of home after many years of wandering.

The Cuban American writer Oscar Hijuelos[29] was the first Latino novelist to win a Pulitzer Prize, for his second novel, *The Mambo Kings Play Songs of Love* (1989), about a pair of brothers who come from Cuba to New York in the late 1940s to start a mambo band. His 2002 novel, *A Simple Habana Melody*, is also about Latin music in the World War II era. The dramatic change in socioeconomic class that often accompanies immigration is addressed in *Empress of the Splendid Season* (1998), which features a female protagonist. *Dark Dude* (2009) is his first novel for young adults, about a Cuban American teenager who leaves behind the urban pressures of New York and hitchhikes to Wisconsin to reinvent his life.

Alvarez is often linked with Mexican American writer Sandra Cisneros. An interest in multiculturalism in the 1980s brought new prominence to Latina writers. *Vanity Fair* featured her with Cisneros, Denise Chavez, and Ana Castillo as "Las Girlfriends" in an article that identified their writing as a new genre.[30] Asked about the group in a 2006 interview, Alvarez said she was embarrassed by the situation, which felt like being promoted as a product, despite the real respect she had for the writers with whom she was grouped.[31]

Cisneros's best-known work, *The House on Mango Street* (1988), is taught in many high school classes. Composed of very brief stories, usually referred to as vignettes, it is a Chicana coming-of-age novel. Cisneros is a poet and short story writer as well as a novelist.[32] Similar themes to those in *Mango Street* and her short stories, *Woman Hollering Creek* (1991), are brought out in poems in *My Wicked Wicked Ways* (1992) and *Loose Woman* (1994). Her multigenerational novel of Mexican American life, *Caramelo*, was published in 2001.

Playwright and fiction writer Denise Chavez comes from the Southwest.[33] Her best-known works are *The Last of the Menu Girls* (1986), a coming-of-age story in seven connected short stories, and *Face of an Angel* (1994), a complex, multivoiced novel that employs techniques similar to Alvarez's and addresses the cultural divide between mainstream American identity and Mexican American heritage.

Ana Castillo, another Mexican American writer born in Chicago,[34] experiments with chronology and point of view, as well as employing magical realism, in her novels. *The Mixquiahuala Letters* (1986), an epistolary novel in which the letters may be read in different sequences for different themes, earned the American Book Award from the Before Columbus Foundation. The magical realist novel *So Far from God* (1993) explores women's lives on the border—geographical, cultural, and spiritual. Her 1996 book of short stories, *Loverboys*, explores a wide range of love relationships. *The Guardians* (2007) employs first-person narratives in alternating chapters to explore the dangerous lives of illegal border-crossers. Her 2005 novel about migrant workers, *Watercolor Women, Opaque Men*, is in verse.

Chilean-born novelist Isabel Allende received critical recognition with her first novel, *The House of the Spirits*, drawing on her family history of political involvement. Her father's cousin, Salvador Allende, was president briefly before General Augusto Pinochet took over the government in a successful U.S.-backed coup. Allende, with other members of her family, was in danger and emigrated to Venezuela, where she lived for 13 years.[35] *The House of the Spirits* began as a letter to her grandfather and grew into the substantial multigenerational novel that won her widespread popularity. It was published in Spain in 1982, translated into English in 1985.[36] Since 1988, she has lived in California. Perhaps her most popular work is *Eva Luna* (1988). Her historical novels are set in North America and Latin America and include *Ines of My Soul* (2006) and *Island Beneath the Sea* (2010). *Daughter of Fortune* (1999) and *Portrait in Sepia* (2001) are multigenerational novels. Recently she has published memoirs as well as fiction.

The Latin American "magical realist" tradition is best known in the United States through the work of Gabriel García Marquez, originally from Colombia, later settling in Mexico after periods of living in Spain and elsewhere.[37] He received the Nobel Prize in Literature in 1982.[38] His best-known novel, now established as a classic, is *One Hundred Years of Solitude* (1967; translated into English in 1970). *The Autumn of the Patriarch* (1975), originally published in Spanish as *El otoño del patriarca*, is a novel about a Caribbean dictator whose country is never identified. Considered a minor work shortly after its publication, its reputation has grown in the decades since its publication, and it is now highly regarded.

The Peruvian novelist Mario Vargas Llosa, author of more than two dozen works of fiction and nonfiction, has written a substantial novel about the Trujillo regime, *The Feast of the Goat* (originally published in Spanish as *Fiesta el Chievo* in 2000, translated into English by Edith Grossman in 2001). Vargas Llosa lived in Europe for 30 years, where he established his international reputation as a novelist.[39] The themes of many of his novels are political, some of them historical, commenting on the turmoil in his nation. In 1990, he himself ran for the presidency, unsuccessfully.[40]

Readers who find the hostage situation of *Saving the World* particularly gripping may also be interested in Ann Patchett's *Bel Canto* (2001), set in an unidentified Latin American country, where a group of terrorists take over a home in which a party of international guests is assembled to honor a Japanese industrialist. Their quarry is the country's president, but he is not at the party, leaving the terrorists with too little leverage to negotiate their demands.

Another notable novelist working in the magical realist tradition, writing in Spanish, is Mexican novelist Laura Esquivel.[41] Her best-known novel, the magical realist novel *Like Water for Chocolate*, is a love story set in the early 20th century, which was made into a movie and released the same year the English translation of the novel was published (1993).[42] Her 2006 novel, *Malinche*, imagines the life of the near-mythic and much-maligned Native American woman who became mistress as well as translator to Cortés, helping to bring about the downfall of the Aztec empire.

A good source of recommendations for books by emerging Latino/Latina authors is the Web site LatinoStories.com, which features book reviews and an annual list of "Top Ten 'New' Authors to Watch (and Read)." A literature page maintained by the Latin American Network Information Center (LANIC) is an index of links to resources and writers in Spanish, Portuguese, and English.[43] The Pura Belpré Award recognizes excellence in books for young readers that represent Latino experience effectively. Award winners and honor books are listed on its Web site.[44] The Américas Book Award for Children's and Young Adult Literature, sponsored by the Center for Latin American and Caribbean Studies, recognizes books in English or Spanish; award winners and resources are listed on its Web site.[45]

Alvarez's 2002 novel for young adults, *Before We Were Free*, which includes a chapter of diary entries written while the protagonist is in hiding, suggests parallels with European Holocaust stories (parallels also suggested in *Finding Miracles*, another novel for young adults). Young readers who have not read Anne Frank's diary will be interested in comparing its depiction of life in hiding, as well as life under a dictator.

Young readers who enjoy *Return to Sender* will be interested in Francisco Jimenez's works, *The Circuit: Stories from the Life of a Migrant Child* (1997), *Breaking Through* (2001), and *Reaching Out* (2008), based on his own experience as a migrant worker born to Mexican parents.

Pam Muñoz Ryan has written over 20 books for young readers, some appropriate for the primary grades, some for the intermediate grades.

Her best works for the latter group are the Pura Belpré Award book, *Esperanza Rising* (2000), about the change in social class that a young immigrant girl experiences when her father is murdered, and *Becoming Naomi Leon*, in which a long-absent mother shows up to initiate a custody battle over her daughter.

Gary Soto has written a number of books for young adult and intermediate readers: novels, short stories, and poems featuring male and female characters and perspectives, on topics ranging from love to jobs to education to sports. His prose is poetic, and plot elements dealing with older protagonists are sometimes tragic. His 1990 *Baseball in April and Other Stories*, for intermediate readers, was a Pura Belpré Honor Book. Victor Martinez's *Parrot in the Oven: mi vida* (1996), a coming-of-age story about a Mexican American boy told in vignettes, won the National Book Award for Young People's Literature.

A strong Caribbean literature emerges from several countries with different languages and traditions, but the immigrant experience, whether islanders migrate to Great Britain or North America, is remarkably similar. Politics is a common topic in South American as well as Caribbean literature. In the early 1980s, it was easier to find novels translated from Spanish by authors from other countries than novels in English by U.S. Latina(o) authors. Fortunately, the new interest in multicultural literature led to publication of many works about Latina(o) culture for readers of all levels and more widespread recognition of their literary value. Thanks to Julia Alvarez as well as other groundbreaking Latina authors, today's readers have far more choices.

NOTES

Preface

1. "Julia Alvarez" Web site, http://www.juliaalvarez.com (accessed October 10, 2010).
2. Alvarez has linked her love of reading with learning English on a number of occasions, making the link clearly in remarks at the National Book Festival on October 1, 2009, Library of Congress, http://www.youtube.com/watch?v=ASbxm-T8-i4 (accessed October 10, 2010).
3. Julia Alvarez, "Of Maids and Other Muses," "So Much Depends," and "Doña Aída, with Your Permission," in *Something to Declare*.

Chapter 1: Julia Alvarez: The Life

1. Alvarez explains her father's first escape from the Dominican Republic, her parents' meeting in North America, and their return in "A Genetics of Justice," in *Something to Declare*, and briefly recapitulates it in *Once Upon a Quinceañera: Coming of Age in the USA*, p. 23.
2. Alvarez recalls family life in the Dominican Republic and her family's hasty departure in "Our Papers," in *Something to Declare*.
3. "A Vermont Writer from the Dominican Republic," *Something to Declare*.
4. "Grandfather's Blessing" and "El Doctor," *Something to Declare*, pp. 7 and 55.
5. "Of Maids and Other Muses," *Something to Declare*, pp. 160–162.
6. "First Muse," *Something to Declare*, pp. 134, 138.
7. Based on 2002 census data; CIA (Central Intelligence Agency), "Literacy," "The World Factbook," https://www.cia.gov/library/publications/the-world-factbook/fields/2103.html (accessed October 10, 2010).

8. "First Muse," pp. 136–139.
9. "Grandfather's Blessing," p. 8.
10. *Once Upon a Quinceañera*, p. 31.
11. "My English," *Something to Declare*, pp. 22–23.
12. "Grandfather's Blessing," pp. 5–6.
13. "My Second Opera," *Something to Declare*, pp. 32–33.
14. Alvarez tells the story in "Our Papers."
15. *Once Upon a Quinceañera*, pp. 23–24.
16. "First Muse," p. 139.
17. Interview, October 27, 2009, "F. Scott Fitzgerald Literary Committee and MCTV," http://www.youtube.com/watch?v=HZ2xe2OFTX8, and "Julia Alvarez: 2009 National Book Festival," October 1, 2009, Library of Congress, http://www.youtube.com/watch?v=ASbxm-T8-i4 (both accessed October 10, 2010).
18. Ibid.
19. *Once Upon a Quinceañera*, p. 23.
20. Ibid., pp. 102, 106.
21. Ibid., p. 82.
22. "Book TV: Julia Alvarez, 2009 National Book Festival," September 30, 2009, http://www.youtube.com/watch?v=FZTxT34fI5Q (accessed October 10, 2010).
23. *The Woman I Kept to Myself*, pp. 29–30.
24. "Of Maids and Other Muses," p. 159.
25. "Julia Alvarez" Web page and "Julia Alvarez, Contemporary Authors Online," 2010, subscription database at http://www.gale.cengage.com/LitRC/.
26. Ibid.
27. "Goodbye, Ms. Chips," *Something to Declare*, pp. 218–219.
28. Ibid., pp. 219–220.
29. Julia Alvarez Web site and "Julia Alvarez, Contemporary Authors Online."
30. Ibid.
31. "Have Typewriter, Will Travel," *Something to Declare*, p. 177.
32. Julia Alvarez Web site and "Julia Alvarez, Contemporary Authors Online."
33. *Once Upon a Quinceañera*, pp. 217–218.
34. "Have Typewriter, Will Travel," p. 179.
35. Ibid., p. 180.
36. Julia Alvarez Web site and "Julia Alvarez, Contemporary Authors Online."
37. "Goodbye, Ms. Chips," p. 213.
38. "Family Matters," *Something to Declare*, p. 123; "So Much Depends," p. 168; and *Once Upon a Quinceañera*, p. 222.
39. "Goodbye, Ms. Chips," p. 213.
40. Julia Alvarez Web site and "Julia Alvarez, Contemporary Authors Online."
41. *Once Upon a Quinceañera*, pp. 194–196.

42. Ibid., pp. 197, 200–202.
43. "Julia Alvarez, Contemporary Authors Online," and "Picky Eater," *Something to Declare,* p. 83.
44. "Picky Eater," p. 83, and *Once Upon a Quinceañera*, p. 12.
45. "Picky Eater," p. 83, and "Briefly, a Gardener," *Something to Declare*, p. 87.
46. All publication information in this paragraph is from Julia Alvarez Web site.
47. Julia Alvarez Web site and "Julia Alvarez, Contemporary Authors Online."
48. "Chasing the Butterflies," *Something to Declare*, p. 197. A longer version of the essay, with additional information on family involvement in the underground and the aftermath of Trujillo's death, is appended to *In the Time of the Butterflies*, pp. 328–335.
49. "Julia Alvarez," Powell's Q&A, 2006, http://www.powells.com/ink/alvarez .html (assessed November 12, 2010).
50. *In the Time of the Butterflies,* IMDb (The Internet Movie Database), http:// www.imdb.com/title/tt0263467/ (accessed October 10, 2010).
51. Information in this paragraph is from the Julia Alvarez Web site.
52. *The Suitor*, Gigantic Pictures, http://www.giganticpictures.com/thesuitor .html (accessed October 10, 2010).
53. "Goodbye, Ms. Chips," pp. 213–214, and Interview, October 27, 2009, F. Scott Fitzgerald Literary Committee and MCTV.
54. Information in this paragraph is from the Julia Alvarez Web site.
55. Information about Café Alta Gracia is from Café Alta Gracia Organic Coffee Web site, http://www.cafealtagracia.com/, and Emily Brady, "Hill of Beans," Smithsonian.com, October 17, 2007, http://www.smithsonianmag .com/people-places/alvarez-coffee.html (both accessed October 10, 2010).
56. From the Julia Alvarez Web site.
57. Ibid.
58. Association for Library Service to Children (ALSC), "About the Pura Belpré Award," 2010, http://www.ala.org/ala/mgrps/divs/alsc/awardsgrants/book media/belpremedal/belpreabout/index.cfm (accessed October 10, 2010).
59. "A Conversation with the Author," *Before We Were Free*, p. 175.
60. "Julia Alvarez: 2009 National Book Festival," October 1, 2009.
61. *Finding Miracles*, p. 9.
62. "Doña Aída, with Your Permission," p. 173, and Interview, October 27, 2009, F. Scott Fitzgerald Literary Committee and MCTV.
63. Interview, October 27, 2009, F. Scott Fitzgerald Literary Committee and MCTV.
64. From the Julia Alvarez Web site.
65. "Julia Alvarez: 2009 National Book Festival," October 1, 2009.
66. From the Julia Alvarez Web site.
67. *Once Upon a Quinceañera*, pp. 6–8, 20.
68. Ibid., pp. 265–267.
69. From the Julia Alvarez Web site.

70. Ibid.
71. *How the García Girls Lost Their Accents*, Miracle Theatre Group, http://www.milagro.org/1-Performance-Presentacion/MiracleMainstage/garcia-girls.html (accessed October 10, 2010).
72. From the Julia Alvarez Web site.
73. "Literary Award Honoree," *F. Scott Fitzgerald Literary Conference*, http://fscottfitzgerald.wordpress.com/f-scott-literary-award/.
74. "Book TV: Julia Alvarez, 2009 National Book Festival," September 30, 2009.

CHAPTER 2: ALVAREZ AND THE NOVEL, ALVAREZ AS POET

1. "First Muse," p. 134.
2. *¡Yo!*, p. 13.
3. "Julia Alvarez," *Bookreporter.com*, September 22, 2000, http://www.bookreporter.com/authors/au-alvarez-julia.asp (accessed October 10, 2010).
4. *How the García Girls Lost Their Accents*, p. 308.
5. Julia Alvarez, "Saving the Writer (With Lots of Helpers): A Short Note from the Author," *Saving the World* (2006; Chapel Hill, NC: Algonquin Books, 2007), p. 371.
6. "A Genetics of Justice," p. 110; "Family Matters," p. 125; "Something to Declare," Salon.com, 2000, http://www.salon.com/life/feature/1998/09/25feature.html (accessed October 10, 2010).
7. "Writing Matters," p. 285.
8. *The Woman I Kept to Myself*, pp. 127–129.
9. *The Other Side/El Otro Lado*.
10. *Homecoming: New and Selected Poems*.
11. *The Woman I Kept to Myself*, pp. 133–134.
12. Ibid., pp. 69–70.
13. Ibid., pp. 41–42.
14. *Merriam-Webster Encyclopedia of Literature*, s.v. "sestina."

CHAPTER 3: *HOW THE GARCÍA GIRLS LOST THEIR ACCENTS*

1. *How the García Girls Lost Their Accents* (1991; New York: Plume, 1992). Quotations are from Plume paperback edition.
2. Ibid., p. 8.
3. Ibid., p. 23.
4. Ibid., p. 67.
5. Ibid., p. 81.
6. Ibid., p. 85.
7. Ibid.

8. Ibid., p. 99.
9. Ibid., p. 103.
10. Ibid., p. 109.
11. Ibid., p. 111.
12. Ibid., p. 118.
13. Ibid., p. 117.
14. Ibid., p. 131.
15. Ibid., p. 142.
16. Ibid., pp. 142–143.
17. Ibid., p. 148.
18. Ibid., p. 167.
19. Ibid.
20. Ibid., p. 191.
21. Ibid., p. 289.
22. Ibid., p. 290.
23. Ibid.
24. "Our Papers," *Something to Declare*, p. 19.
25. BBC, "Santeria: Religions," http://www.bbc.co.uk/religion/religions/santeria/ (accessed October 10, 2010).

CHAPTER 4: *IN THE TIME OF THE BUTTERFLIES*

1. *In the Time of the Butterflies* (1994; New York: Plume, 1995). Quotations are from Plume paperback edition.
2. "Chasing the Butterflies," *Something to Declare*, pp. 197–198.
3. Ibid., pp. 198–199. Information about Alvarez's research process and sources comes from this essay.
4. Ibid., p. 203.
5. Ibid., p. 205, and Julia Alvarez, "A Postscript," *In the Time of the Butterflies*, p. 323.
6. "Mirabal Sisters of the Dominican Republic," The Real DR: Dominican Republic Travel Guide, Real Planet Group, 2007, http://www.therealdr.com/mirabal-sisters-of-the-dominican-republic.html (accessed October 10, 2010).
7. Ibid.
8. Ibid.
9. Birthdates for Patria, Minerva, and María Teresa appear in the front matter in all editions of *In the Time of the Butterflies*; characterizations of the sisters are based on Alvarez's depiction rather than biographical sources.
10. *In the Time of the Butterflies*, p. 65.
11. "Dominican Republic," Country Studies, Library of Congress, http://lcweb2.loc.gov/frd/cs/ (accessed October 10, 2010).
12. *In the Time of the Butterflies*, p. 116.
13. Ibid., p. 29.

14. Ibid., p. 171.
15. Ibid., p. 281.
16. Ibid., p. 308.
17. Ibid., p. 311.
18. Ibid., pp. 312–313.
19. Ibid., p. 324.
20. Organization of American States, "History of CIM," Inter-American Commission of Women, 2007, http://www.oas.org/cim/English/History8.htm (accessed October 10, 2010).
21. United Nations, "International Day for the Elimination of Violence Against Women," Dag Hammarskjöld Library, http://www.un.org/depts/dhl/violence/ (accessed October 10, 2010).

Chapter 5: *¡Yo!*

1. *¡Yo!* (New York: Plume, 1997). Quotations are from Plume paperback edition.
2. Ibid., p. 3.
3. Ibid., p. 13.
4. Ibid., p. 18.
5. Ibid., p. 33.
6. Ibid., p. 36.
7. Ibid., p. 96.
8. Ibid., p. 131.
9. Ibid., p. 169.
10. Ibid., p. 266.
11. Ibid., p. 268.
12. Ibid., p. 293.
13. Ibid., p. 294.
14. Ibid., p. 296.
15. Ibid., p. 309.
16. "Why I Write," *The Woman I Kept to Myself*, pp. 153–154.

Chapter 6: *In the Name of Salomé*

1. *In the Name of Salomé* (2000; New York: Plume, 2001). Quotations are from Plume paperback edition.
2. "Dominican Republic," Country Studies.
3. Ibid.
4. *In the Name of Salomé*, p. viii.
5. Ibid., p. 238.
6. Ibid., p. 39.
7. Ibid., p. 2.

8. Ibid., p. 13.
9. Ibid., p. 30.
10. Ibid., p. 35.
11. Ibid., p. 45.
12. Ibid., p. 77.
13. Ibid., p. 55.
14. Ibid., p. 119.
15. Ibid., p. 125.
16. Ibid., p. 200.
17. Ibid., p. 277.
18. Ibid., p. 318.
19. Ibid., p. 316.
20. Ibid., p. 327.
21. Ibid., p. 330.
22. Ibid., p. 331.
23. Ibid., p. 4.
24. Ibid., pp. 337–338.
25. Ibid., p. 320.
26. Ibid., p. 187.
27. Ibid., p. 281.
28. Ibid., p. 219.
29. Ibid., p. 187.
30. Ibid., p. 268.
31. Ibid., p. 269.
32. "Salomé Ureña de Henríquez," Poesía Dominicanas, http://www.fortunecity .cs/felices/margarita/3/cultura/poesia/salome.html (accessed October 10, 2010).
33. Dominican Republic, Country Studies.
34. *In the Name of Salomé*, p. 347.
35. Ibid., p. 312.
36. Ibid., p. 331.

CHAPTER 7: *SAVING THE WORLD*

1. *Saving the World* (2006; Chapel Hill, NC: Algonquin Books, 2007). Quotations are from the paperback edition.
2. "A Short Note from the Author," *Saving the World*, p. 371.
3. *Saving the World*, p. 22.
4. Ibid., p. 56.
5. Ibid., p. 1.
6. Ibid., p. 11.
7. Ibid., p. 23.
8. Ibid., p. 1.
9. Ibid., p. 28.

10. Ibid., p. 41.
11. Ibid., p. 10.
12. Ibid., p. 48.
13. Ibid., p. 56.
14. Ibid., pp. 83–84.
15. Ibid., pp. 10, 178.
16. Ibid., p. 89.
17. Ibid., p. 93.
18. Ibid., p. 292.
19. Ibid., p. 327.
20. Ibid., pp. 224, 245.
21. Ibid., p. 32.
22. Ibid., p. 81.
23. Ibid., p. 90.
24. Ibid., p. 226.
25. Ibid., p. xi.
26. Ibid.
27. Ibid., p. 239.
28. Ibid., p. 242.
29. Ibid., pp. 317, 322, 331.
30. Ibid., p. xiii.
31. Ibid., p. 32.
32. Ibid., p. 41.
33. Ibid., p. 80.
34. Ibid., p. 90.
35. Ibid., p. 359.
36. Ibid., p. 357.
37. Ibid.
38. Ibid., p. 363.
39. Ibid., p. 327.
40. Emily Dickinson, "After great pain, a formal feeling comes," *The Poems of Emily Dickinson*, edited by R. W. Franklin (Cambridge: Harvard University Press, 1999) PoetryFoundation.org, http://www.poetryfoundation.org/archive/poem.html?id=177118 (accessed October 10, 2010).
41. *Saving the World*, p. 277.
42. Ibid., p. 353.
43. Ibid., p. 195.
44. Ibid., p. 363.

CHAPTER 8: BOOKS FOR YOUNG READERS

1. ALSC (Association for Library Services to Children), "Pura Belpré Award Home Page," 2010, http://www.ala.org/ala/mgrps/divs/alsc/awardsgrants/bookmedia/belpremedal/index.cfm (accessed October 10, 2010).

2. *Before We Were Free* (2002; New York: Laurel Leaf, 2004). Quotations are from the Laurel Leaf edition.
3. Ibid., p. 66.
4. Ibid., p. 161.
5. Ibid., p. 135.
6. Ibid., p. 111.
7. From the Julia Alvarez Web site.
8. "A Conversation with Julia Alvarez," *Before We Were Free*, p. 176.
9. *Finding Miracles* (2004; New York: Laurel Leaf, 2006). Quotations are from the Laurel Leaf edition.
10. Ibid., p. 15.
11. Ibid., p. 9.
12. Ibid., p. 106.
13. Ibid., p. 136.
14. *Return to Sender* (New York: Knopf, 2009).
15. "Number of Illegal Immigrants Plunges by 1M," CBSNews.com, February 11, 2010, http://www.cbsnews.com/stories/2010/02/11/national/main 6197466.shtml (accessed November 13, 2010).
16. Brad Knickerbocker, "Illegal Immigrants in the U.S.: How Many Are There?," *The Christian Science Monitor*, May 16, 2006, http://www .csmonitor.com/2006/0516/p01s02-ussc.html (accessed November 13, 2010).
17. *A Cafecito Story* (White River Junction, VT: Chelsea Green, 2001).
18. Bill Eichner, Afterword, *A Cafecito Story*, p. 39.
19. Belkis Ramírez's Web page, http://je1su.tripod.com/belkis2html (accessed November 13, 2010), and the Julia Alvarez Web site.
20. *How Tía Lola Came to ~~Visit~~ Stay* (New York: Knopf, 2001).
21. "A Brief History of Baseball and the Dominican Republic," dr1.com, 2010, http://dr1.com/articles/baseball.shtml (accessed November 13, 2010).
22. Independent Television Service, "Dominican Ball Players," *The New Americans*, Independent Lens, 2010, http://www.pbs.org/independentlens/ newamericans/newamericans/dominican_intro.html (accessed November 13, 2010).
23. *The Secret Footprints* (New York: Knopf, 2000).
24. *A Gift of Gracias* (New York: Knopf, 2005).
25. "About the Story," *A Gift of Gracias*, n.p.
26. *El major regalo del mundo: La leyenda de la Vieja Belén/The Best Gift of All: The Legend of La Vieja Belén*, bilingual edition with Rhina P. Espaillat (2008; Miami: Santillana/Alfaguaro, 2009).
27. Ibid., p. 12.
28. The Beatriz Vidal Web site, http://www.beatrizvidal.com/ (accessed November 13, 2010).
29. "Rhina P. Espaillat," The Poetry Foundation Web site, http://www .poetryfoundation.org/archive/poet.html?id=2072 (accessed November 13, 2010).

Chapter 9: Nonfiction

1. *Something to Declare* (1998; New York: Plume, 1999). Quotations are from Plume paperback edition.
2. Ibid., p. xiv.
3. Ibid.
4. Ibid., p. 27.
5. Ibid., p. 29.
6. Ibid., p. 61.
7. Ibid., p. 71.
8. Ibid., p. 99.
9. Ibid., p. 111.
10. Ibid.
11. Ibid., p. 123.
12. Ibid., p. 125.
13. "William Carlos Williams," Contemporary Authors Online, 2004, subscription database at http://www.gale.cengage.com/LitRC/.
14. *Something to Declare*, p. 175.
15. Ibid., p. 185.
16. Ibid., p. 202.
17. Ibid., p. 209.
18. Ibid., p. 259.
19. *Once Upon a Quinceañera: Coming of Age in the USA* (New York: Plume, 2007).
20. LitMinds Blog and Interviews: Julia Alvarez, August 9, 2007, http://www.litminds.org/blog/2007/08/julia_alvarez_talks_about_stor.html, and Interview, *LatinaLista*, November 28, 2007, http://www.youtube.com/watch?v=bRbLeRwCnVc (both accessed November 13, 2010).
21. *Once Upon a Quinceañera*, p. 5.
22. Julia Alvarez Web site.
23. *Once Upon a Quinceañera*, p. v.
24. Ibid., p. vii.
25. Ibid., p. 2.
26. Ibid., p. 5.
27. Ibid., p. 6.
28. Ibid.
29. Ibid., p. 14.
30. Ibid., p. 51.
31. Ibid., p. 84.
32. Ibid., p. 86.
33. Ibid., p. 101.
34. Ibid., p. 107.
35. Ibid., p. 181.
36. Ibid., p. 165.
37. Ibid., p. 175.

38. Ibid., p. 207.
39. Ibid., p. 215.
40. Ibid., p, 248.
41. U.S. Census Bureau, "Hispanic Population of the United States," 2010, http://www.census.gov/population/www/socdemo/hispanic/hispanic_pop_presentation.html (accessed November 13, 2010).
42. Ibid.
43. *Once Upon a Quinceañera*, p. 268.

CHAPTER 10: POETRY

1. "Of Maids and Other Muses," *Something to Declare*, p. 148.
2. *Homecoming: New and Selected Poems*, revised and expanded edition (New York: Plume, 1996). Originally published as *Homecoming* (New York: Grove Press, 1984).
3. *The Other Side/El Otro Lado* (New York: Dutton, 1995).
4. *The Woman I Kept to Myself* (Chapel Hill, NC: Algonquin, 2004).
5. *Homecoming*, pp. 7–8.
6. "Ironing Their Clothes," *Homecoming*, p. 26.
7. "Rolling the Dough," *Homecoming*, pp. 27–28.
8. "Grounds for Fiction," p. 266.
9. "Something to Declare to My Readers," *Something to Declare*, pp. xiii–xiv.
10. The sonnets titled "33" and "Redwing Sonnets" are unnumbered but here they are assigned roman numerals for ease of reference.
11. Walt Whitman, "So Long," *Leaves of Grass* 182, 1900, Bartleby.com, http://www.bartleby.com/142/182.html (accessed November 13, 2010).
12. Poems are assigned roman numerals here for ease of reference.
13. W. H. Auden, "In Memory of W. B. Yeats," *Another Time* (New York: Random House, 1940), Poets.org, Academy of American Poets, http://www.poets.org/viewmedia.php/prmMID/15544 (accessed November 13, 2010).
14. Joan Didion, "Why I Write," *New York Times Book Review*, December 5, 1976.

CHAPTER 11: JULIA ALVAREZ AND CONTEMPORARY ISSUES

1. From Book TV: Julia Alvarez, 2009 National Book Festival.
2. *Finding Miracles*, p. 232.
3. "Doña Aída, with Your Permission," p. 173.
4. Ibid.
5. Ibid.
6. *Once Upon a Quinceañera*, p. 232.
7. Ibid.

8. Ibid., p. 233.
9. From Café Alta Gracia Organic Coffee Web site.
10. *Saving the World*, p. 174.
11. Ibid., p. 275.
12. Ibid.
13. Ibid., pp. 275–276.
14. "The Other Side," XIX: 39–42.
15. From Café Alta Gracia Organic Coffee Web site.
16. *¡Yo!*, p. 37.
17. *Once Upon a Quinceañera*, p. 176.
18. "Imagining Motherhood," *Something to Declare*, p. 99.
19. *Once Upon a Quinceañera*, p. 240.
20. Ibid., p. 241.
21. Ibid., p. 257.
22. Ibid., p. 202.
23. Ibid.
24. Kingston, *The Woman Warrior*, p. 3.
25. "Family Matters," *Something to Desire*, p. 122.
26. Ibid., p. 127.
27. From Julia Alvarez: 2009 National Book Festival.
28. *In the Name of Salomé*, p. 347.
29. From Café Alta Gracia Organic Coffee Web site.
30. "Julia Alvarez," Bookreporter.com Web site.
31. From Book TV: Julia Alvarez, 2009 National Book Festival.

CHAPTER 12: JULIA ALVAREZ AND THE INTERNET

1. From "Julia Alvarez," Bookreporter.com.
2. From Julia Alvarez Web site.
3. Brady, "Hill of Beans."
4. From Book TV: Julia Alvarez, 2009 National Book Festival, September 30, 2009, and Julia Alvarez: 2009 National Book Festival, October 1, 2009.
5. Interview, F. Scott Fitzgerald Literary Committee and MCTV.
6. Interview with Julia Alvarez, National Coalition Against Censorship, 2008, http://www.ncac.org/literature/20080129~USA~Interview_With_Julia_Alvarez.cfm (accessed November 13, 2010).
7. *In the Time of the Butterflies*. The Big Read. National Endowment for the Humanities, 2010, http://www.neabigread.org/books/timeofthebutterflies/ (accessed November 13, 2010).
8. El Bohío Dominicano: A Visual Archive of the Dominican Republic, Mirabal sisters Web site, http://www.el-bohio.com/mirabal/ (accessed November 13, 2010).
9. Dedé Mirabal interview, http://www.youtube.com/watch?v=c3TEJyjlWHM &NR=1 (accessed November 13, 2010).

10. Spanish interview at http://www.youtube.com/watch?v=LsEX5knyM6c &NR=1 (accessed November 13, 2010).
11. International Day for the Elimination of Violence Against Women on the anniversary of the Mirabal sisters' deaths, November 25. http://www .oas.org/cim/English/Int.%20Violence%20Ag.%20Women%20Day.htm (accessed November 13, 2010).
12. "Magill's Survey of American Literature, Julia Alvarez," Salem Press Web site, http://salempress.com/Store/samples/survey_american_lit/survey_american_ lit_alvarez.htm (accessed November 10, 2010).
13. Julia Alvarez interview with Robert Birnbaum.
14. Powell's Q&A, http://www.powells.com/ink/alvarez.html (accessed November 13, 2010).
15. Kerri Miller, "Author Julia Alvarez Thrives in Two Worlds," MPR [Minnesota Public Radio] News, April 13, 2006, http://minnesota.publicradio.org/ display/web/2006/04/12/juliaalvarez/ (accessed November 13, 2010).
16. LatinaLista interview, http://www.youtube.com/watch?v=bRbLeRwCnVc (accessed November 13, 2010).
17. "Julia Alvarez," Bookreporter.com.

CHAPTER 13: JULIA ALVAREZ AND THE MEDIA

1. "First Muse," pp. 138–139.
2. "Of Maids and Other Muses," pp. 160–162.
3. "Grandfather's Blessing," pp. 3–4, and "El Doctor," pp. 47–48.
4. From Julia Alvarez: 2009 National Book Festival.
5. "Mami and Gauguin," *The Other Side/El Otro Lado* (New York: Dutton, 1995), pp. 12–14.
6. *Saving the World*, pp. 222, 224, 245.
7. From Julia Alvarez: 2009 National Book Festival.
8. *¡Yo!*, pp. 3, 227.
9. *Return to Sender*, p. 256.
10. *Finding Miracles*, p. 106.
11. *Saving the World*, pp. 19–22.
12. "Julia Alvarez," Bookreporter.com.
13. From Julia Alvarez Web site.
14. *The Suitor*, Gigantic Pictures, http://www.giganticpictures.com/thesuitor .html (accessed November 13, 2010).
15. *In the Time of the Butterflies,* IMDb (The Internet Movie Database), http:// www.imdb.com/title/tt0263467/ (accessed November 13, 2010).
16. Ibid.
17. Ibid.
18. *In the Time of the Butterflies,* directed by Mariano Barosso (MGM [Metro-Goldwyn-Mayer], 2001).
19. Julia Alvarez, "A Postscript," *In the Time of the Butterflies*, p. 324.

20. *The Suitor*, directed by Julia Solomonoff (Gigantic Pictures, 2001).
21. From Julia Alvarez: 2009 National Book Festival.
22. "Julia Alvarez," Bookreporter.com.

CHAPTER 14: WHAT DO I READ NEXT?

1. See, for example, "So Much Depends," "Grounds for Fiction," and "Writing Matters" in *Something to Declare* and "Julia Alvarez," Powell's Q&A, 2006, http://www.powells.com/ink/alvarez.html (accessed November 13, 2010).
2. Alvarez expresses this succinctly in her poem, "Passing On," *The Woman I Kept to Myself*, pp. 139–140.
3. "First Muse," pp. 133–134.
4. See "Of Maids and Other Muses," pp. 159–160, and *Once Upon a Quinceañera*, pp. 182–183.
5. "Of Maids and Other Muses," pp. 148–149.
6. See "So Much Depends" and "Doña Aída, with Your Permission," in *Something to Declare* and *Once Upon a Quinceañera*, p. 222.
7. Ibid. Also see "Family Matters" in *Something to Declare*, p. 123, and *Once Upon a Quinceañera*, p. 13.
8. "So Much Depends," p. 168.
9. Ibid.
10. "Doña Aída, with Your Permission," p. 173.
11. "So Much Depends," p. 164.
12. "Ten of My Writing Commandments," *Something to Declare,* p. 260, and "Of Maids and Other Muses," p. 149.
13. "Writing Matters," p. 285.
14. "Julia Alvarez," Powell's Q&A.
15. "Jean Rhys," Contemporary Authors Online, 2004, subscription database at http://www.gale.cengage.com/LitRC/.
16. "Paule Marshall," Contemporary Authors Online, 2009.
17. "Maryse Condé," Contemporary Authors Online, 2010.
18. "Jamaica Kincaid," Contemporary Authors Online, 2004.
19. "Edwidge Danticat," Contemporary Literary Criticism Select, 2008, http://www.gale.cengage.com/LitRC/.
20. "Cristina García," Contemporary Authors Online, 2008.
21. From the Cristina García Web site, http://www.cristinagarcianovelist.com/ (accessed November 13, 2010).
22. "Rosario Ferré," Contemporary Literary Criticism Select, 2008.
23. "Judith Ortiz Cofer," Poets.org, Academy of American Poets, 2010, http://www.poets.org/poet.php/prmPID/738 (accessed November 13, 2010).
24. Ibid.
25. Maria Helena Lima, "Andrea Levy," *Twenty-First Century "Black" British Writers*, edited by R. Victoria Arana, 2009, http://www.gale.cengage.com/LitRC/.

26. From Junot Díaz Web site, http://www.junotdiaz.com/ (accessed November 13, 2010).
27. "Derek Walcott—Biography," Nobelprize.org, http://nobelprize.org/nobel_prizes/literature/laureates/1992/walcott-bio.html (accessed November 13, 2010).
28. "V. S. Naipaul—Biography," Nobelprize.org, http://nobelprize.org/nobel_prizes/literature/laureates/2001/naipaul-bio.html (accessed November 13, 2010).
29. "Oscar Hijuelos," Contemporary Authors Online, 2010.
30. Alvarez discussed the article with Elizabeth Coonrod Martinez in "Julia Alvarez: Progenitor of a Movement: This Dominican-American Writer Weaves Passionate Sensibilities through Her Works with the Gift of Seeing through Others' Eyes." *Américas* [English ed.], March–April 2007, pp. 6–13, http://www.gale.cengage.com/LitRC/.
31. Julia Alvarez with Robert Birnbaum.
32. From the Sandra Cisneros Web site, http://www.sandracisneros.com (accessed November 13, 2010).
33. "Denise (Elia) Chávez," Contemporary Authors Online, 2008.
34. "Ana Castillo," Contemporary Authors Online, 2008.
35. "Isabel Allende," Contemporary Authors Online, 2009.
36. Ibid.
37. "Gabriel García Marquez," Contemporary Authors Online, 2010.
38. Ibid.
39. "Mario Vargas Llosa," Contemporary Authors Online, 2008.
40. Ibid.
41. "Laura Esquivel," Contemporary Authors Online, 2010.
42. Ibid.
43. Latin American Network Information Center, http://lanic.utexas.edu/ (accessed November 13, 2010)
44. Pura Belpré Award Web page, http://www.ala.org/ala/mgrps/divs/alsc/awardsgrants/bookmedia/belpremedal/index.cfm (accessed November 13, 2010).
45. Center for Latin American and Caribbean Studies. University of Wisconsin–Milwaukee, http://www4.uwm.edu/clacs/ (accessed November 13, 2010).

BIBLIOGRAPHY

BOOKS BY JULIA ALVAREZ

Fiction

Alvarez, Julia. *Before We Were Free*. New York: Knopf, 2002.

Alvarez, Julia. *A Cafecito Story*. White River Junction, VT: Chelsea Green, 2001.

Alvarez, Julia. *Finding Miracles*. New York: Knopf, 2004.

Alvarez, Julia. *How the García Girls Lost Their Accents*. Chapel Hill, NC: Algonquin, 1991.

Alvarez, Julia. *How Tía Lola Came to ~~Visit~~ Stay*. New York: Knopf, 2001.

Alvarez, Julia. *How Tía Lola Learned to Teach*. New York: Knopf, 2010.

Alvarez, Julia. *In the Name of Salomé*. Chapel Hill, NC: Algonquin, 2000.

Alvarez, Julia. *In the Time of the Butterflies*. Chapel Hill, NC: Algonquin, 1994.

Alvarez, Julia. *Return to Sender*. New York: Knopf, 2009.

Alvarez, Julia. *Saving the World*. Chapel Hill, NC: Algonquin, 2006.

Alvarez, Julia. *¡Yo!* Chapel Hill, NC: Algonquin, 1997.

Nonfiction

Alvarez, Julia. *Once Upon a Quinceañera: Coming of Age in the USA*. New York: Viking, 2007.

Alvarez, Julia. *Something to Declare*. Chapel Hill, NC: Algonquin Books, 1998.

Poetry

Alvarez, Julia. *Homecoming: New and Collected Poems*. New York: Plume, 1996.

Alvarez, Julia. *The Other Side/El Otro Lado.* New York: Dutton, 1995.
Alvarez, Julia. *The Woman I Kept to Myself.* Chapel Hill, NC: Algonquin Books, 2004.

Picture Books

Alvarez, Julia. *The Best Gift of All: The Legend of La Vieja Belén/El major regalo del mundo: la leyenda de La Vieja Belén.* Translated by Rhina P. Espaillat. Illustrated by Ruddy Nuñoz. Miami: Santillat/Alfaguara Infantil, 2008.
Alvarez, Julia. *A Gift of Gracias: The Legend of Altagracia.* Illustrated by Beatriz Vidal. New York: Knopf, 2005.
Alvarez, Julia. *The Secret Footprints.* Illustrated by Fabian Negrin. New York: Knopf, 2000.

WORKS CITED AND SELECTED RESOURCES

Alvarez, Julia. "An American Childhood in the Dominican Republic." *American Scholar* 56 (1987): 71–85.
Alvarez, Julia. "A Note on the Loosely Autobiographical." *New England Review: Middlebury Series* 21, no. 4 (Fall 2000): 165–166.
Alvarez, Julia. "On Finding a Latino Voice: A Collection from the *Washington Post BookWorld.*" In Marie Arana, ed., *The Writing Life: Writers on How They Think and Work.* New York: PublicAffairs, 2003: 128–133.
Alvarez, Julia, and Juanita Heredia. "Citizen of the World: An Interview with Julia Alvarez." In Bridget Kevane and Juanita Heredia, eds., *Latina Self-Portraits: Interviews with Contemporary Women Writers.* Albuquerque: University of New Mexico Press, 2000: 15–32. Reprinted in Jeffrey W. Hunter, ed., *Contemporary Literary Criticism.* Vol. 274. Detroit: Gale, 2009. Subscription database at http://www.gale.cengage.com/LitRC/.
Association for Library Service to Children (ALSC). "About the Pura Belpré Award." 2010. http://www.ala.org/ala/mgrps/divs/alsc/awardsgrants/book-media/belpremedal/belpreabout/index.cfm (accessed November 13, 2010).
Auden, W. H. "In Memory of W. B. Yeats." In *Another Time.* New York: Random House, 1940. Poets.org. Academy of American Poets. http://www.poets.org/viewmedia.php/prmMID/15544 (accessed November 13, 2010).
Ayala, Jennifer. "*Once Upon a Quinceañera: Coming of Age in the USA.*" *NWSA Journal* 21, no. 3 (2009): 202–206.
Barak, Julie. "'Turning and Turning in the Widening Gyre': A Second Coming into Language in Julia Alvarez's *How the García Girls Lost Their Accents.*" *MELUS* 23, no. 1 (1998): 159–176.
Belkis Ramírez's Web Page. http://je1su.tripod.com/belkis2html (accessed November 13, 2010).
Bess, Jennifer. "Imploding the Miranda Complex in Julia Alvarez's *How the García Girls Lost Their Accents.*" *College Literature* 34 (2007): 78–105.

Bing, Jonathan. "Julia Alvarez: Books that Cross Borders." *Publishers Weekly* (December 16, 1996): 38–39.

Blackford, Holly. "The Spirit of a People: The Politicization of Spirituality in Julia Alvarez's *In the Time of the Butterflies*, Ntozake Shange's *sassafrass, Cypress & Indigo*, and Ana Castillo's *So Far from God*." In Kristina K. Groover, ed., *Things of the Spirit: Women Writers Constructing Spirituality*. Notre Dame, IN: University of Notre Dame Press, 2004: 224–255.

Book TV: Julia Alvarez, 2009 National Book Festival. September 30, 2009. http://www.youtube.com/watch?v=FZTxT34fI5Q (accessed November 13, 2010).

Brady, Emily. "Hill of Beans." Smithsonian.com. October 17, 2007. http://www.smithsonianmag.com/people-places/alvarez-coffee.html (accessed November 13, 2010).

"A Brief History of Baseball and the Dominican Republic." dr1.com. 2010. http://dr1.com/articles/baseball.shtml (accessed November 13, 2010).

Brown, Isabel Zakrzewski. "Historiographic Metafiction in *In the Time of the Butterflies*." *South Atlantic Review* 64 (Spring 1999): 98–112.

Café Alta Gracia Organic Coffee Web site. 2010. http://www.cafealtagracia.com (accessed November 13, 2010).

Caminero-Santangelo, Marta. *On Latinidad: U.S. Latino Literature and the Construction of Ethnicity*. Gainesville: University Press of Florida, 2007.

Central Intelligence Agency (CIA). "Literacy." "The World Factbook." http://www.cia.gov/library/publications/the-world-factbook/fields/2103.html (accessed November 13, 2010).

Contemporary Authors Online. Subscription database at http://www.gale.cengage.com/LitRC/.

Coonrod Martinez, Elizabeth. "Julia Alvarez: Progenitor of a Movement: This Dominican-American Writer Weaves Passionate Sensibilities through Her Works with the Gift of Seeing through Others' Eyes." *Americas* [English ed.] (March–April 2007): 6–13.

Coonrod Martinez, Elizabeth. "Teaching Spanish Caribbean History through *In the Time of the Butterflies*: The Novel and the Showtime Film." *Journal of Hispanic Higher Education* 5, no. 2 (April 2006): 107–126.

Cowart, David. *Trailing Clouds: Immigrant Fiction in Contemporary America*. Ithaca, NY: Cornell University Press, 2006.

Cox, Karen Castellucci. "A Particular Blessing: Storytelling as Healing in the Novels of Julia Alvarez." In Margarite Fernández Olmos and Lizabeth Paravisini-Gebert, eds., *Healing Culture: Art and Religion as Curative Practices in the Caribbean and Its Diaspora*. New York: Palgrave, 2001: 133–148

Criniti, Steve. "Collecting Butterflies: Julia Alvarez's Revision of North American Collective Memory." *Modern Language Studies* 36, no. 2 (Winter 2007): 42–63.

D'alleo, Raphael, and Elena Machado Saez. "Writing in a Minor Key: Postcolonial and Post-Civil Rights Histories in the Novels of Julia Alvarez." In *The Latino/a Canon and the Emergence of Post-Sixties Literature*. New York: Palgrave Macmillan, 2007: 134–157.

Dickinson, Emily. "After Great Pain, a Formal Feeling Comes." In R. W. Franklin, ed., *The Poems of Emily Dickinson*. Cambridge: Harvard University Press, 1999. Also found on Poetry Foundation Web site, http://www.poetryfoun dation.org/archive/poem.html?id=177118 (accessed November 13, 2010).

Didion, Joan. "Why I Write." *New York Times Book Review*. December 5, 1976.

"Dominican Republic." Country Studies. Library of Congress. http://lcweb2.loc .gov/frd/cs/ (accessed November 13, 2010).

Frever, Trinna S. "'Oh! You Beautiful Doll!': Icon, Image, and Culture in Works by Alvarez, Cisneros, and Morrison." *Tulsa Studies in Women's Literature* 28, no. 1 (Spring 2009): 121–139. Also available at Project MUSE, http://muse .jhu.edu/journals/tulsa_studies_in_womens_literature/v028/28.1.frever .html (accessed November 14, 2010).

Gómez Vega, Ibis. "Hating the Self in the 'Other' or How Yolanda Learns to See Her Own Kind in Julia Alvarez's *How the García Girls Lost Their Accents*." *Intertexts* 3, no. 1 (1999): 85–96.

Gómez Vega, Ibis. "Radicalizing Good Catholic Girls: Shattering the 'Old World' Order in Julia Alvarez's *In the Time of the Butterflies*." *Confluencia: Revista Hispanica de Cultura y Literature* 15, no. 2 (Spring 2004): 94–108. Reprinted in Jeffrey W. Hunter, ed., *Contemporary Literary Criticism*. Vol. 274. Detroit: Gale, 2009.

Hewett, Cami. "Critiquing the Bourgeois Family: Julia Alvarez's *In the Time of the Butterflies*." *EAPSU Online: A Journal of Critical and Creative Work* 1 (Fall 2004): 93–108. Available on EAPSU Web site, http://www.eapsu.net/ PDFs/vol1.pdf (accessed November 14, 2010).

Hickman, Trenton. "Coffee and Colonialism in Julia Alvarez's *Cafecito Story*." In Elizabeth M. DeLoughrey, Renée K. Gosson, and George B. Handley, eds., *Caribbean Literature and the Environment: Between Nature and Culture*. Charlottesville, VA: University of Virginia Press, 2005: 70–82.

Hickman, Trenton. "Hagiographic Commemorafiction in Julia Alvarez's *In the Time of the Butterflies* and *In the Name of Salomé*." *MELUS* 31, no. 1 (2006): 99–121.

Hoffman, Joan M. "'She Wants to Be Called Yolanda Now': Identity, Language, and the Third Sister in *How the García Girls Lost Their Accents*." *Bilingual Review/La Revista Bilingue* 23, no. 1 (1998): 21–27.

Hoffman, Joan M. "'That Much I Learned from My Mother': Shaping the Mother-Daughter Relationship in Julia Alvarez's *In the Name of Salomé*." *Hispanic Journal* 23, no. 2 (Fall 2002): 119–131.

In the Time of the Butterflies. The Big Read. National Endowment for the Humanities. 2010. http://www.neabigread.org/books/timeofthebutterflies/ (accessed November 14, 2010).

In the Time of the Butterflies. IMDb (The Internet Movie Database), http:// www.imdb.com/title/tt0263467/ (accessed November 14, 2010).

In the Time of the Butterflies. Directed by Mariano Barosso. MGM (Metro-Goldwyn-Meyers), 2001.

Independent Television Service. "Dominican Ball Players." *The New Americans.* Independent Lens. 2010. http://www.pbs.org/independentlens/newameri cans/newamericans/dominican_intro.html (accessed November 14, 2010).

Ink, Lynn Chun. "Remaking Identity, Unmaking Nation: Historical Recovery and the Reconstruction of Community in *In the Time of the Butterflies* and *The Farming of Bones.*" *Callaloo* 27, no. 3 (Summer 2004): 788–807. Reprinted in *Contemporary Literary Criticism Select.* Detroit: Gale, 2008.

Inter-American Commission of Women. Organization of American States. 2007. http://www.oas.org/cim/English/Int.%20Violence%20Ag.%20Women%20Day.htm (accessed November 14, 2010).

"An Interview with Julia Alvarez." BostonLatinoTV. January 18, 2007. http://www.youtube.com/watch?v=IDvFGbGC3uA (accessed November 13, 2010).

Irizarry, Guillermo. "Travelling Textualities and Phantasmagoric Originals: A Reading of Translation in Three Recent Spanish-Caribbean Narratives." *Ciberletras* 4 (January 2001). http://www.lehman.cuny.edu/ciberletras/v04/ Irizarry.html (accessed November 14, 2010).

Jacques, Ben. "Julia Alvarez Real Flights of Imagination." *Americas* [English ed.] (January 2001): 22.

Johnson, Kelli Lyon. *Julia Alvarez: Writing a New Place on the Map.* Albuquerque: University of New Mexico Press, 2005.

Julia Alvarez Web site. 2010. http://www.juliaalvarez.com (accessed October 10, 2010).

Julia Alvarez: 2009 National Book Festival. October 1, 2009. Library of Congress. http://www.youtube.com/watch?v=ASbxm-T8-i4 (accessed October 10, 2010).

"Julia Alvarez." Bookreporter.com. September 22, 2000. http://www.book reporter.com/authors/au-alvarez-julia.asp (accessed October 10, 2010).

"Julia Alvarez." Contemporary Authors Online. 2010. Subscription database at http://www.gale.cengage.com/LitRC/.

"Julia Alvarez." In Jeffrey W. Hunter, ed., *Contemporary Literary Criticism.* Vol. 274. Detroit: Gale, 2009.

Julia Alvarez. Interview at Montgomery College. F. Scott Fitzgerald Literary Committee and MCTV. October 27, 2009. http://www.youtube.com/ watch?v=HZ2xe2OFTX8 (accessed November 13, 2010).

Julia Alvarez. Interview by LatinaLista. November 28, 2007. http://www.you tube.com/watch?v=bRbLeRwCnVc (accessed November 13, 2010).

Julia Alvarez. Interview with La Bloga. August 6, 2007. http://labloga.blogspot. com/2007/08/interview-with-julia-alvarez.html (accessed November 14, 2010).

Julia Alvarez. Interview with National Coalition Against Censorship. 2008. http://www.ncac.org/literature/20080129~USA~Interview_With_Julia_ Alvarez.cfm (accessed November 14, 2010).

Julia Alvarez. Interview with Robert Birnbaum. Identitytheory.com. 2006. http:// www.identitytheory.com/interviews/birnbaum171.php (accessed November 14, 2010).

Julia Alvarez. LitMinds Blog and Interviews. August 9, 2007. http://www
.litminds.org/blog/2007/08/julia_alvarez_talks_about_stor.html (accessed
November 13, 2010).
"Julia Alvarez." Powell's Q&A. 2006. http://www.powells.com/ink/alvarez.html
(accessed October 10, 2010).
Junot Díaz Web site. http://www.junotdiaz.com/ (accessed November 13,
2010).
Kellman, Steven G. *Switching Languages: Translingual Writers Reflect on Their
Craft*. Lincoln: University of Nebraska Press, 2003.
Kingston, Maxine Hong. *The Woman Warrior*. New York: Knopf, 1975, 1977.
Kirschner, Luz Angélica. "History and Its Vicissitudes in Alvarez's *In the Time
of the Butterflies* and Atwood's *The Handmaid's Tale*." *CLCWeb: Com-
parative Literature and Culture* 8, no. 4 (December 2006). http://docs.lib
.purdue.edu/clcweb/ (accessed November 14, 2010).
Knadler, Stephen. "'Blanca from the Block': Whiteness and the Transnational
Latina Body." *Genders* 41 (2005): 37. http://www.genders.org/g41/g41_
knadler.html (accessed November 14, 2010).
"Las Hermanas Mirabal—The Mirabal Sisters." El Bohío Dominicano: A Visual
Archive of the Dominican Republic. http://www.el-bohio.com/mirabal/
(accessed November 14, 2010).
Lima, Maria Helena. "Andrea Levy." In R. Victoria Arana, ed., *Twenty-First
Century "Black" British Writers*. 2009. Subscription database at http://
www.gale.cengage.com/LitRC/.
Lindner, April. "Younger Women Poets of the New Formalism." In Jonathan
N. Barron and Bruce Meyer, eds., *New Formalist Poets. Dictionary of
Literary Biography*. Vol. 282. Detroit: Gale, 2003.
Lovelady, Stephanie. "Walking Backwards: Coming of Age in *My Antonia* and
How the García Girls Lost Their Accents." *Modern Language Studies* 35,
no. 1 (Spring 2005): 28–37.
Luis, William. "A Search for Identity in Julia Alvarez's *How the García Girls
Lost Their Accents*." *Callaloo* 23, no. 3 (Summer 2000): 839–849.
Lyons, Bonnie, and Bill Oliver. "A Clean Windshield: An Interview with Julia
Alvarez." In *Passion and Craft: Conversations with Notable Writers*.
Urbana: University of Illinois Press, 1998: 128–144.
Marciniak, Katarzyana. "Accented Bodies and Coercive Assimilation: The
Trespasses of the García Girls." In *Alienhood*. Minneapolis: University of
Minnesota Press, 2006: 57–75. Reprinted in Jeffrey W. Hunter, ed., *Con-
temporary Literary Criticism*. Vol. 274. Detroit: Gale, 2009.
Mardorossian, Carine M. *Reclaiming Difference: Caribbean Women Rewrite
Postcolonialism*. Charlottesville: University of Virginia Press, 2005.
Mayock, Ellen C. "The Bicultural Construction of Self in Cisneros, Alvarez,
and Santiago." *Bilingual Review/La Revista Bilingue* 23, no. 3 (1998):
223–229.
McCallum, Shara. "Reclaiming Julia Alvarez: *In the Time of the Butterflies*."
Women's Studies: An Interdisciplinary Journal 29, no. 1 (February 2000):
93–117.

McClellen, Hilary. "In the Name of the Homeland." *Atlantic Unbound*. July 19, 2000. Available at The Atlantic Online, http://www.theatlantic.com/past/docs/unbound/interviews/ba2000-07-19.htm (accessed November 14, 2010).

McCracken, Ellen. "The Postmodern Self of Julia Alvarez's ¡Yo!: Identity, Memory, and Community." In Laura P. Alonso Gallo and Antonia Domínguez Miguela, eds., *Evolving Origins, Transplanting Cultures: Literary Legacies of the New Americans*. Huelva, Spain: Universidad de Huelva, 2002: 223–228. Reprinted in Jeffrey W. Hunter, ed., *Contemporary Literary Criticism*. Vol. 274. Detroit: Gale, 2009.

Merriam-Webster Encyclopedia of Literature. Springfield, MA: Merriam-Webster, 1995.

Miller, Kerri. "Author Julia Alvarez Thrives in Two Worlds." *MPR* [Minnesota Public Radio] News. April 13, 2006. http://minnesota.publicradio.org/display/web/2006/04/12/juliaalvarez/ (accessed November 14, 2010).

"Mirabal Sisters of the Dominican Republic." The Real DR: Dominican Republic Travel Guide. Real Planet Group, 2007. http://www.therealdr.com/mirabal-sisters-of-the-dominican republic.html (accessed November 14, 2010).

Mitchell, David T. "The Accent of 'Loss': Cultural Crossings as Context in Julia Alvarez's *How the García Girls Lost Their Accents*." In Timothy B. Powell, ed., *Beyond the Binary: Reconstructing Cultural Identity in a Multicultural Context*. New Brunswick, NJ: Rutgers University Press, 1999: 165–184.

Mujcinovic, Fatima. *Postmodern Cross-Culturalism and Politicization in U.S. Latina Literature: From Ana Castillo to Julia Alvarez*. New York: Peter Lang, 2004.

Muratori, Fred. "Traditional Form and the Living, Breathing American Poet." *New England Review and Bread Loaf Quarterly* (Winter 1986): 231–232.

Nas, Loes. "Border Crossings in Latina Narrative: Julia Alvarez's *How the García Girls Lost Their Accents*." *Journal of Literary Studies* 15, no. 2 (2003): 125–136.

Nobelprize.org. http://nobelprize.org/nobel_prizes/literature/laureates/ (accessed November 14, 2010).

"Number of Illegal Immigrants Plunges by 1M." CBSNews.com. February 11, 2010, http://www.cbsnews.com/stories/2010/02/11/national/main6197466.shtml (accessed November 14, 2010).

Oliver, Kelly. "'One Nail Takes Out Another': Power, Gender, and Revolution in Julia Alvarez's Novels." In Benigno Trigo, ed., *Foucault and Latin America: Appropriations and Deployments of Discursive Analysis*. New York: Routledge, 2002: 235–246. Reprinted in Jeffrey W. Hunter, ed., *Contemporary Literary Criticism*. Vol. 274. Detroit: Gale, 2009.

Organization of American States. "History of CIM." Inter-American Commission of Women. 2007, http://www.oas.org/cim/English/History8.htm (accessed November 14, 2010).

Ortiz, Lisa M. "'Becoming a Butterfly': Julia Alvarez's *In the Time of the Butterflies* as Autoethnography." *A/B: Auto/Biography Studies* 20, no. 2 (Winter 2005): 230–245.

Patterson, Richard E. "Resurrecting Rafael: Fictional Incarnations of a Dominican Dictator." *Callaloo* 29, no. 1 (Winter 2006): 223–237.

Poets.org. Academy of American Poets. 2010. http://www.poets.org/poet.php/prmPID/738 (accessed November 14, 2010).

"The Reluctant Celebrity: At Heart, Julia Alvarez Says, She's a 'Worker.' Her Job Is to Tell Stories." *Publishers Weekly* (March 2006): 49–50.

Rich, Charlotte. "Talking Back to El Jefe: Genre, Polyphony, and Dialogic Resistance in Julia Alvarez's *In the Time of the Butterflies*." *MELUS* 27, no. 4 (2002): 165–182.

Rivera-van Schagen, Judy. "Mininarratives: Subversive Discourse in Julia Alvarez's Works." *Hispanic Journal* 23, no. 1 (Spring 2002): 151–159.

Romagnolo, Catherine. "Recessive Origins in Julia Alvarez's García Girls." In Brian Richardson, ed., *Narrative Beginnings: Theories and Practices*. Lincoln: University of Nebraska Press, 2008.

Rosario-Sievert, Heather. "Anxiety, Repression, and Return: The Language of Julia Alvarez." *Readerly/Writerly Texts: Essays on Literature, Literary/Textual Criticism, and Pedagogy* 4, no. 2 (1997): 125–139.

Ruiz Cameron, Christopher David. "How the García Cousins Lost Their Accents." In Richard Delgado and Jean Stefancic, eds., *The Latino/a Condition: A Critical Reader*. New York: New York University Press, 1998: 579–582.

"Salomé Ureña de Henríquez." Poesía Dominicanas. http://www.fortunecity.es/felices/margarita/3/cultura/poesia/salome.html (accessed November 14, 2010).

Sandra Cisneros Web site. 2010. http://www.sandracisneros.com (accessed October 10, 2010).

"Santeria." Religions. BBC. http://www.bbc.co.uk/religion/religions/santeria/ (accessed October 10, 2010).

Schaefer, Andrea. "Julia Alvarez." In Jay Parini, ed., *American Writers: A Collection of Literary Biographies*, Supplement 7. New York: Charles Scribner's Sons, 2001.

Schultermandl, Silvia. "Rewriting American Democracy: Language and Cultural (Dis)locations in Esmeralda Santiago and Julia Alvarez." *Bilingual Review* 28, no. 1 (2004): 3–15.

Sirias, Silvio. *Julia Alvarez: A Critical Companion*. Critical Companions to Popular Contemporary Writers. Westport, CT: Greenwood, 2005.

Socolovsky, Maya. "Patriotism, Nationalism, and the Fiction of History in Julia Alvarez's *In the Time of the Butterflies* and *In the Name of Salomé*." *Latin American Literary Review* 34, no. 68 (July–December 2006): 5–24.

"Something to Declare." Salon.com. 2000, http://www.salon.com/life/feature/1998/09/25feature.html (accessed October 10, 2010).

Stefanko, Jacqueline. "New Ways of Telling: Latinas' Narratives of Exile and Return." *Frontiers: A Journal of Women Studies* 17, no. 2 (July 1996): 50–69.

Suarez, Lucia M. "Julia Alvarez and the Anxiety of Latina Representation." *Meridians: Feminism, Race, Transnationalism* 5, no. 1 (2004): 117–145.

Subramanian, Shreerekha. "Insouciance as Resistance: Transformative Powers of Loss and Mourning." In Joyce C. Harte, ed., *Come Weep with Me: Loss and Mourning in the Writings of Caribbean Women Writers*. Newcastle upon Tyne, England: Cambridge Scholars, 2007: 221–242.

The Suitor. Gigantic Pictures. http://www.giganticpictures.com/thesuitor.html (accessed November 14, 2010).

Tate, Julee. "My Mother, My Text: Writing and Remembering in Julia Alvarez's *In the Name of Salomé*." *Bilingual Review* 28, no.1 (January 2004): 54–60.

United Nations. "International Day for the Elimination of Violence Against Women." Dag Hammarskjöld Library, http://www.un.org/depts/dhl/violence/ (accessed November 14, 2010).

U.S. Census Bureau. "Hispanic Population of the United States." 2010. http://www.census.gov/population/www/socdemo/hispanic/hispanic_pop_presentation.html (accessed November 14, 2010).

Valerio-Holguin, Fernando. "Julia Alvarez (1950–)." In Alan West-Duran, Maria Herrera-Sobek, and Cesar A. Salgado, eds., *Latino and Latina Writers, I: Introductory Essays, Chicano and Chicana Authors; II: Cuban and Cuban American Authors, Dominican and Other Authors, Puerto Rican Authors*. Scribner Writers Series. New York: Scribner's, 2004: 783–801.

Vela, Richard. "Daughter of Invention: The Poetry of Julia Alvarez." *Postscript: Publication of the Philological Association of the Carolinas* 16 (1999): 33–42. http://www2.unca.edu/postscript/postscript16/ps16.4.pdf (accessed November 14, 2010).

Wall, Catharine E. "Bilingualism and Identity in Julia Alvarez's Poem 'Bilingual Sestina'." *MELUS* 28, no. 4 (2003): 125–143.

Whitman, Walt. "So Long." *Leaves of Grass* 182. 1900. Bartleby.com. http://www.bartleby.com/142/182.html (accessed November 13, 2010).

Yitah, Helen Atawube. "'Inhabited by Un Santo': The Antojo and Yolanda's Search for the 'Missing' Self in *How the García Girls Lost Their Accents*." *Bilingual Review* 27, no. 3 (2003): 234–243.

INDEX

Abraham: in ¡Yo!, 51, 54, 55
AIDS, 47, 124; in Saving the World, 68–72, 76
Alighieri, Dante, 19, 97, 144; in Saving the World, 67–68, 72; in The Woman I Kept to Myself, 115
American Library Association (ALA), 4, 5, 77, 80
Anzaldúa, Gloria, 113
Arabian Nights, The (The Thousand and One Nights), 2, 11, 53, 80, 98, 135. See also Scheherazade
Ariadne, 73, 75, 118
Auden, W. H., 19, 118
Austen, Jane, 19, 118

baseball, 91
Batista, Fulgencio, 38, 62, 125. See also Castro, Fidel; Castro, Raúl; Cuba
Before We Were Free, vii, 7, 31, 77, 78–81, 126, 128, 129, 135, 149
Bendición, 54; "La Bendición" (section of Once Upon a Quinceañera), 104–105
Best Gift of All, The: The Legend of La Vieja Belén/El mejor regalo el mundo: la leyenda de La Vieja Belén, 7, 93–94
biculturalism, 3, 4, 121, 122, 144: in How the García Girls Lost Their Accents, 22, 24; in Something to

Declare, 95, 98; in ¡Yo!, 51. See also spanish language
Big Read, The, 133
"Bilingual Sestina," 17, 111. See also spanish language
bird, 19, 24, 58, 63, 64, 73, 88–90, 110–111
Bishop, Elizabeth, 17, 117, 144
blood, 18, 129, 138, 139; in Before We Were Free, 79, 80; in How the García Girls Lost Their Accents, 28; in In the Time of the Butterflies, 35. See also menstruation
Butterflies, 78–79. See also In the Time of the Butterflies; Mirabal sisters

Café Alta Gracia, 7, 124–125, 132
Cafecito Story, A, viii, 7, 77, 88–91, 122, 124, 128, 131, 132
cage: in How the García Girls Lost Their Accents, 25; in In the Time of the Butterflies, 35, 126; in The Other Side/El Otro Lado, 113
cancer: in In the Time of the Butterflies, 41; in Saving the World, 68, 71, 74; in The Woman I Kept to Myself, 113
Carla (character): in Before We Were Free, 78, 79; in How the García Girls Lost Their Accents, 23, 24, 25, 26, 29

Castro, Fidel: in *In the Name of Salomé*, 58, 61, 65, 66, 125; in *In the Time of the Butterflies*, 38
Castro, Raúl, 38
censorship, 3, 98, 125, 126, 132; in *Before We Were Free*, 78; of Alvarez's books, 133
Chucha (character): in *Before We Were Free*, 79, 80; in *How the García Girls Lost Their Accents*, 15, 28, 31
Cisneros, Sandra, 143, 147
Ciudad Trujillo (Santo Domingo), 1, 36, 58, 59, 63, 114, 116
Cold War, 27, 112
Cuba, 6, 12, 134, 145, 147: in *In the Name of Salomé*, 57, 58, 61–65, 121, 125, 128; in *In the Time of the Butterflies*, 38

Dante. *See* Alighieri, Dante
darkness, 3, 38, 40, 58, 61, 83, 115, 116, 138, 144; in *Saving the World*, 68, 69, 70, 72, 73. *See also* light; racism
diary, 16, 20, 77, 128, 141, 145, 149: in *Before We Were Free*, 78, 80–81; in *In the Time of the Butterflies*, 35–36, 39, 43; in *Return to Sender*, 87; in *Saving the World*, 68; in *¡Yo!*, 47. *See also testimonio*
Dickinson, Emily, 17, 19, 135, 143, 144; in *In the Name of Salomé*, 58; in *Saving the World*, 74, 76
dictator, vii, 1, 7, 9, 11, 77, 122, 125, 134, 137, 140, 148, 149; in *Before We Were Free*, 78–81; in *Finding Miracles*, 82–83, 125; in *How the García Girls Lost Their Accents*, 22, 26, 27, 126; in *In the Name of Salomé*, 57, 60, 62, 65; in *In the Time of the Butterflies*, 33, 38, 40, 41, 42, 126; in *Something to Declare*, 97–98; in *¡Yo!*, 54. *See also* Trujillo, Rafael
Dr. Payne (character): in *How the García Girls Lost Their Accents*, 24; in *Saving the World*, 68

dreams, 118; in *Before We Were Free*, 79; in *A Gift of Gracias*, 92–93

Eichner, Bill, viii, 5, 7, 88, 90, 99, 124, 132
Eliot, George, 19, 143
Eliot, T. S., 144; in *Saving the World*, 74
Espaillat, Rhina, 17, 93–94, 134

F. Scott Fitzgerald Award, vii, 9, 132
fairy tale, 98, 113; in *Once Upon a Quinceañera*, 100, 102–105, 126
familia (family), viii, 1–3, 5–7, 12–13, 15–16, 125, 126–128, 139, 140, 145, 148; in *Before We Were Free*, 78–81; in *Finding Miracles*, 81–84; in *Homecoming*, 107–109, 111; in *How the García Girls Lost Their Accents*, 21–31; in *How Tía Lola Came to ~~Visit~~ Stay*, 91–92; in *In the Name of Salomé*, 57–66; in *In the Time of the Butterflies*, 34–43; in *Once Upon a Quinceañera*, 100–105; in *The Other Side/El Otro Lado*, 112, 114–115; in *Return to Sender*, 84–87; in *Something to Declare*, 95–98; in *The Woman I Kept to Myself*, 115–116; in *¡Yo!*, 45–47, 50–54. *See also* marriage; patriarchy
Fifi (Sofía) (character), 12–13, 126; in *How the García Girls Lost Their Accents*, 23–26, 28; in *¡Yo!*, 46
Finding Miracles, 7, 8, 81–84, 122, 123, 125, 128, 135, 136, 149
Frost, Robert, 17, 110, 117, 144

Gauguin, Paul, 112, 135
Gift of Gracias, A: The Legend of Altagracia, 7, 92–93
Gladys (character): in *How the García Girls Lost Their Accents*, 29; in *The Other Side/El Otro Lado*, 111, 112; in *Something to Declare*, 98
globalization, 85, 123
Goya, Francisco, 73
Guevara, Che, 38

Hamlet, 119

Heaney, Seamus, 144; in *Saving the World*, 74

Hispanic Heritage Award for Literature, vii

Homecoming, 5, 18, 107–111, 122, 127

"Housekeeping" poems, 98

How the García Girls Lost Their Accents, vii, 4, 5, 6, 7, 8, 9, 12, 14–15, 17, 20, 21–31, 34, 45, 46, 50, 54, 58, 78, 98, 122, 126, 127, 132, 133, 135, 136, 140; adaptation for stage, vii, 9, 136, 140

How Tía Lola Came to Visit Stay, 7, 91–92, 132, 134

Hughes, Langston, 3, 129, 132

immigration, vii, viii, 4, 7–8, 21, 22, 31, 77, 84–88, 95, 96, 99, 100, 103, 110, 112, 121, 123, 126, 132, 136, 138, 146, 147, 149, 150

In the Name of Salomé, vii, 6, 12, 13–14, 16, 57–66, 67, 121, 122, 125, 128, 129, 134, 135

In the Time of the Butterflies, vii, 5, 12, 13, 14, 15, 16, 33–43, 98, 121, 125, 133, 136; adaptation for television, vii, 6, 136–140

insomnia, 30, 41, 49, 118

International Day Against Violence Against Women, 42, 133, 139

Joan of Arc, 80

Kingston, Maxine Hong, 4, 73, 98, 128, 143–144

library, 3, 4, 116, 132

light, 40, 48, 60–61, 64, 73, 83, 104, 110, 113, 137, 138

literacy, viii, 71, 121, 128, 129, 132, 135; in *A Cafecito Story*, 89–91; in *In the Name of Salomé*, 66; in *¡Yo!*, 48, 51. *See also* oral culture; reading; storytelling

Lucinda (character), 12, 126; in *Before We Were Free*, 78, 79; in *How the*

García Girls Lost Their Accents, 22; in *¡Yo!*, 47, 50

maid, 29, 30, 47, 51, 61, 78, 80, 98, 108, 111, 112, 128, 135. *See also* Gladys; Sarita; Tivisita

marriage, 4, 5, 97, 98, 101, 104, 109, 121–122, 126, 127, 138, 139, 140; in *Before We Were Free*, 79; in *A Cafecito Story*, 89, 90, 91; in *Finding Miracles*, 83; in *Homecoming*, 107, 108; in *How the García Girls Lost Their Accents*, 15, 23, 24; in *In the Name of Salomé*, 59, 60, 62–63; in *In the Time of the Butterflies*, 26, 36–41; in *The Other Side/El Otro Lado*, 114; in *Saving the World*, 68, 70, 72; in *The Woman I Kept to Myself*, 117; in *¡Yo!*, 48, 49, 51–52

menstruation, 129; in *Before We Were Free*, 79–80; in *In the Time of the Butterflies*, 35, 41

Middlebury College, 1, 3, 4, 5, 6, 61, 99

Milosz, Czeslaw, 115, 144

Milton, John, 74, 135. *See also Paradise Lost*

Mirabal sisters (*Las Mariposas*, the Butterflies), 5–6, 13, 15, 16 17, 79, 98, 99, 121, 125, 126, 127, 128, 133, 141; in *In the Time of the Butterflies*, 33–42; in *In the Time of the Butterflies*, adaptation for television, 136–140

Morison, Toni, 144

Mundín (character), 12, 126; in *Before We Were Free*, 78, 79; in *How the García Girls Lost Their Accents*, 29; in *¡Yo!*, 48, 51

National Book Critics Circle Award, 5, 8, 33, 100

ode, 17, 19, 116

Once Upon a Quinceañera: Coming of Age in the USA, viii, 7, 8–9, 15, 95, 100–105, 123, 126–127, 128, 133, 134

oral culture, viii, 2, 11, 134, 135, 146.
    See also literacy; reading; storytelling
Other Side, The/El Otro Lado, 5, 17,
    107, 111–115, 122, 124, 127

Pandora: in *Finding Miracles*, 82, 83;
    in *¡Yo!*, 52, 54
Paradise Lost, 74. *See also* Milton,
    John
patriarchy, viii, 22, 26, 28, 30, 41, 63,
    98, 105, 108, 121, 126
Plato: in *Homecoming*, 109, 110; in
    Once Upon a Quinceañera, 100,
    103, 126; in *The Other Side/El Otro
    Lado*, 114
point of view, 11, 12, 15, 20, 77, 136,
    137, 139, 147, 148; in *How the
    García Girls Lost Their Accents*,
    15–16, 22, 28; in *In the Name of
    Salomé*, 16, 58, 64; in *In the Time of
    the Butterflies*, 16, 34, 40; in *Return
    to Sender*, 84–85, 87; in *Saving the
    World*, 16–17; in *¡Yo!*, 45, 46, 50,
    51, 52, 54, 55
prejudice, viiii, 3, 20, 101–102, 112,
    116, 126, 128, 144; in *How the
    García Girls Lost Their Accents*, 24,
    27, 30. *See also* racism
Pura Belpré Award, vii, 7, 77, 80, 146,
    149, 150

quinceañera, 9, 100–105, 127. *See also*
    *Once Upon a Quinceañera: Coming
    of Age in the USA*

racism, 3, 24, 63, 107, 114, 127, 129, 144
rain, 37, 40, 49, 91
Ramirez, Belkis, 88, 90, 131
reading, viii, 2, 3, 4, 9, 11, 17, 23,
    25, 34, 49, 80, 97, 108, 113, 114,
    115, 116, 117, 118, 126, 128, 131,
    132, 133, 134, 143, 144, 146; in *A
    Cafecito Story*, 89; in *In the Name
    of Salomé*, 60, 61, 66; in *Saving the
    World*, 67, 74. *See also* literacy
Return to Sender, vii, 7, 77, 84–88,
    122, 123, 128, 135, 136, 149

Rilke, Rainer Maria, 114, 144
role models, vii, 3, 4, 98, 102, 104,
    126–127, 128, 143

saint, 31, 36, 48, 54, 80
Sandi (character): in *How the García
    Girls Lost Their Accents*, 12, 23, 25,
    27, 29
Santería, 28, 31
Sarita (character), 47, 50
Saving the World, vii, 8, 12, 14, 15,
    16, 67–76, 122, 124, 128, 133–134,
    135, 136, 139
Scheherazade (character), 54, 80, 98.
    See also The Arabian Nights
Secret Footprints, The, 6, 77, 92
sestina, 17, 20, 111
Seven Trees, 5, 19, 115–116
sewing, 91, 108
Shakespeare, William, 18, 19, 109,
    135. *See also Hamlet*
silence, viii, 4, 22, 30, 33, 34, 42,
    53, 54, 62, 80, 85, 97, 110, 113,
    114, 115, 119, 122, 137. *See also*
    dictator; patriarchy; *testimonio*;
    Trujillo, Rafael
smallpox: in *Saving the World*, 67, 69,
    70, 73, 75, 76
snow, 27, 79, 112
Sofía (character). *See* Fifi
Something to Declare, viii, 6, 17, 31,
    95–100, 126, 127, 128, 143
sonnet, 17–19, 24, 109–111
spanish language, vii, viii, 2, 8, 13,
    17, 58, 66, 81, 82, 87, 91, 92, 117,
    129, 133, 140, 146, 148, 149, 150;
    in *How the García Girls Lost Their
    Accents*, 22, 25, 27, 31; in *The
    Other Side/El Otro Lado*, 111–112,
    115; in *Something to Declare*, 96,
    97, 98–99, 100; in *¡Yo!*, 45, 52.
    See also "Bilingual Sestina"
storytelling, vii, viii, 8, 9, 11, 80, 86,
    89, 93–94, 95, 109, 113, 117, 121,
    122, 128, 135, 137, 146; in *Finding
    Miracles*, 82, 83, 84; in *How the
    García Girls Lost Their Accents*,

12–13, 15, 22, 23–24, 30; in *How Tía Lola Came to ~~Visit~~ Stay*, 91, 92; in *In the Name of Salomé*, 13–14; in *In the Time of the Butterflies*, 13, 16–17, 34, 41, 43; in *Once Upon a Quinceañera*, 102, 103, 104; in *Saving the World*, 69, 70, 72, 73, 75, 76; in *Something to Declare*, 98, 99; in *¡Yo!*, 12, 14, 46, 50, 51, 53–54, 55

"The Suitor," adaptation for television, 136, 140

sustainability, viii, 7, 121, 122, 124, 125, 128, 132

teaching, 1, 3, 4, 6, 17, 49, 51, 60, 62, 63, 65, 66, 91, 96, 99, 100, 103–104, 105, 115, 121, 122, 126, 128

testimonio, viii, 41, 81, 83, 122, 128

Tivisita (character), 61, 63, 64

Trujillo, Rafael, viii, 1–2, 5–6, 7, 9, 11, 46, 53, 62, 65, 97, 111, 116, 121, 125, 126, 129, 132, 133, 134, 146, 148; in *Before We Were Free*, 78–81; in *How the García Girls Lost Their Accents*, 28; in *In the Time of the Butterflies*, 33–42; in *In the Time*

of the Butterflies, adaptation for television, 136–140

tuberculosis, 39

United Nations, 9, 42

Virgin Mary (*Virgencita*), 36, 99, 126; in *Finding Miracles*, 83; in *A Gift of Gracias*, 92–98; in *How the García Girls Lost Their Accents*, 29–30; in *Saving the World*, 73–75

voodoo, 2, 96, 114

Whitman, Walt, 3, 17, 25, 26, 58, 109, 110, 118, 135, 143

Williams, William Carlos, 98, 114, 144

Woman I Kept to Myself, The, 5, 8, 19, 107, 115–119, 126, 127

Wordsworth, William, 19, 116

Yo (Yolanda, Yoyo) (character), 12, 14–15, 20, 23, 25–29, 45–55, 122, 126, 127, 128, 129, 135, 140

¡Yo!, 6, 8, 12–13, 14–15, 16, 20, 45–55, 78, 121, 122, 127, 128, 136

About the Author

ALICE L. TRUPE is associate professor of English and directs the writing center at Bridgewater College in Bridgewater, Virginia. Dr. Trupe is the author of *Thematic Guide to Young Adult Literature*.